THE SHIPWRECK DECODER

A Handbook for Divers and Maritime Enthusiasts

by Ashton East

ISBN 978-1-909455-42-9

Copyright © 2025, 2026 Ashton East. All intellectual property and associated rights are hereby asserted and reserved by the author in full compliance with UK, European and international law. No part of this book may be copied, reproduced, stored in any retrieval system, ingested or relied upon for the purposes of artificial intelligence, or transmitted in any form or by any means, including in hard copy or via the internet, without the prior written permission of the publishers to whom all such rights have been assigned worldwide. The moral right of the author to be identified as author of this work is hereby asserted in accordance with the Copyright, Designs and Patents Act 1998.

All photographs and illustrations are the copyright of the author (subject to the same conditions above) except where stated otherwise, or where attempts to ascertain copyright were unsuccessful.

Cover Design © 2025 Dived Up.

A CIP catalogue record for this book can be obtained from the British Library.

Manufacturer (for compliance purposes):
Waterside Press, Hook, United Kingdom.

EU Authorised Representative:
Easy Access System Europe, Mustamäe tee 50, 10621 Tallinn, Estonia, easproject.com, gpsr.requests@easproject.com

First Published 2025
Reprinted with Revisions 2026

DIVED UP

Dived Up Publications
Bournemouth • United Kingdom
Email info@divedup.com
Web DivedUp.com

10 9 8 7 6 5 4 3 2

For Helen, who caught me working on this text when it was merely a consolidation exercise for my own understanding and insisted on sending it to a publisher.

THE SHIPWRECK DECODER

INTRODUCTION

Shipwreck diving holds a special attraction that is difficult to explain. For me it is the challenge of exploration, the contrast of a technological artefact within an alien environment, and its role as a time-capsule of the past. This book was prepared to help divers "read" the features of a shipwreck. It will help them to better place a vessel within its historical context, learn something of its function and maybe connect that to its story. Every item on a shipwreck adds to the richness of the story.

This guide is intended as a primer and briefing aid to show divers what they are looking for before a dive, and to begin to interpret observations. The book does not and cannot include every technology and item that might be found on a shipwreck, as that would include the entire history of man-made items and would not be possible.

Marine engineering is a highly specialised field that is often simultaneously at the cutting edge of technological development and deeply rooted in tradition. This guide is intended to help a layman understand the factors and technological developments in form and function that shape a generic historic vessel and its equipment. Much has been omitted for simplification and brevity, but readers are encouraged to dig deeper into more specialised sources for areas of interest.

The locations on a vessel indicated for different structures and components in this guide are the most likely placements, but they are not and cannot be absolute for all vessels. The location indicators serve to direct readers to the general vicinity in which they might find an item of interest, and to orient a diver on a shipwreck. For example, a diver arriving at a triple expansion engine in bad visibility can orient themselves towards the bow or stern by knowing that of the three pots the one with the largest diameter will be at the stern end of the engine.

It might seem strange to include such mundane objects as kitchen implements in a guide such as this, but seeing the shapes in connection with other items likely to be found together helps reinforce associations and pattern recognition. Hopefully spotting a ladle on a shipwreck will trigger the diver to look for oven bricks and other galley associations, helping to build out the story.

There is enormous variation in the way materials respond to different environments. Structures made of wood are rapidly degraded by wood-boring animals in warm tropical waters, but appear pristine after hundreds of years in anoxic cold waters. Light metal structures rapidly degrade in saltwater but heavier structures can persist and acquire dense marine growth. Shallow wrecks are more exposed to storms and more likely to be broken up into wreckage fields than deeper wrecks. These reactions are unfortunately beyond the scope of this book.

Grey boxes appear throughout this book at the start of chapters and sections. These highlight the key points to look for and what they might tell us about a vessel and its context. For example, the presence of metal reinforcements incorporated into a large wooden hull suggests the ship was constructed in a period when the abundance and affordability of refined metals was increasing but had not yet displaced wood as a primary construction material for hulls. In Europe this would suggest the vessel was constructed in the early 19th century.

The timelines indicated for different technologies and styles indicate the earliest known year, and in some cases the major regional timeline differences or more likely periods of maritime use. If a technology is observed on a shipwreck, then the timeline indicates the earliest date the vessel could have been lost. For example, solid porcelain bathtubs could not be produced before 1890, so finding one on a shipwreck means the vessel was lost no earlier than that year. This is not the same as indicating the vessel was launched after 1890 because the bathtub might have been a later addition. This guide attempts to show a simplified timeline for the evolution of maritime technologies so that a diver observing the features of a shipwreck can place the vessel in its historical context.

Take this guide to a maritime museum and spend some time with the exhibits and historic vessels to familiarise yourself with the appearance and logic of maritime architectural components. Gaining this familiarisation without the time restrictions of a dive will make it easier to read shipwrecks underwater. I cannot recommend enough the book, *Ship: 5,000 Years of Maritime Adventure* by Brian Lavery (2017), in which the story of maritime history is beautifully told and illustrated.

This guide does not discuss specific dive sites where the various

structures and machines can be seen, but there are several areas that divers can visit with good representative wrecks for different ages and functions:
- Ancient vessels in the Aegean and eastern Mediterranean;
- Cannon-era warships off the coasts of Europe;
- Age of Sail vessels with wooden hulls and masts are common in the Great Lakes regions of the United States and Canada;
- Age of Steam vessels with metal hulls, boilers and steam engines are somewhat ubiquitous;
- German warships from the First World War in Scapa Flow, to the north of the United Kingdom;
- Warships, cargo ships and militarised passenger liners from the Second World War in the islands of the south west Pacific or the Mediterranean Sea; and
- Combustion engine and Cold War-era vessels are often available as purpose sunk dive sites.

Another way to enhance your understanding of shipwrecks is to take advantage of the educational resources made available by the Nautical Archaeology Society (NAS), see www.nauticalarchaeologysociety.org. NAS offers introductory e-learning courses, foundational practical courses, and regular online and in-person short courses on specialised topics.

When exploring a wreck, treat it as an underwater cultural monument: removing artefacts not only erases history for future researchers and visitors but may also expose you to serious legal penalties.

A note regarding repetition: There is a degree of unavoidable repetition where terms relevant to different chapters are explained using similar wording.

THE SHIPWRECK DECODER

TABLE OF CONTENTS

Dedication   *iii*

Introduction   *v*

1. **ORIENTATION AND CORE STRUCTURES** 14
   - Orientation   *14*
   - Core structures   *16*
   - Decks   *17*

2. **HULL** 18
   - Wooden hulls   *18*
     - Hull shape   *18*
     - Internal structures   *19*
     - Construction methods   *20*
     - Joining methods   *22*
     - Structural reinforcements   *25*
     - Hull sheathing   *26*
     - Ballast   *27*
   - Metal hulls   *28*
     - Hull shape   *28*
     - Metal hull types   *30*
     - Metal keel types   *31*
     - Naval armour   *32*
   - Concrete hulls   *34*
   - Fibreglass hulls   *34*

3. **BOW AREA** 35
   - Basic shapes   *35*
   - Naval rams and bulbous bows   *38*
   - Icebreaker bow   *39*
   - Sailing bow   *40*
   - Towing point   *41*
   - Bow thruster   *41*

TABLE OF CONTENTS

    Anchors   *42*

        Stone and composite anchors   *42*

        Modern anchors   *44*

    Anchor mechanism   *46*

    Permanent moorings   *48*

4. STERN: PROPULSION/STEERING 49

    Basic shapes   *49*

    Rudder   *52*

        Rudder assembly   *53*

        Rudderstock positions   *53*

        Mounting types   *54*

        Rudder layouts   *55*

        Rudder types   *55*

    Steering assembly   *56*

    Leeboard   *60*

    Reduction gearbox   *60*

    Paddlewheel   *61*

    Propeller   *62*

        Propeller types   *63*

        Propeller assembly   *65*

        Propeller configurations   *66*

    Voith Schneider propeller   *68*

    Propeller guards   *68*

    Lifting screw   *69*

    Stern (kedge) anchor   *69*

5. BRIDGE AREAS 70

    Command, steering and navigation   *70*

    Instruments and gauges   *72*

    Navigation and steering (direction)   *75*

    Engine speed control   *78*

    Communications   *80*

6. FITTINGS AND EQUIPMENT 82

    Ship's bell *82*

    Winches *82*

    Deck fittings for mooring *83*

    Ventilation *84*

    Bilge pumps *84*

        Hand-operated pumps *85*

        Motorised pumps *86*

    Sensor and communication masts *87*

    Fishing rigs *89*

    Maintenance *90*

    Galley (kitchen) *92*

    Head (bathroom) *94*

    Deck lighting *95*

        Navigation and anchor lights *96*

    Gunports and portholes *96*

    Searchlights *98*

    Safety devices *99*

        Davits and small boats *99*

    Computers and electronics *100*

    Gangway *101*

    Movement between decks *102*

7. ROWED VESSELS 103

    Types of rowing *103*

    Rowing positions *103*

    Rowing equipment *103*

8. WIND-POWERED VESSELS 105

    Mast structure *105*

    Multiple masts *107*

    Mast stack *107*

    Rigging *108*

    Sails *109*

    Types of sailing vessel *110*

TABLE OF CONTENTS

    Bipod and tripod masts   *111*

    Mast/boom crutch   *111*

9. **STEAM-POWERED VESSELS**..112

    Feedwater system   *112*

    Coal or oil fuel supply   *113*

    Marine boilers   *114*

    Donkey boiler   *120*

    Exhaust funnel   *120*

    Steam whistle   *121*

    Steam engine   *121*

        Steam engine concepts   *122*

        Basic steam engine assembly   *123*

        Newcomen engine   *124*

        Watt engine   *126*

        Cornish (walking beam) engine   *127*

        Side-lever and grasshopper engine   *128*

        Dual-action pot   *129*

        Compound engine   *130*

        Engine configurations   *131*

    Steam turbine engine   *132*

10. **COMBUSTION-POWERED VESSELS**...133

    Combustion engine   *133*

    Four stroke engine cycle   *135*

    Two stroke engine cycle   *136*

    Gas turbine engine cycle   *137*

11. **ELECTRIC-POWERED VESSELS**..138

    Electric engine   *138*

    Electric generator   *139*

    Diesel-electric   *140*

    Turbo-electric   *140*

12. CARGO STORAGE AND HANDLING 141

    Cargo hold   *141*

    Solid cargo   *142*

    Solid cargo handling   *143*

    Landing deck and hangar   *146*

    Explosive cargo "magazine"   *147*

    Bulk cargo handling   *148*

    Liquid cargo handling   *150*

    Gaseous cargo handling   *152*

13. CANNON-AGE ARMAMENT 153

    Bore   *155*

    Muzzle   *156*

    Chase   *157*

    Reinforce   *157*

    Vent field   *159*

    Cascabel   *159*

    Cannon types   *160*

        Material   *161*

        Muzzle or breech-loading   *162*

        Classification and trajectory   *162*

        Calibre   *163*

        Key types   *164*

        Mouldings   *166*

    Cannon carriage   *167*

        Recoil system   *168*

    Cannon assemblage   *168*

    Projectiles   *170*

    Wreck site layouts   *171*

14. MODERN ARMAMENT 173

    Modern naval guns   *173*

    Key developments   *174*

    Anti-aircraft guns   *177*

    Light arms   *178*

TABLE OF CONTENTS

  Ordnance *179*
    Gun ammunition *179*
    Sea mines *181*
    Torpedoes *182*
    Depth charges *184*
    Rockets and missiles *187*

15. SUBMARINES 189
  Bow *190*
  Midships *192*
  Stern *194*
  Armaments *195*
    Missiles *195*
    Mines *195*

Select Bibliography *196*
About the author *197*
Acknowledgements *198*
Index *199*

CHAPTER 1
ORIENTATION AND CORE STRUCTURES

This chapter introduces orientation terms and the basic structural components of a vessel.

- Hull material
- Number of decks
- Number and position of cargo holds
- Size and position of superstructure
- Basic dimensions
    - Length (longitudinal distance between the ends of bow and stern at vessel's longest point)
    - Beam (lateral distance across the hull at its widest point)
    - Freeboard (height above the waterline of the highest continuous deck/upper deck)
    - Draught (depth below the waterline of the keel)
    - Superstructure height (above the deck)

The basic hull shape of a vessel is determined by intended function. The hull of a cargo vessel must be as full bodied as possible to maximise carrying capacity. The hull of a military vessel must usually be narrow to improve speed and manoeuvrability, and low to the waterline to present a smaller target profile. The hull of a passenger vessel usually carries high superstructure to maximise the enclosed accommodation and living spaces.

Orientation

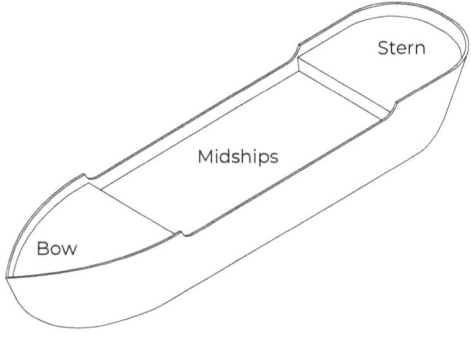

ORIENTATION AND CORE STRUCTURES

- **Bow:** the front or forward part of a vessel, pointing in the direction of movement through water.
- **Midships:** the central part of a vessel, equidistant from bow and stern.
- **Stern:** the back or rear part of a vessel, opposite the bow.

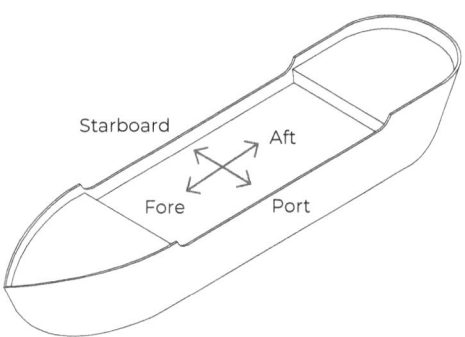

- **Port:** the left side of a vessel when facing the bow, marked with a red navigation light at night.
- **Starboard:** the right side of a vessel when facing the bow, identified by a green navigation light at night.
- **Fore:** the front part of a ship ahead of midships, or the direction facing towards the bow.
- **Aft:** the rear part of a ship behind midships, or the direction facing towards the stern.
- **Longitudinal:** the imaginary line running along the length of the vessel from bow to stern, aligning with the vessel's forward motion.
- **Lateral:** the imaginary line running across the width of the vessel from port to starboard, perpendicular to the vessel's forward motion.

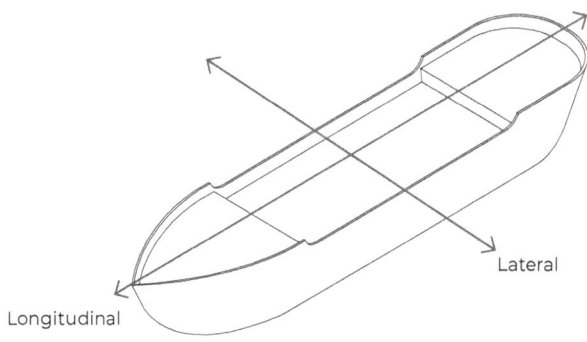

THE SHIPWRECK DECODER

Core structures

- **Superstructure:** enclosed or partially enclosed structures built atop the main deck.
- **Forecastle:** an enclosed structure at the bow formed between the partial forecastle deck and main deck.
- **Poop:** an enclosed structure at the stern formed between the partial poopdeck and main deck.
- **Hold:** a large storage space below the main deck.

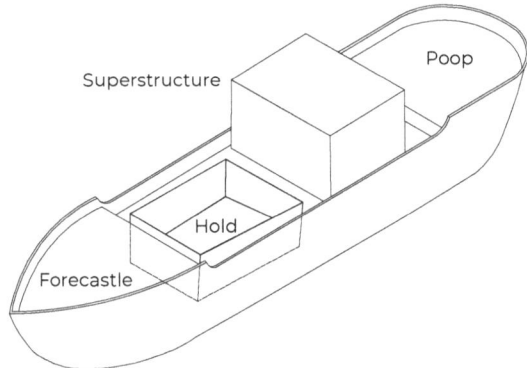

- **Gunwale:** the upper edge of the hull, forming a protective barrier along the top deck perimeter for shelter and safety.
- **Keel:** the central spine running along the bottom of the hull for stability and structural integrity.
- **Frames:** the heavy lateral ribs that give the vessel shape.

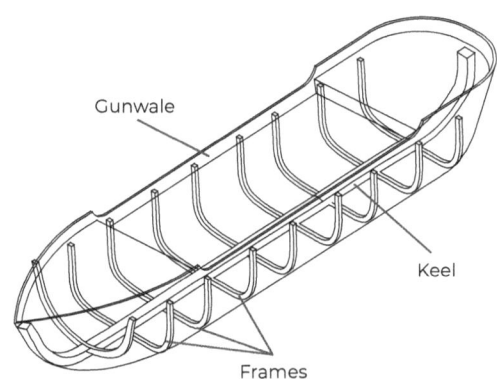

ORIENTATION AND CORE STRUCTURES

Decks

- **Main deck:** highest deck extending the full length of the vessel.

Above the main deck:
- **Forecastle deck:** partial length deck above the main deck at the bow.
- **Poopdeck:** highest partial length deck at the stern.
- **Quarterdeck:** partial length deck immediately above the main deck at the stern.
- **Upper deck:** partial length deck above the main deck amidships; or a partial deck extending from amidships to either the bow or stern.
- **Superstructure deck:** partial length deck above the main, upper, forecastle or poopdeck and not extending the full width of the ship.

Below the main deck:
- **Second deck:** full length deck immediately below the main deck, sequentially lower full length decks are third deck, fourth deck, etc.
- **Half deck:** partial length deck between the main deck and lowest full length deck.
- **Platform deck:** partial length deck below the lowest full length deck, sequentially lower platform decks are second platform deck, third platform deck, etc.
- **Orlop deck:** the lowest deck in a vessel with three or more decks.

!Warning! Deck naming conventions vary between maritime traditions and over time. The names in this section are a best attempt at generic rules.

CHAPTER 2
HULL

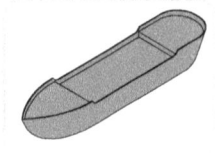

This chapter focuses on understanding a generic hull as the most basic component of a vessel. The main sections are separated by construction material (wood, metal, concrete, and fibreglass) because each has different structural elements and joining methods.

- Note whether the hull is made from wood, metal, a combination of wood and metal components, fibreglass, or (rarely) concrete. The material and features can quickly suggest the technological and economic context of a vessel's construction.
- If lighter decking material has deteriorated away, the number of decks may be determined by the remaining stanchion and beam structure.

Wooden hulls

Hull shape

To understand the shape and major components of a wooden hull we can build the picture from the keel up. The keel forms the backbone of the vessel. Adding the stem and sternpost defines the ends of the vessel. From the keel the vessel's hull can be built up from planks and frames by either hard shell or frame-first construction.

- **Keel:** the main longitudinal timber from which the hull is built up. The keel may be a single piece or built up from parts to add length or reinforcement. The keel provides rigidity, reducing rolling and lateral drift.
- **Stem:** the central timber connecting the two sides of the bow. The stem projects vertically up and forward from the bow end of the keel.
- **Sternpost:** the central timber connecting the two sides of the stern unless the vessel has a transom instead. The sternpost projects vertically up from the stern end of the keel.
- **Transom:** the flat surface connecting the two sides of the stern.
- **Frame:** heavy lateral timbers providing reinforcement and/or shape to the hull. Can be single piece or built up of sections called futtocks.
- **Plank:** longitudinal timbers providing the watertight skin of the hull. Each full line of planks is called a strake. Strakes are counted from

HULL

the keel to the gunwales, so that the plank closest to the keel is the first strake (aka garboard strake).
- **Bulwark:** protective extension of hull planking above the main deck.
- **Timberhead:** top section of a frame, or separate vertical timber, extending above the uppermost deck to stiffen the bulwark.

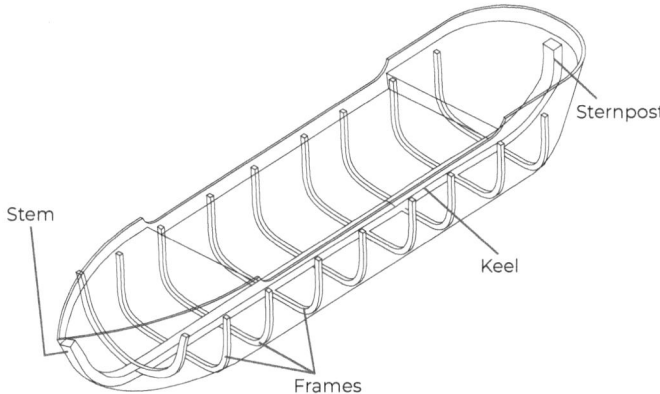

Internal structures

Once the skeleton and skin of the hull are complete, we can add the internal structure of stanchions and beams.
- **Ceiling:** internal planking of a vessel such as decks.
- **Beam:** horizontal and lateral timbers that support deck planks above. Beams in contact with the hull are supported by a notch cut from, or a knee added to, the inside edge of the frames. Stanchions may be used to support beams within the hull.
- **Carling:** horizontal and longitudinal timbers that reinforce beams and deck openings.
- **Stanchion:** vertical or angled posts to support beams.
- **Thwart:** horizontal beam providing lateral structural rigidity for a vessel without decks.

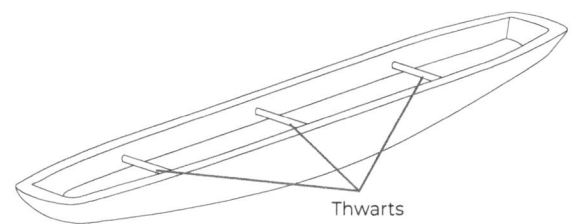

THE SHIPWRECK DECODER

Construction methods

- Heavy planks with light or no frames ➤ Hard shell
- Flat bottom of heavy, flush laid planks, without any keel ➤ Bottom based
- Heavy frames with light planks ➤ Frame first
- Notched frames and overlapping planks with rows of fasteners ➤ Clinker
- Smooth frames with flush planks ➤ Carvel
- Planks attached to both sides of frames ➤ Double planked

> **Pre-history** Clinker
> **1400 BCE** Carvel
> **1900** Double diagonal

The basic hull construction methods are hard shell and frame first depending on which component provides the main structural strength. The hull is built from the keel or bottom up to the gunwales. Each strake of planks is laid above the previous strake either flush using sewn or mortise and tenon joinery techniques, overlapping and nailed together in the clinker style, or abutting and nailed to the frames in the carvel style, or a combination.

- **Hard shell:** heavy outer planking provides the shape and main strength of the hull with any frames inserted last as lateral reinforcement. Planks may be flush (sewn or mortise and tenon joined), or clinker (nailed). The hull may be bottom-based or built up from a keel. The planks are not bent around frames so they must be cut and shaped to achieve curvature, a process which is relatively labour intensive and wasteful of timber.

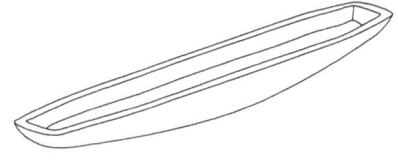
Hard shell (dugout canoe)

- **Bottom based:** construction starts from a base of heavy flush-laid planks, before building up the sides. Bottom-based vessels have no keel and are usually only suitable for confined waters.
- **Frame first:** heavy frames joined to the keel provide the basic hull shape like a skeleton to which the planks are nailed as a waterproof

HULL

skin. Planks are usually carvel but clinker is possible. In frame-first construction planks can be incrementally bent around frames to achieve curves. The keel provides the main longitudinal strength for frame-first vessels.

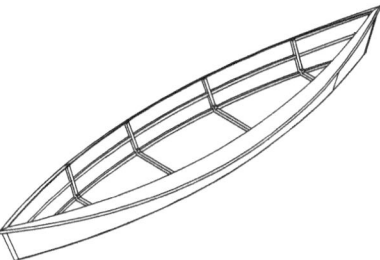

Frame first (frame canoe)

- **Clinker:** the bottom edge of each plank is fitted over the top edge of the plank immediately below, with the two planks nailed together at the overlap. The effect is a series of longitudinal ridges. Frames are notched to closely fit the overlap between each strake.

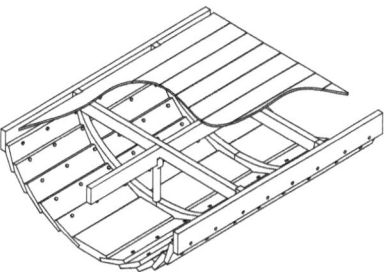

Clinker

- **Carvel:** the bottom edge of each plank is joined to the upper edge of the plank immediately below. The outer edge of the frames will be smooth. The effect is a smooth hull.

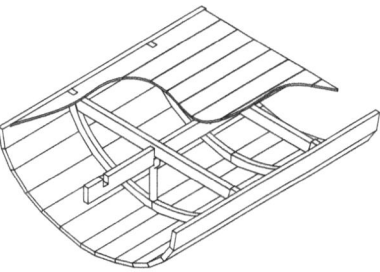

Carvel

- **Double planked:** the hull has an inner and outer layer of planking for additional waterproofing.
- **Double diagonal:** two layers of carvel planking laid diagonally between the keel and gunwales. Used on some smaller 20th century wooden vessels such as minesweepers.

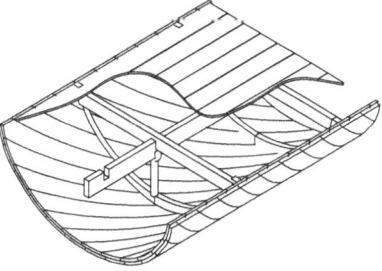

Double diagonal

THE SHIPWRECK DECODER

Joining methods

- Flush hull planking, without frames or with light frames only, may be pegged or unpegged ➤ Mortise and tenon joint ➤ Vessel constructed with labour intensive woodworking techniques
- Wooden planking with hole sequences around the edges and grooves cut between paired holes ➤ Sewn planking ➤ Vessel made with primitive techniques
- Circular patches of different (usually darker) coloured wood ➤ Trenails ➤ Vessel made by a society with woodworking tools advanced enough to achieve the necessary accuracy and precision in hole and cylinder diameters
- Copper or bronze fasteners ➤ Vessel made before iron became available to originating society

> **6000 BCE** Copper
> **3300 BCE** Bronze
> **3000 BCE (technology available)** Iron
> **Post-1783 (likely)** Iron

The fastening techniques used for wooden-hulled boats follow a pattern of technological progression as more advanced tools and materials become available in the area. The progression from sewn planking, to trenails, to metal nails and rivets is not by clean separation of periods. Multiple techniques may be present in the same vessel for reasons of tradition and economics.

Mortise and tenon

A woodworking technique where two sections of wood are held together by tightly fitting a wooden tab (the tenon) into a recessed slot (the mortise). In more advanced versions of the technique the tenon is secured by perpendicular

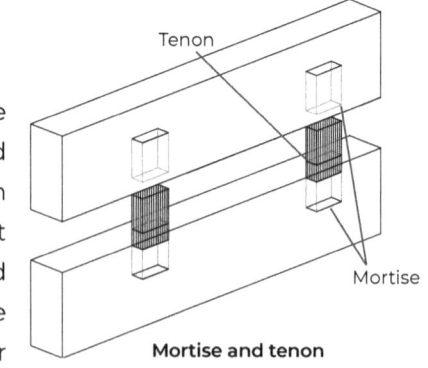
Mortise and tenon

wooden pegs passed through both the tenon and mortise. The tenon may be a different species of wood that is harder than the mortise. Use of mortise and tenon produces flush hull planking but is only suitable for smaller vessels.

Sewn planking

Sewn planking has been used worldwide from pre-history to the present day, depending on the economic and technological development of the region. In sewn plank construction, a flexible material (the ligature), e.g. fibre cord, saplings, vines, bamboo, etc., is woven between adjacent holes across the gap between wooden planks.

Sewn planking can be confirmed if the ligature material survives. Empty holes could have been originally filled with either flexible material, trenails or metal fasteners that deteriorated at a different rate to the wooden planks.

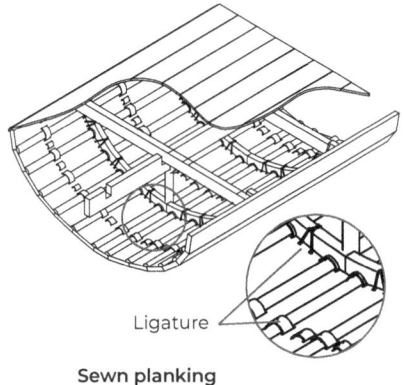

Sewn planking

The ligature can be used for lashings or lacing. Ligature holes may penetrate the full thickness or partway through the plank. Grooves may be cut between paired holes so that the ligature can be recessed for protection.

- **Lashing:** stitches are made individually between pairs of holes like a staple. This technique joins the planks together but does not provide any longitudinal strength.
- **Lacing:** a continuous thread of ligatures joins holes along the length of the edge like the stitched seams of a wetsuit. The diagonal stitch between adjacent hole pairs provides longitudinal strength.

The gap between planks and ligature holes must be made watertight using a filler material (e.g. gum, tar, moss, etc.).

Wedges or a wadding material that expands when wet may be inserted under the stitches to tighten them.

THE SHIPWRECK DECODER

Trenails

Trenails are cylindrical wooden pins used to fasten layers of wood together. The trenail is tightly fitted through overlapping holes in each layer. The connection may be strengthened by insertion of a wedge into the ends of the trenail.

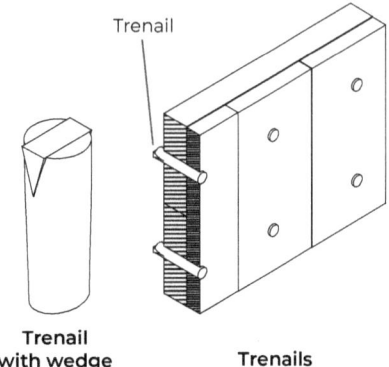

Metal fasteners

Copper, bronze and iron became available in different parts of the world at different times as metalworking technologies spread or were independently developed. Copper is quite soft and bronze is relatively expensive, so the presence of either metal in fasteners suggests the vessel was built before iron became available. Metal fasteners may take the form of a nail, rivet, or rivet with rove.

- **Nail:** metal shaft with a sharp end to penetrate the wood without a pre-existing hole, and a broadened end to lock the nail in place.
- **Rivet:** metal shaft passed through aligned holes with:
  (a) a broadened end that sits flush against one side of the structure; and
  (b) a headless end that is heated and beaten until flat against the other side of the structure; so that the rivet is locked in place from both ends fixing the structure together.
- **Rivet with rove:** the rove is a metal plate or washer placed over the headless end of a rivet before it is beaten out to protect the underlying wood.

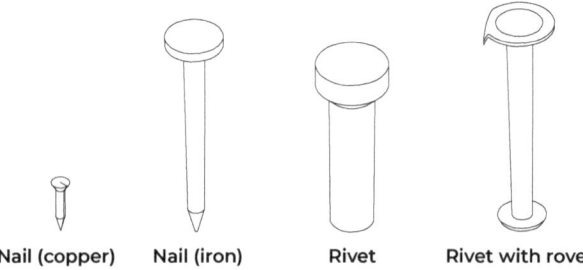

HULL

Structural reinforcements

- Metal reinforcement in wooden hull ➤ Vessel may be constructed in the transition period between wood and metal hulls

> **c.1800** Iron knees, fastenings, reinforcing parts in otherwise wooden hull
> **1840** Wooden hull built on iron frames

- **Knee:** angular brackets used to reinforce the point of intersection between surfaces meeting at an angle.
- **Diagonal riders:** internal frames placed diagonally to stiffen the hull.
- **Hogging truss:** bow to stern cables on raised supports located midship, preventing the ends of the vessel from dropping relative to midship ("hogging"), and operating on the same principle as a suspension bridge. Hogging occurs where the keel has insufficient strength to prevent relatively lower buoyancy at the bow and stern from causing the ends of the vessel to drop lower in the water compared to the middle. The hogging truss compensates by pulling the ends of the vessel together from the top.
- **Sagging arch:** bow-to-stern arch to redistribute weight from the supports hanging in the centre of the arch to the feet of the arch, preventing the middle of the vessel from dropping relative to the ends of the vessel ("sagging"), and operating on the same principle as an arch

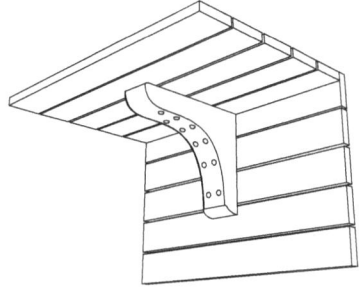
Wood knee

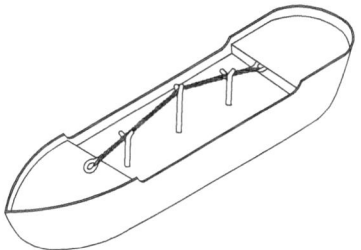
Hogging truss

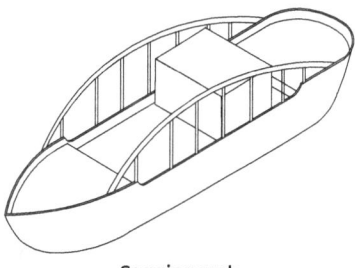
Sagging arch

bridge. Sagging occurs when the keel has insufficient strength to counter relatively lower buoyancy at midships (e.g. from heavy cargo) from causing the middle of the vessel to drop lower in the water compared to the ends. The sagging arch compensates by pushing the ends of the vessel apart from the top.

In the transition period, wooden hulls begin to use more metal parts such as iron knees, fastenings, and reinforcing parts. Later wooden hull planks were built onto iron frames. Finally, wood hull planking was replaced with iron plates completing the transition to metal hulls.

Hull sheathing

- Thin metal sheeting perforated around edges → Sheathing for wooden hull

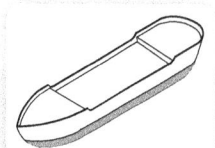

389 BCE–1770 Lead
1761–1832 Copper
1832 Muntz metal

Wooden hulls are vulnerable below the waterline to attack and fouling by marine organisms. Organisms such as shipworm and gribbles eat into the timbers causing damage (attack). Growth of organisms such as seaweed and barnacles can drastically reduce the speed and manoeuvrability of the hull ("fouling"). Sheathing the hull with metal reduces the rate of attack and fouling, but the metal itself can attack the hull's iron fastenings through galvanic corrosion. Soft metals will also be gradually abraded away by moving water.

Ancient and medieval vessels sometimes used lead, but lead is

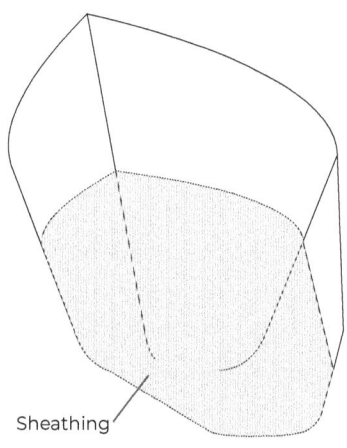

Sheathing

heavy and vulnerable to both corrosion and abrasion. Copper sheathing was first introduced by the British Admiralty in 1761 and is less heavy and corrosive than lead. Muntz metal (60% copper and 40% zinc) was invented in 1832 and was quickly adopted for sheathing wooden hulls as it is cheaper and more resistant to corrosion and abrasion than copper. Distinguishing between copper and Muntz metal requires metallurgical analysis.

Ballast

- Patches of gravel or stone that do not match the surrounding environment ➜ Ballast

Ballast is weight placed in the bottom of the hull to lower the centre of gravity and improve stability. The weight may be a heavy material such as gravel, stone, pig iron, inoperable cannon, etc., or water tanks for liquid ballast.

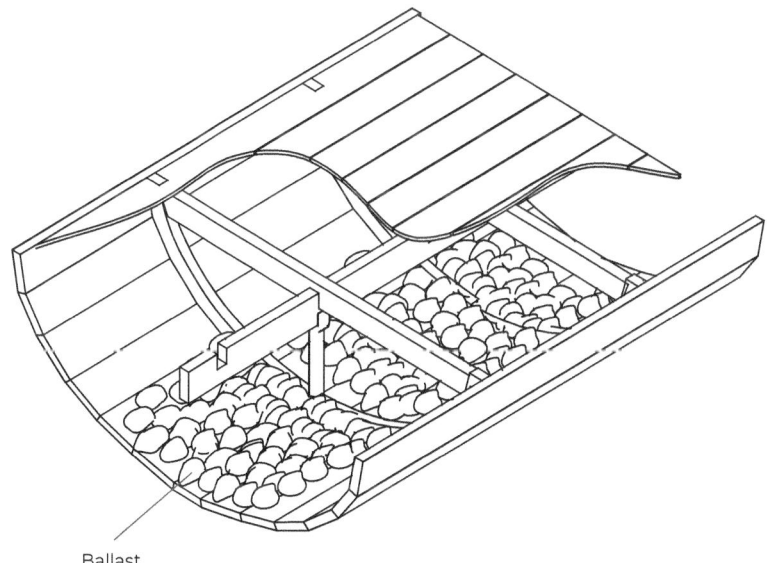

Ballast

Metal hulls

Hull shape

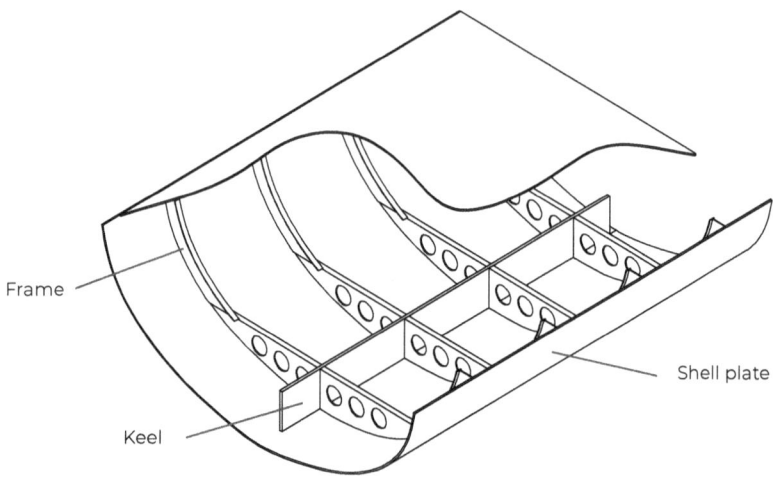

Metal hull

- **Shell plates:** longitudinal runs of metal plates providing the watertight skin of the hull. Each full line of plates is called a strake. Strakes are counted from the keel to the gunwale, so that the one closest to the keel is the first strake (aka garboard strake).
- **Frames:** lateral vertical plate or girder providing reinforcement and shape to the hull.
- **Stringers:** longitudinal vertical plate or girder laid within the frames providing reinforcement to the hull.
- **Stern frame:** the central bar or girder connecting the two sides of the stern below the waterline, usually incorporating the rudder post.
- **Stem:** the central bar or rolled plate connecting the two sides of the bow at the forward-most edge of the bow. The stem projects vertically up and forward from the bow end of the keel.
- **Bulwark:** protective extension of the shell plates above the main deck.
- **Bulwark stay:** top section of a frame, or separate vertical metal bar, extending above the uppermost deck to stiffen the bulwark.
- **Watertight bulkheads and hatches:** vertical partitions to divide the hull into compartments strong enough to contain flooding.

- **Minor bulkheads:** screens or lightweight bulkheads subdividing compartments for use but not providing structural strength or significant flood containment.

Construction method
Metal hulls use frame-first construction and may be assembled from prefabricated sections.
- **Prefabrication:** beyond installing prefabricated components whole ships are assembled by joining prefabricated sections at the shipyard, e.g. hull sections, stern and bow structures, superstructure, etc.

Joining methods
- **Rivet:** metal shaft passed through aligned holes with:
  (a) a broadened end that sits flush against one side of the structure;
  (b) a headless end that is heated and beaten until flat against the other side of the structure; so that the rivet is locked in place from both ends fixing the structure together.

Riveted

Welded

- **Welding:** metal parts are fused together by melting a metal rod at their adjoining edges/surfaces and mixing the interface at high temperatures.
- **Combination:** in the transition period from rivets to welding, when the new welding technology was not fully understood or trusted. Hulls from this transition period may be:
  (a) riveted below the waterline and welded above the waterline;
  (b) riveted for strength and welded for watertightness; or
  (c) riveted with welded repairs.

THE SHIPWRECK DECODER

Metal hull types

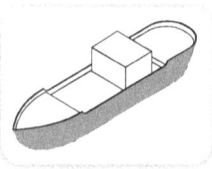

- Green crust, shiny yellow core ➜ Copper or bronze
- Thick red/brown crust (rust), black intermediate layer, matt grey core ➜ Iron
- White crust, matt grey core ➜ Aluminium
- Untarnished surface, shiny grey core ➜ Stainless steel

1787 Iron
1858 Steel
1865 Aluminium
1913 Stainless Steel
1917 Combination rivets and welded
1920 Fully welded

- **Single bottom (aka open floor):** the hull is composed of a single outer skin of shell plating mounted to the keel and frames with no inner skin of plating.
- **Double bottom:** the hull is composed of an outer skin of shell plating mounted to the keel and frames, and a parallel/horizontal inner bottom of shell plating above the keel.
- **Double side:** the hull is composed of an outer skin of shell plating mounted to the keel and frames, and parallel/vertical inner walls of shell plating above the keel.
- **Double hull:** the hull is composed of an outer skin of shell plating mounted to the keel and frames, and a parallel inner skin of shell plating within the keel and frames.

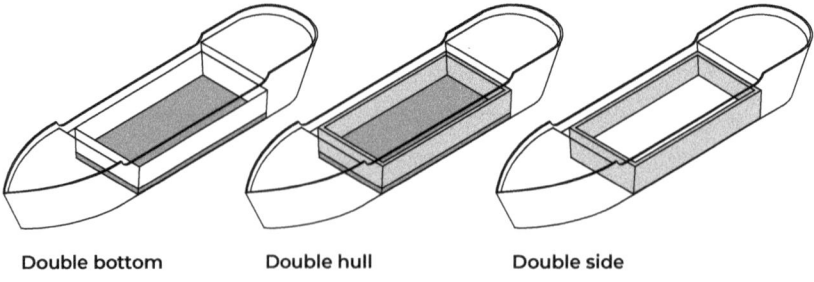

Double bottom   **Double hull**   **Double side**

HULL

Metal keel types
- **Flat plate keel:** horizontal longitudinal metal plate along the lowest point of the hull, thicker than adjacent hull plates. In a single bottom hull the flat plate keel is reinforced by a vertical longitudinal metal plate (keelson plate) and completed with an inner horizontal longitudinal metal plate (ridder plate). In a double bottom hull the flat plate keel is reinforced by a longitudinal metal girder (centre girder) and completed with the bottom metal plate of the inner hull.

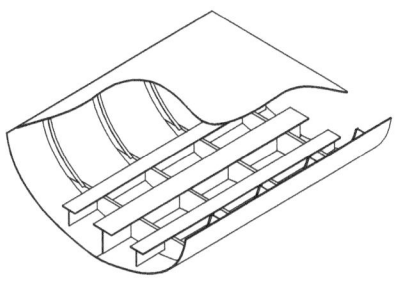

Flat plate keel

- **Bar keel:** longitudinal flat metal bar (stronger and heavier than a plate). Usually found on smaller, single bottom hulls where grounding is a risk.

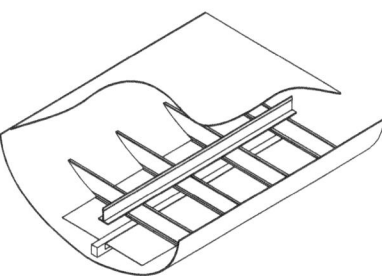

Bar keel

- **Duct keel:** a watertight passage formed by longitudinal plates welded into a box shape, usually found on larger, double bottom hulls, from the bow to the forward engine room bulkhead. The box is formed by welding a perpendicular centre girder to each side of a flat keel plate, topped with the bottom metal plate of the inner hull. The space within the duct keel may be used to house ballast, pipes and cables, and is likely to have fittings and fixtures to enable crew access.

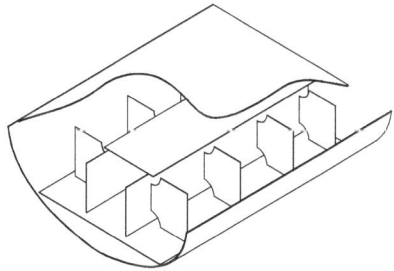

Duct keel

THE SHIPWRECK DECODER

Naval armour

- Naval armour → Warship
- Armour coverage → Critical areas, priorities and expected threats

> **1413** Metal armoured deck (Korea)
> **1859** Metal deck armour (Europe)
> **1862–1933** Casemate
> **1908–1945** Torpedo belt
> **1914–1930** Torpedo bulge

Naval armour is extremely heavy so full coverage is rarely possible, and the additional mass cuts into speed and engine efficiency. Armour coverage is prioritised for vessel survivability, mission critical areas, and expected threats. Warships usually prioritise the engine room and navigation within a citadel. Gunships protect the cannon loading area though to ammunition storage as mission critical.

- **Armour plate:** heavy metal plate using strength and thickness to absorb the energy of a projectile strike and/or explosion.
- **Sloped armour:** heavy plates angled to present a longer penetration distance for incoming projectiles.
- **Belt armour:** a layer of vertical armour plate installed against the outer hull.
- **Armoured deck:** a layer of horizontal armour plate installed atop a deck.
- **Casemate:** armoured box enclosing one or more gun positions.

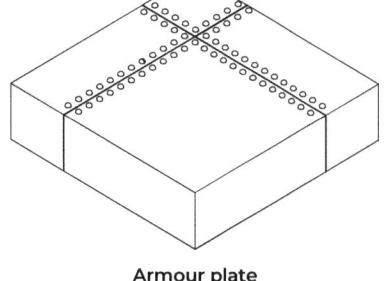

Armour plate

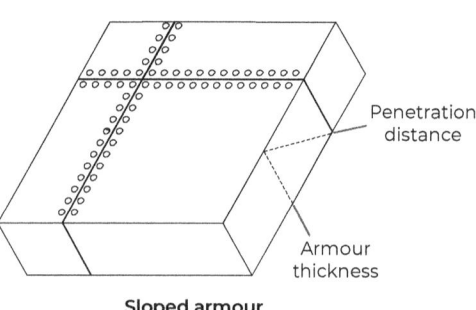

Sloped armour

HULL

- **Armoured citadel:** armoured box enclosing the engine room and magazine.
- **Torpedo bulge:** projecting sponson installed against each side of the vessel's hull at and below the waterline, consisting of partially flooded compartments intended to absorb the explosion from torpedo attack before it reaches the hull.
- **Torpedo belt:** an evolution of the torpedo bulge where layers of lightly armoured and internally partitioned compartments extend outward from the hull at the waterline.

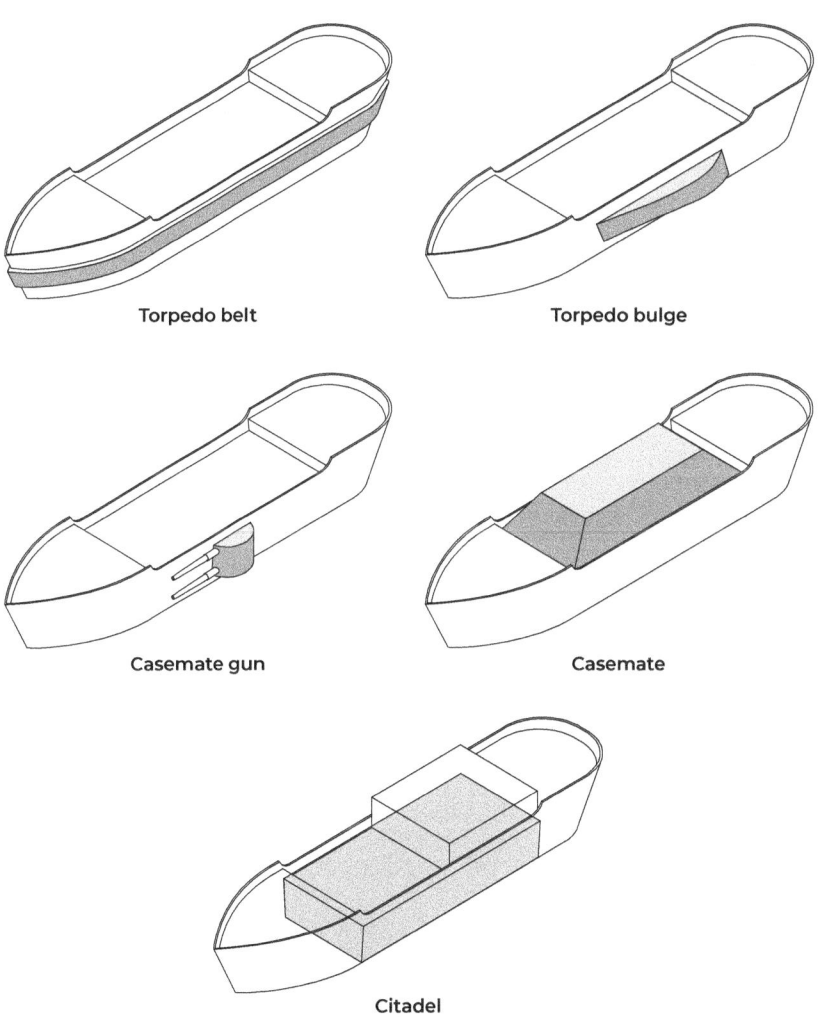

Torpedo belt

Torpedo bulge

Casemate gun

Casemate

Citadel

THE SHIPWRECK DECODER

Concrete hulls

1848 Concrete hull

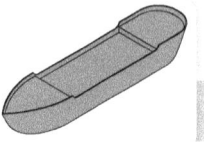

Concrete is occasionally used as an inexpensive hull construction material. Hull sections are formed from concrete poured into a wooden mould, with steel rods that are inserted for structural reinforcement. Separate hull sections are joined by steel I-beams, like the joints of a bridge surface. Concrete hulls need to be much thicker than steel to achieve the same resilience.

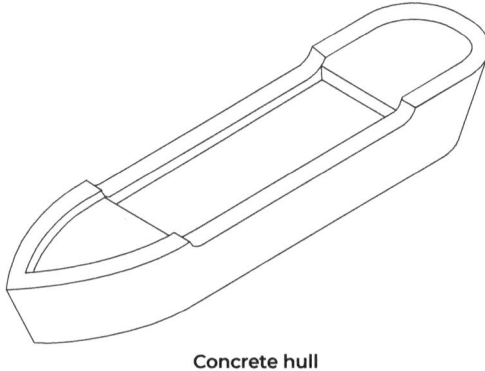

Concrete hull

Fibreglass hulls

1947 Fibreglass hull

Fibreglass is a widely used material in hull construction due to its durability and ease of fabrication. Hull sections are formed by layering woven glass fibre sheets and resin within a mould, creating a strong, lightweight composite. The resin hardens, binding the fibres into a rigid structure that resists corrosion and impact damage. Unlike concrete or steel, fibreglass does not require internal reinforcement, relying instead on its layered composition for strength. Hull sections are joined seamlessly using additional resin and glass fibre layers, forming a continuous, chemically bonded watertight surface. The result is a hull that is both flexible and resilient, ideal for small to mid-sized vessels.

CHAPTER 3
BOW AREA

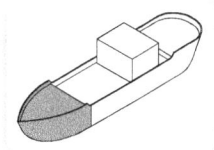

A bow's basic form is dictated by operational needs and hydrodynamic principles. Designers must balance water resistance (affecting speed and turning) with effects like roll (side-to-side rocking), pitch (front-to-back rocking), yaw (side-to-side turning), slamming (wave impact on the hull), and greenwater (water washing over the deck).

Basic shapes

- Cross-section shape
    - U-shape ➤ Less speed loss, heavy slamming and high pitch
    - V-shape ➤ Speed loss, reduced slamming and pitch
- Profile fullness
    - Round and short horizontal profile ➤ Bluff bow: slow speed, abrupt wave impacts, less greenwater, more pitch
    - Pointed and long horizontal profile ➤ Fine bow: fast speed, smooth wave cutting, more greenwater, less pitch
    - Square horizontal profile ➤ Square bow: intended for flat water and slow speeds, or specialist shore landing applications
- Stem angle
    - Straight vertical ➤ Plumb bow: less manoeuvrability and yaw, more greenwater
    - Inclined forward ➤ Rake bow: more manoeuvrability and yaw, less pitch and slamming
    - Inclined backwards ➤ Reverse bow: less manoeuvrability and yaw, very little slamming, very wet foredeck

The basic shape of the bow area is a compromise between buoyancy, stability, hydrodynamic efficiency and length. It can tell the story of its operational speed, manoeuvrability, and stability requirements.
- **Cross-section shape:** the transverse cross-section at the bow determines how buoyancy changes at each level of submersion. U-shaped sections have a consistent buoyancy profile at each level. U-sections suffer less speed loss in waves but suffer heavier slamming as the bow

strikes the surface all at once. V-shaped sections increase buoyancy linearly as more of the bow is submerged. V-sections cut into waves gradually, reducing peak impact forces but suffering more speed loss from deeper immersion.

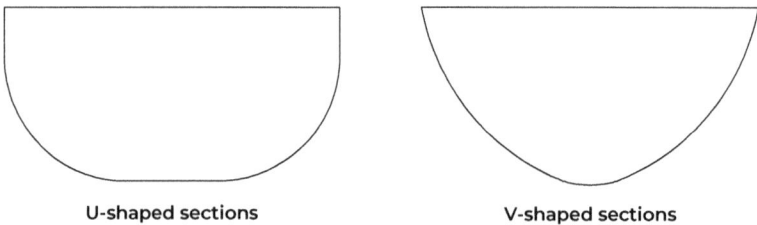

U-shaped sections   V-shaped sections

- **Profile fullness:** the horizontal shape where the port and starboard sides of the hull meet at the bow. Fine (sharp) bows have a narrow water entry and slice through water with low resistance making them better for fast operating speeds, but less forward buoyancy allows the bow to submerge deeper into waves putting more water over the foredeck. Bluff (rounded) bows have more forward buoyancy that lifts the bow faster on a wave, keeping the foredeck dryer but increasing pitch. Square bows maximise forward buoyancy and usable space at the cost of water resistance and pitch.

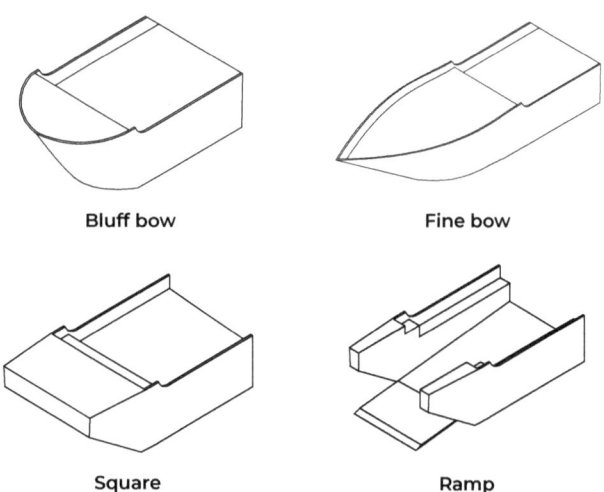

Bluff bow   Fine bow

Square   Ramp

BOW AREA

- **Stem angle (rake)**: the vertical angle of a ship's stem (leading edge). Raked (forward overhung) stems lean forward creating overhang and raising the buoyancy profile of the bow. Raked stems reduce water resistance to turning for better manoeuvrability but at the expense of greater yaw requiring more corrections to maintain a straight-line heading. Longer overhangs allow a raked bow to meet waves with gradually increasing buoyancy to reduce pitch and slamming. A spoon bow is a type of raked bow that is curved on the underside. Plumb (vertical) stems present a constant buoyancy profile. Reverse (back sloping) stems lean backwards, lowering the buoyancy profile of the bow. Reverse stems have greater water resistance to turning for reduced yaw but less manoeuvrability. Reverse stems let waves wash over the top reducing pitch and slamming but have very wet foredecks.

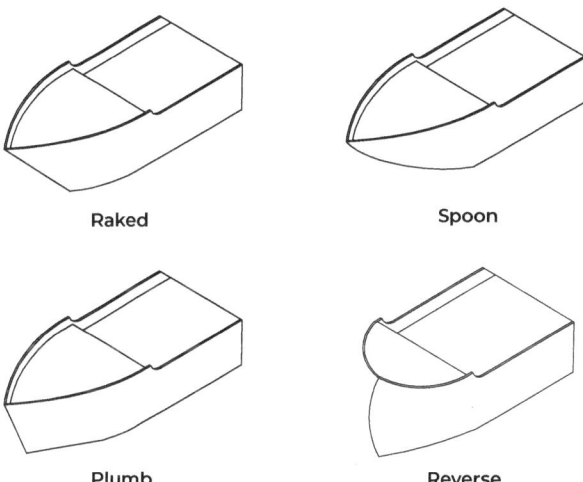

- **Bow flare:** an outward spreading curve of the bow sides above the waterline. Flare high on the bow increases foredeck width and deflects waves outward to keep water from washing over the decks. The high additional buoyancy volume resists deep plunging of the bow but excessive flare can cause slamming in heavy seas.
- **Foredeck camber:** the curvature of the foredeck if the centre is higher than the sides. Camber helps water drain off the foredeck to recover from submersion and water washing over the deck.

THE SHIPWRECK DECODER

Naval rams and bulbous bows

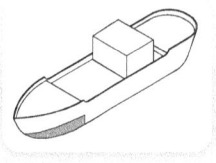

- Wood hull with metal sheathed protrusion below waterline at the bow ➤ May be ram on a rowed vessel pre-dating gun technologies
- Metal hull with solid metal protrusion below waterline at the bow ➤ May be a ram on an engine-powered vessel, constructed after 1862 and pre-dating modern heavy naval guns
- Metal hull with rounded protrusion from the bow ➤ Bulbous bow

> **c.550 BCE–c.1571** Naval ram (ancient)
> **1862–1906** Naval ram (modern)
> **1910** Bulbous bow

Naval rams and bulbous bows are located at the leading edge of the bow, at or below the waterline. Ancient naval rams were timber with heavy metal sheathing and were intended to puncture the hull of target vessels in a deliberate collision. Using a ram effectively requires the manoeuvrability to accurately strike the target vessel and then reverse, letting water flood the damaged hull. The manoeuvrability requirement means that naval rams are only suitable for vessels powered by oar or motor and not by sail.

Use of a ram requires survivability to close with the target vessel before incurring disabling damage. Rams on wooden-hulled vessels became ineffective under sufficient weight, volume and accuracy of cannon fire. The expansion of naval gunnery made ramming obsolete in Europe by 1571. Naval rams briefly returned as weapons of naval warfare in 1862 with the introduction of armoured steam warships, but were only effective while gunnery was unable to penetrate armoured hulls.

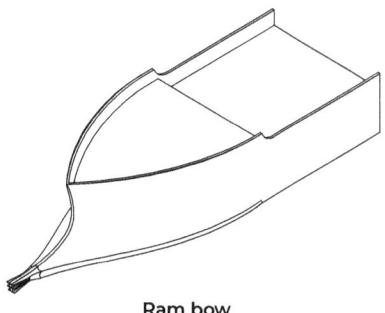

Ram bow

The modern naval ram quickly became obsolete as a weapon, but a

BOW AREA

projection before the bow does have hydrodynamic benefits and large vessels began to carry a bulbous bow.

When a vessel is moving forward the leading edge of the bow pushes up a wave that the length of the hull must pass through. The wave pattern has more surface area of water in contact with the hull and therefore more drag acting to slow the forward speed. Adding a bulbous bow as a projection ahead of the bow creates a second wave at 180 degrees to the first wave, cancelling out both waves to reduce drag.

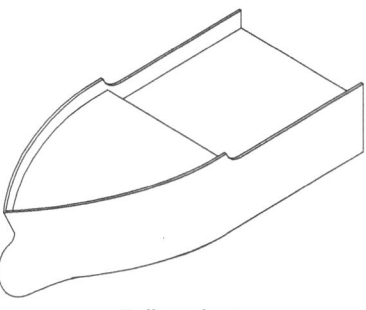
Bulbous bow

Icebreaker bow

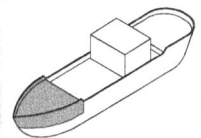

- Heavy sloping bow → Icebreaker

> **1864** European-style icebreaking bow
> **1888** American-style icebreaking bow with single bow propeller
> **1933** Runeberg bow
> **1956** American-style icebreaking bow with twin bow propellers

Icebreakers are designed with sloping and reinforced bows. The vessel pushes the heavy bow on top of the ice plate, using the downward force of its weight to split the ice. American-style icebreakers include one or more propellers at the bow. European-style icebreakers do not have propellers at the bow. The Runeberg bow is designed to break ice using a sharp cutting edge instead of the weight of the vessel.

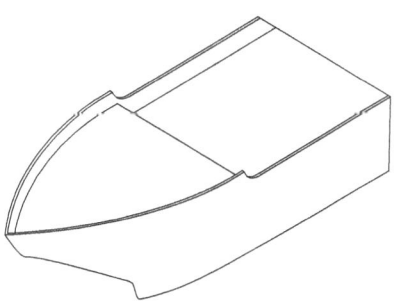
Icebreaker bow

THE SHIPWRECK DECODER

Sailing bow

- The subject of a bow decoration can indicate the civilisation it came from:
  - Lotus flower → Egyptian
  - Horse → Phoenician
  - Wolf or boar → Greek and Roman
  - Dragon or serpent → Viking (700–800)
  - Lion and dragon → Norman (1000–1100)
  - Swan → Northern Europe (1200–1300)
  - Mythical creature, human or animal → Western Europe (1500–1900)

1500–1800 Beakhead

- **Bowsprit:** spar projecting beyond the bow. The bowsprit provides an anchor for the ropes supporting the foremast, and may hold a spritsail.
- **Beakhead:** structure projecting forward of the bow beneath the bowsprit for sailors working on the bowsprit.
- **Figurehead:** a decorative element included for superstition or prestige. They are usually human or animal figures carved from or attached to the top of the bow stem and below the bowsprit (if present). Figureheads survived for a while on the bows of motorised iron vessels but went out of fashion by the early 20th century.

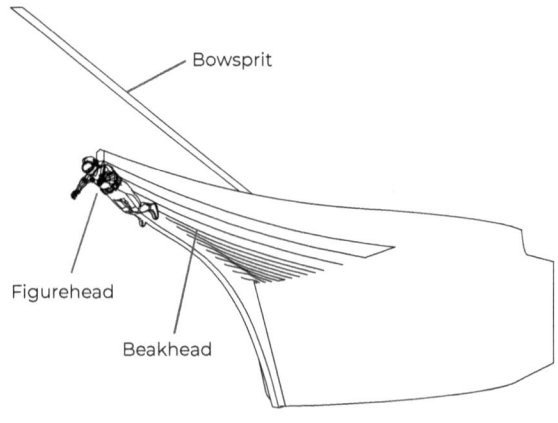

BOW AREA

Towing point

- Towing points (bit or pad eye) located at the apex of a sharp bow, or at either edge of a broad bow ➔ Intended to be wholly or partly propelled by being towed behind another vessel

Vessels designed to be towed will have one or more heavy bits, or pad eyes, located at the bow. If the towing cable needs to pass through the gunwale there will be a heavy guidance hole along the line of the cable.

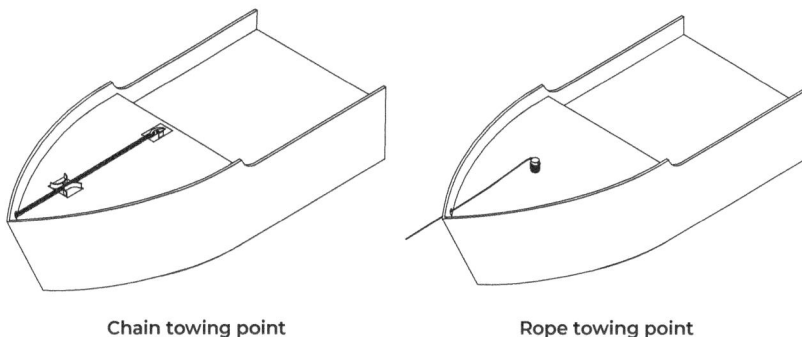

Chain towing point   Rope towing point

Bow thruster

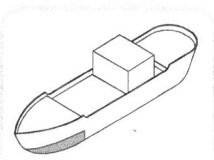

- Bow thruster ➔ Motorised vessel

A lateral propeller fitted within a tube located towards the bow to aid manoeuvring on motorised vessels.

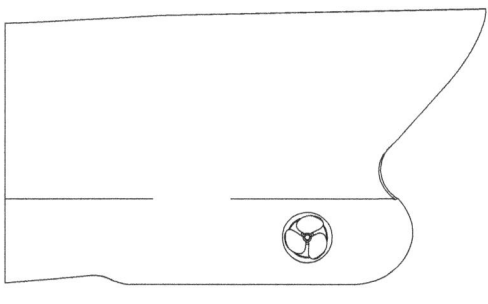

Bow thruster

41

THE SHIPWRECK DECODER

Anchors

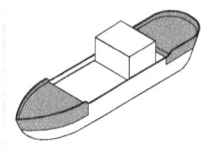

The anchor is a device weighted and shaped to connect the vessel to the seabed in order to prevent it from drifting. Holding force is provided by a combination of weight, friction, and contact or embedding in the seabed. Anchors are usually located at the bow, and occasionally supplemented by additional anchors at the stern.

- **Pre-history** Stone
- **700 BCE** Hook (one-arm), wood with stone stock (Mediterranean)
- **500 BCE** Lead-cored wood stock (Mediterranean)
- **500 BCE** Two-arm, wood with stone stock (Mediterranean)
- **300 BCE** Iron shank (Mediterranean)
- **300 BCE** Cast lead stock (Mediterranean)
- **50** Iron shank (Northern Europe)
- **900** Two-arms, wood with stone stock (East Asia)
- **1320** Grapnel with iron shank and arms (East Asia)
- **1450** Admiralty longshank, straight arms
- **1815** Admiralty pattern (fisherman), curved arms and wood/metal stock
- **1852** Trotman (articulated admiralty)
- **1886** Hall (stockless)
- **1933** CQR (plough)
- **1939** Danforth (spade)
- **1972** Bruce (claw)

The anchor must be shaped to provide maximum resistance while in use, but also be recoverable. Pre-19th century anchors can be dated by the mix of materials (stone, wood, metal) used. Designs from the 19–20th century can be specifically dated from records of their invention and patenting.

Stone and composite anchors
- **Stone ring anchor:** stone shaped into a circle with a single hole to pass a rope through.

BOW AREA

- **Simple stone anchor:** stone shaped with a single hole to pass a rope through.
- **Composite anchor:** stone shaped into a triangle with a single hole to pass a rope through at the apex, and one or two holes or rectangular slots for wooden flukes at the base.
- **Far-Eastern stone anchor:** stone shaped into a squat rectangular block with a continuous shallow recess around four faces to hold a cinched rope loop.
- **Indo-Arabian stone anchor:** stone shaped into a long rectangular block, tapering at one end. The narrow end has a single hole to pass a rope through. The wider end has a rectangular slot on each face for a wooden fluke.
- **Hook (one-armed anchor):** a wooden arm, as simple as a natural tree branch, digs into the seabed for improved holding. The stone stock mounted on the arm side gives the anchor a better chance of landing hook-down, perpendicular to the arm, keeping it vertical until it digs in, and weighted (stone or lead) to help push the arm into the bottom.
- **Two-armed anchor (wood and stone or metal):** a stock mounted perpendicular to the arms, forces the anchor to rotate into a position where one arm digs in, improving holding power and stability on the bottom.

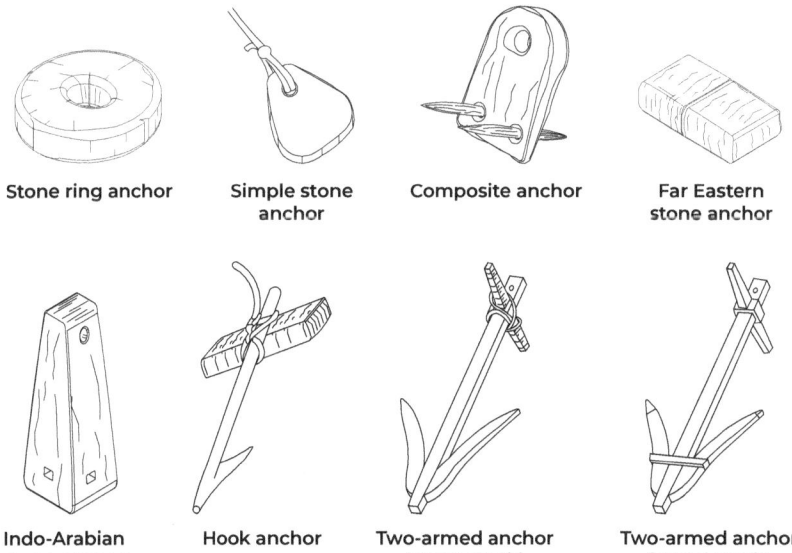

Stone ring anchor | Simple stone anchor | Composite anchor | Far Eastern stone anchor

Indo-Arabian stone anchor | Hook anchor | Two-armed anchor (stone stock) | Two-armed anchor (metal stock)

THE SHIPWRECK DECODER

Modern anchors

- **Ring or shackle:** attachment point for the anchor line. Ring suggests the anchor was used with rope. Shackle suggests the anchor was used with chain.
- **Stock:** wood or metal (lead, iron, steel) crosspiece located at the ring end of the shank and oriented perpendicular to the arms. The stock orients the arms to dig into the seabed.
- **Shank:** central shaft of the anchor between the ring and the crown.
- **Crown:** point where the arms join the shank. The crown may be fixed or hinged.
- **Arms:** shaped to dig into the seabed and provide resistance. Most marine anchors have two arms. Curved arms improve the mechanics of the initial set (tendency to bury under own weight) and break-out (reduced resistance) compared to straight arms.
- **Fluke:** pointed or shaped end of the arm that sets (i.e. buries) in the seabed.
- **Grapnel anchor:** an anchor designed with four or five arms.
- See also Stern (kedge) anchor in the Stern chapter, on page 69.

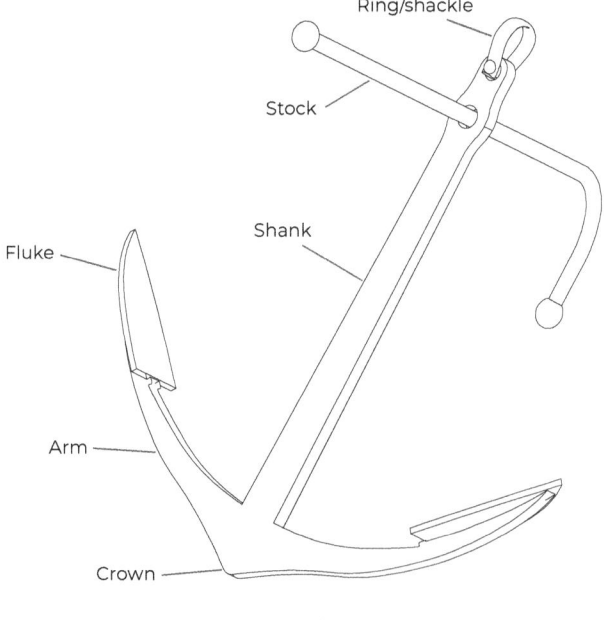

Generic anchor

BOW AREA

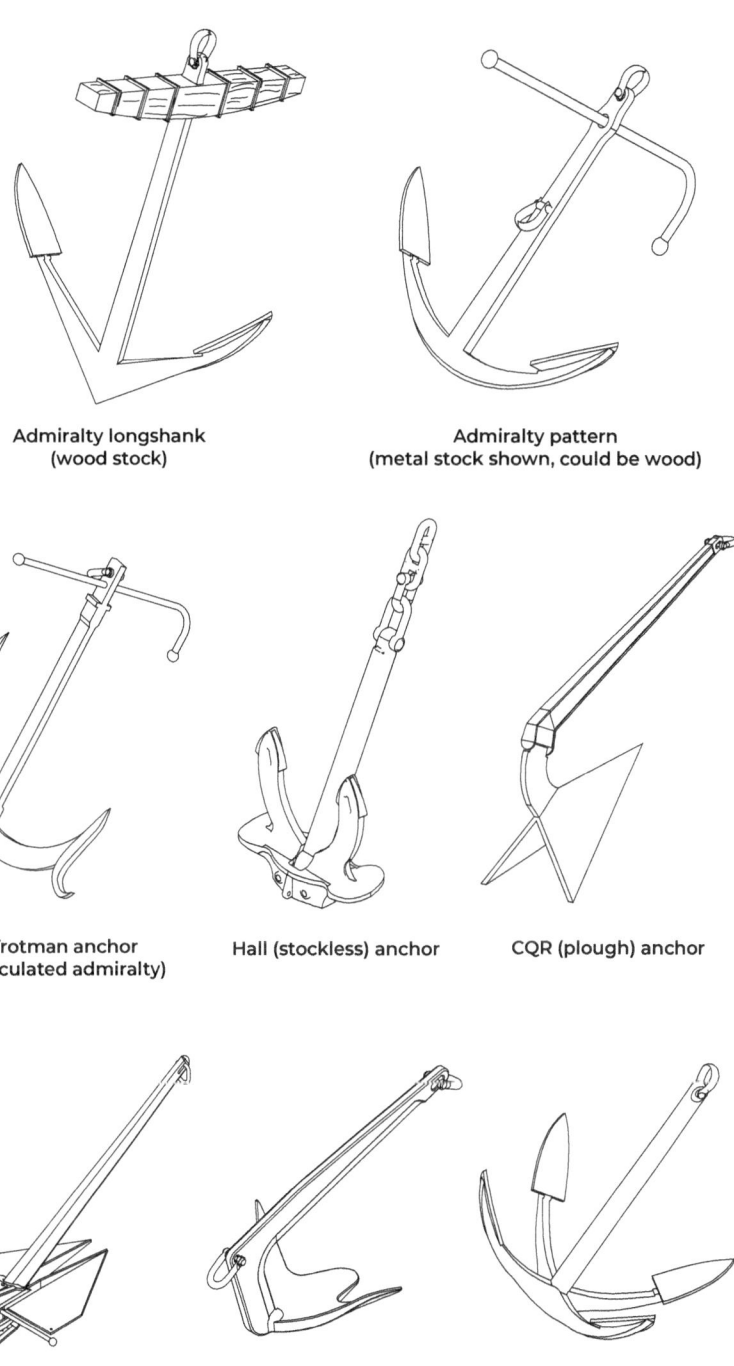

Anchor mechanism

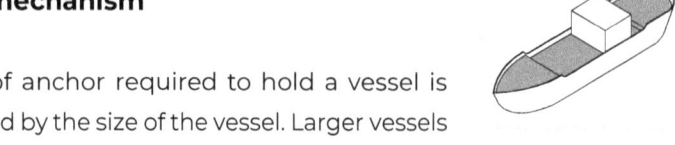

The size of anchor required to hold a vessel is determined by the size of the vessel. Larger vessels require larger anchors and thicker anchor lines. In small vessels it is possible to raise an anchor by hand, but for larger vessels, anchors can weigh several tonnes and will require mechanical assistance.

Pre-steam sailing vessels used large capstans (see page 82) worked by several men to raise the anchors. The capstan was located midships, usually on the main or gun deck. With engine technology, anchors are raised by large windlasses located on the forecastle. The engine may be located adjacent to or on the deck beneath the windlass.

The anchor cable is pulled in through the hawse hole/pipe by the windlass and stored in the chain locker. Stocked anchors were then stowed hanging from a cathead or derrick, and later stockless anchors are stowed directly in the end of the hawse pipe.

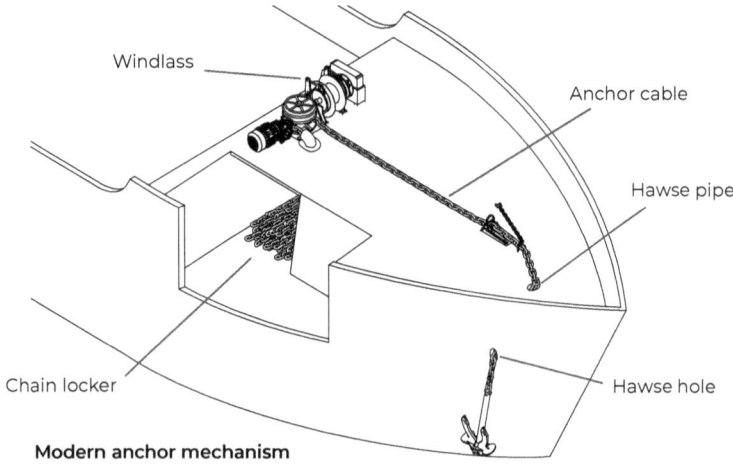

Modern anchor mechanism

- **Anchor cable (rode or warp):** chain, rope, or a combination of both strong enough to connect the anchor to the vessel and absorb the energy of vessel movement without breaking. Rope is capable of absorbing energy by stretching and contracting. Metal chain provides additional weight and friction resistance, and by applying weight at the anchor shackle will reduce the angle between the shank and seabed. If used in combination, the chain will be connected between the anchor shackle and cable. The anchor cable includes any connections such as a swivel or shackle.

- **Hawse hole:** holes through the hull on the forecastle through which the anchor line passes. When chain began to be used for anchor lines it became necessary to reinforce and extend hawse holes to prevent the chain sawing away the wooden hull. They became metal tubes.
- **Hawse pipe:** metal tube between the hawse hole and winching mechanism. When used with stockless anchors the hawse pipe may end in a recessed and shielded area on the outer hull where the anchor is stored with the shaft drawn fully inside the hawse pipe.
- **Chain locker:** compartment located in the bow for storage of the anchor chain. Will have drainage holes to release water, and may still contain piles of heavy rope and chain.
- **Cathead:** heavy wooden beam projecting out at an angle from the bow a little behind the hawse hole and supporting a heavy tackle block. The cat tackle is attached to the anchor ring and used to hoist and secure the stock end of the anchor from the hawse hole to the cathead ('catting'). The fish tackle is attached to an arm and used to lift the anchor to its horizontal storage position ('fishing'). When the anchor is needed the process is reversed.

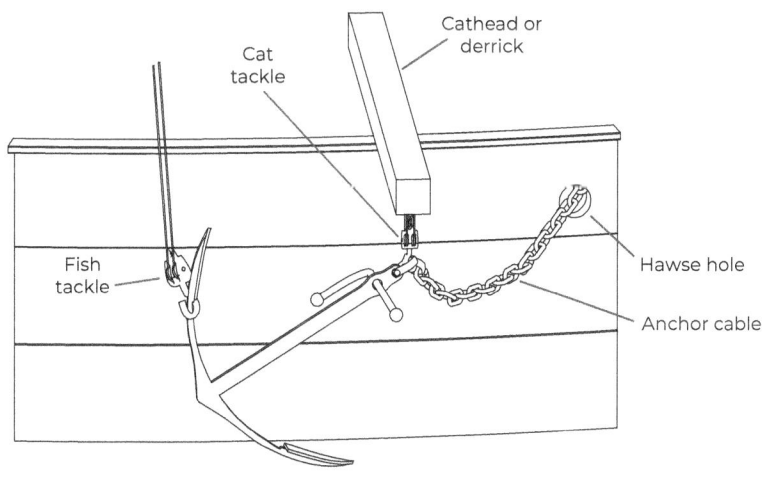

Cathead anchor mechanism

- **Derrick:** ships constructed in the intermediate period where metal parts were increasingly used on otherwise wooden hulled vessels, but still using stocked anchors, may have used a metal derrick to secure the anchor instead of the wooden cathead.

Permanent moorings

Permanent moorings are anchors that do not need to be easily recoverable.
- **Single fluke anchor:** this anchor is more difficult to set but once in place it is less at risk of being dragged out of place.
- **Mushroom anchor:** this anchor has a bowl shaped head with centrally fixed shank that can set at any angle.

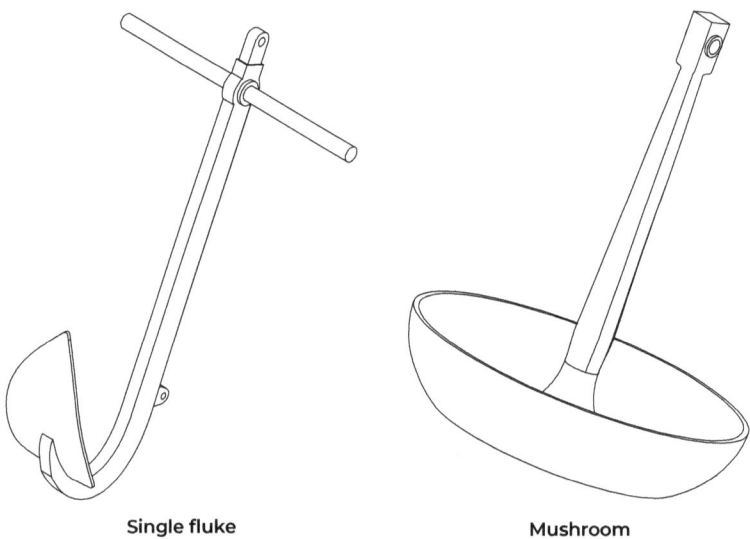

Single fluke   Mushroom

CHAPTER 4
STERN: PROPULSION/ STEERING

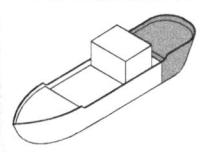

The design and equipment of a vessel's stern are shaped by operational needs and hydrodynamic principles. Primary functions of propulsion and manoeuvring—including midship systems for completeness—are integrated while balancing key effects like wake size, slamming (as defined in Chapter 3), and squatting.

- Transom shape
  - Flat ➤ More wake and drag (less efficient speed), more buoyancy, more deck space
  - Taper/point ➤ Less wake and drag (more efficient speed), less buoyancy, less deck space
  - Round/elliptical ➤ Compromise between wake, buoyancy and deck space
- Transom angle
  - Vertical ➤ Plumb stern: more space, worse squatting and slamming
  - Inclined forward ➤ Raked stern: better speed, reduced squatting and slamming

- **Wake size:** the wave created by the closure of water behind a moving vessel leading to turbulence and drag.
- **Squatting:** the change of trim a vessel experiences when it moves through the water where the flow speed under the hull sucks the stern downward.

Basic shapes

The basic shape of the stern area is a compromise between buoyancy, hydrodynamic efficiency, operational space requirements, and length. The design can tell a story of its prioritisation between speed efficiency and operational space requirements. The stern's shape determines the flow of water as it leaves the hull, with implications for the size of the wake and the flow of water past the rudder(s) and any propeller(s). Higher wakes create more drag so the stern should be designed to reduce the wake. Turbulent water flowing past the rudders and propellers degrades their performance, so the stern should be designed to channel water cleanly past these features.

- **Transom shape:** the horizontal shape where the port and starboard sides of the hull meet at the stern. The vessel may have a discrete transom at and below the waterline, and a counter above the waterline. A flat transom provides more buoyancy to reduce squatting but causes more wake. It also provides more deck space. A tapered stern produces a smoother water flow, less wake and drag, but has less buoyancy to resist submergence from following waves (pooping). A round or elliptical stern is a compromise between reducing wake and maximising deck space.
- **Transom angle (rake):** the vertical angle of the transom. A raked (backward overhung) design reduces squatting and slamming by letting the stern submerge gradually. A long counter stern (overhang) can help distribute the stern wave over a longer length, increasing waterline length at speed for better efficiency. A plumb (vertical) stern maximises waterline length for efficiency, but increases squatting and slamming.
- **Counter/overhang:** the overhang behind the rudder and above the waterline. Provides additional reserve buoyancy and deck space.
- **Stern flare:** an outward spreading curve of the stern sides above the waterline. Flare high on the stern increases poopdeck width, helps the stern lift over following waves and reduces squatting. Excessive flare can cause slamming in heavy seas.
- **Poopdeck camber:** the curvature of the poopdeck if the centre is higher than the sides. Camber helps water drain off the poopdeck.

STERN: PROPULSION/STEERING

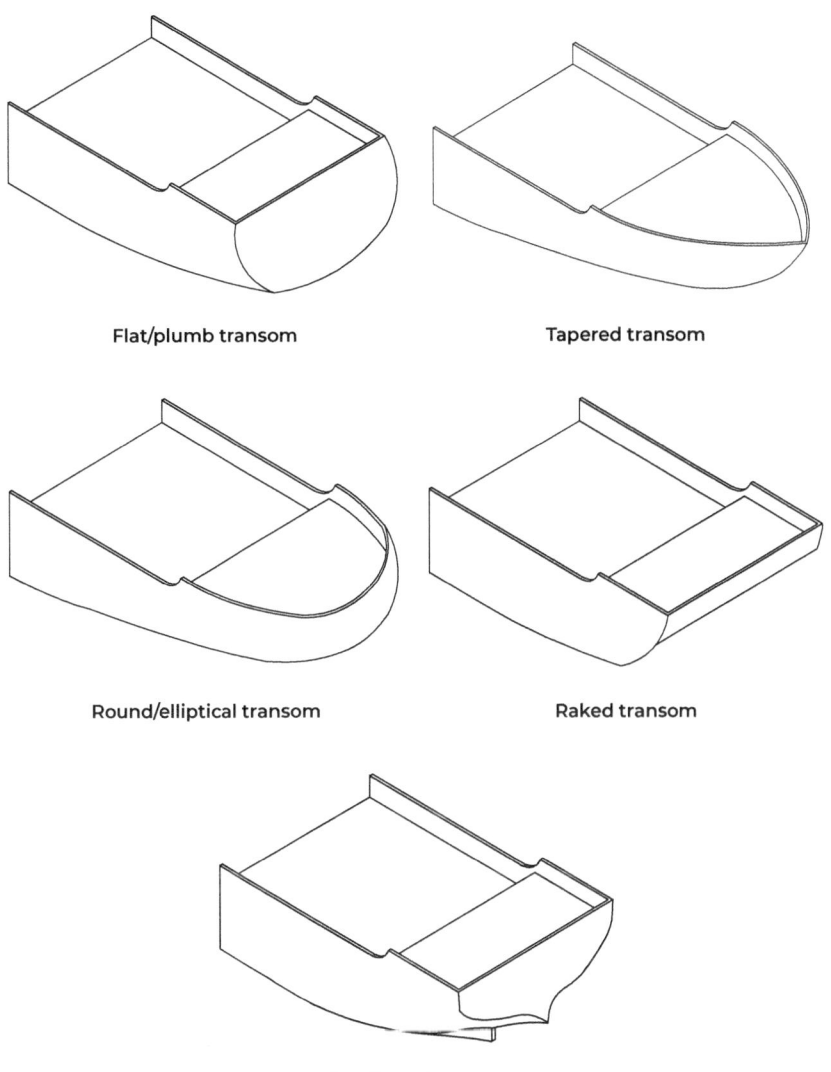

Flat/plumb transom

Tapered transom

Round/elliptical transom

Raked transom

Overhung transom

Rudder

- Number of rudders
- Location relative to hull
- Location relative to propeller
- Profile shape
- Cross-section shape
- Width at leading edge, trailing edge, widest point
- Height at leading edge, trailing edge, highest point
- Position of stock, balance

c.25 Stern mounted rudder (China)
1150 Pintle and gudgeon stern rudder (Europe)
Pre-1200 Greco-Roman rudder
c.1200 Medieval rudder (Europe)
1833 Balanced stern rudder

The rudder is a plane surface that can be angled to turn the vessel. When the rudder is at an angle to the direction of flow, water striking the side with the smaller angle relative to the hull will have higher pressure compared to the side with the greater angle. The pressure difference moves the rudder towards the lower pressure side and away from the new direction of travel. The force on the rudder pulls the stern out of the line of travel so that the hull pivots around the bow until it is facing the new direction. This is why a ship is steered from the back.

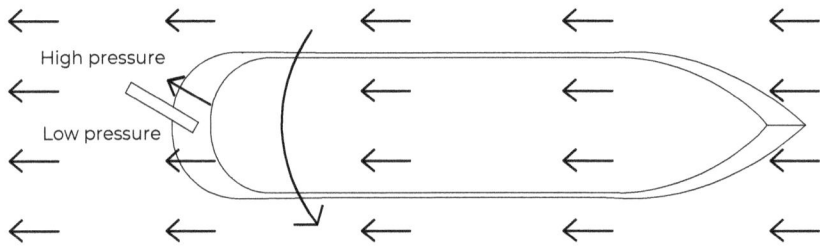

Effect of rudder position on vessel

STERN: PROPULSION/STEERING

Rudder assembly
- **Rudder plate/blade:** the main part of the rudder that provides the surface area to deflect water flow. A rudder plate is a flat board while a rudder blade is a shaped hydrofoil.
- **Rudder post:** a vertical beam or post that is the fixed structural component of the hull to which the rudder is attached, i.e. where gudgeons are mounted or a pintle is held.
- **Rudderstock:** a vertical shaft connected to or passing through the rudder blade and rotated by the steering assembly. This is the component that pivots the rudder blade.
- **Rudder trunk:** sheath around the rudderstock between the hull and the top of the rudder blade.

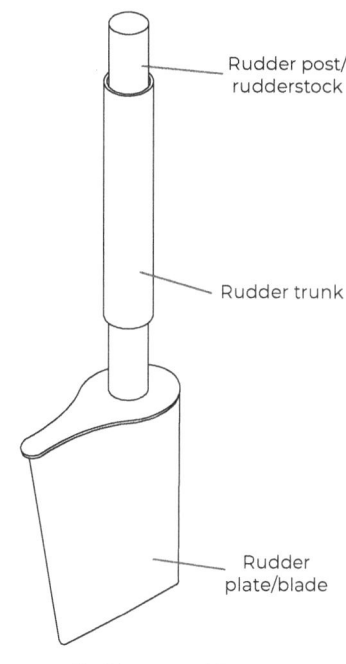

Rudder assembly

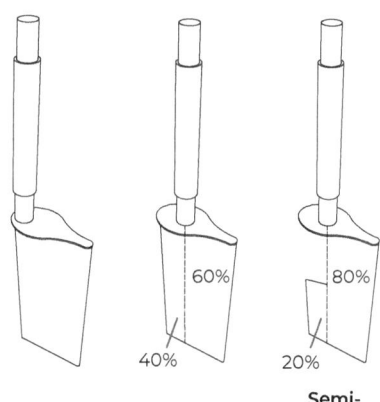

Unbalanced   Balanced   Semi-balanced

Rudderstock positions
- **Unbalanced:** the rudder blade is completely behind the rudderstock. Requires more torque to turn.
- **Balanced rudder:** 20–40% of the rudder blade is forward of the rudderstock. A balanced rudder does not require torque to keep specific angles, and requires less torque around those angles.
- **Semi-balanced:** up to 20% of the rudder blade is forward of the rudderstock. This may be achieved by placement of the rudderstock

towards but not at the leading edge of the rudder, or by combining an unbalanced top half with a balanced bottom half of the rudder blade. A semi-balanced rudder requires less torque to keep specific angles.

Mounting types
- **Pintle:** a support bolt or pin with a bearing located along the length of the rudder. There may be one or more pintles.
- **Pintle and gudgeon stern rudder:** an interim technology before the invention of metal rudderstocks. In this design the rudder is mounted at the stern, using a metal ring (gudgeon) and bolt (pintle) hinge.

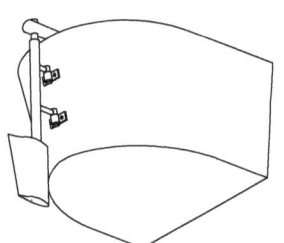
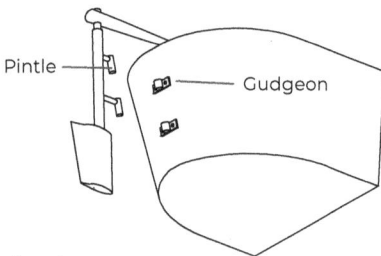

Pintle and gudgeon

- **Spade/hanging rudder:** the rudderstock is attached by a single pintle at the top.
- **Lower pintle rudder:** the rudderstock is attached by pintles at the top and bottom.
- **Mariner rudder:** the rudderstock is attached by a single pintle towards the centre of the rudder.

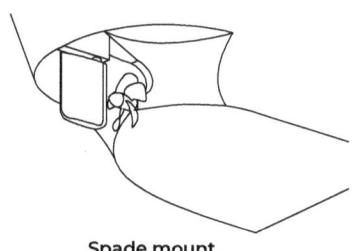

Spade mount

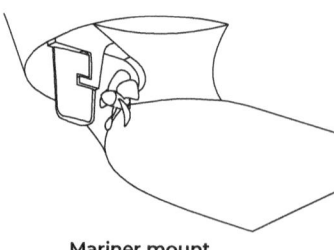

Mariner mount

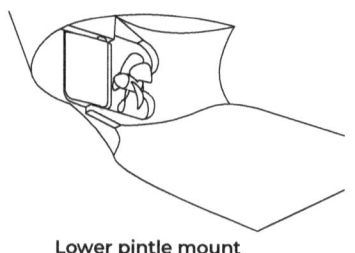

Lower pintle mount

STERN: PROPULSION/STEERING

Rudder layouts
- **Quarter-rudder:** the rudder is mounted via a rudder post on the side of the hull in the stern quarter. The earliest large vessels of antiquity used this rudder system.

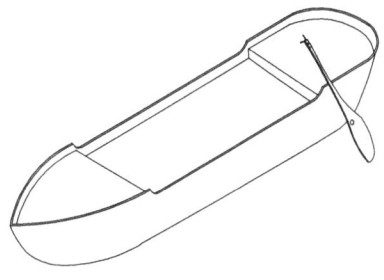
Quarter-rudder

- **Stern mounted rudder:** the rudder is mounted via a rudderstock at the stern.
- **Twin rudders:** two rudders mounted at the stern provide a lot of turning force where manoeuvrability is required (e.g. harbour tugs).

Rudder types
- **Greco-Roman rudder:** the rudder post is centrally located on the flat rudder plate, like an oversized paddle. Used in the quarter-rudder layout.
- **Medieval rudder:** the rudder post is located at the leading edge of the rudder plate (unbalanced). Used in the quarter-rudder layout. Due to being thicker than the rudder plate the rudderstock began to act as a hydrofoil, improving performance. May taper towards the trailing edge.
- **Norse rudder:** the rudder post is centrally located on the foil-shaped rudder blade. The rudder blade may have a sharp or extended point at the bottom of the trailing edge to reduce turbulence. Used in the quarter-rudder layout.
- **Modern stern rudder:** foil-shaped rudder blade with rudderstock used in the stern-mounted or twin layout.

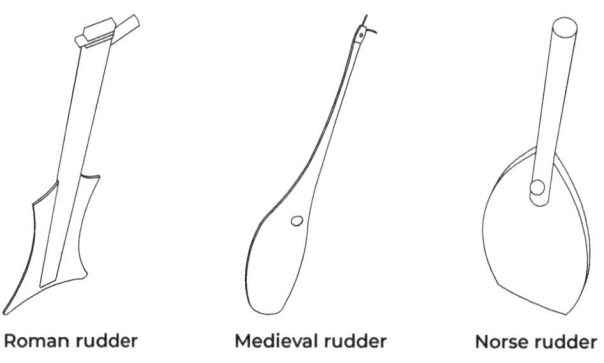
Roman rudder   Medieval rudder   Norse rudder

Steering assembly

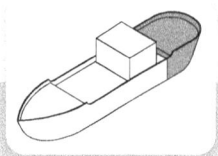

- 1628 Whipstaff and rowl
- 1705 Ship's wheel
- 1740 Double ship's wheel
- 1771 Quadrant
- c.1800 Ship's wheel and screw
- 1866–1930 Steam engine
- 1944 Hydraulic ram
- 1952 Hydraulic rotary vane

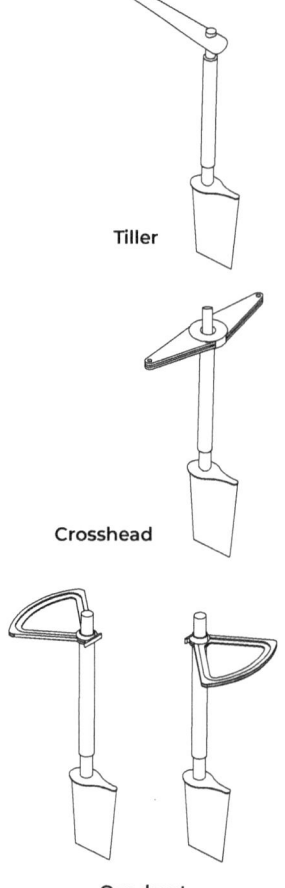

Tiller

Crosshead

Quadrant

- **Tiller:** horizontal bar lever used to turn the rudder. The rudder end of the tiller is the tillerhead, which attaches to the rudderhead, extending the axis of the rudder beyond the rudder post. The other end of the tiller is operated by the helmsman.
- **Crosshead:** horizontal bar lever used to turn the rudder. The center of the crossbar is attached to the rudderhead, perpendicular to the axis of the rudder. Force can be applied to either end of the crosshead.
- **Quadrant:** arc lever used to turn the rudder. The convergent point of the arc attaches to the rudderhead. The arc can be forward or aft of the rudderstock. The use of an arc ensures constant line tension around the arc of rudder positions.
- **Whipstaff and rowle:** an interim European technology used in the period between (a) when ships became too tall for a helmsman at the tiller at the stern to receive direct communications from the officer of the deck, and (b) when the steering wheel was invented. The whipstaff is a

STERN: PROPULSION/STEERING

vertical lever operated by a helmsmen, passing down through one or more decks, pivoting on a bearing (the rowle), and attached to the tiller on a lower deck.

- **Ship's wheel and barrel:** developed as ships became too tall and rudders too large for a whipstaff and rowle. The ship's wheel is immediately forward of the barrel and they share a common axle. The barrel is likely to have a protective case. Port and starboard lines or chains are wrapped around the barrel in opposite directions. The lines run down to the level of the tiller, spread out to pulleys on each side, and then attach to either side of the tiller. When the ship's wheel is turned to starboard the barrel wraps in the starboard line and lets out the port line, pulling the tiller to starboard so that the rudder and vessel turn to port. The ship's wheel can be operated by two people, one on either side. The pulleys may be compounded to increase mechanical advantage for turning larger rudders.

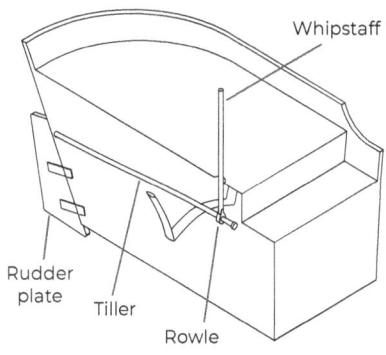

Whipstaff and rowle

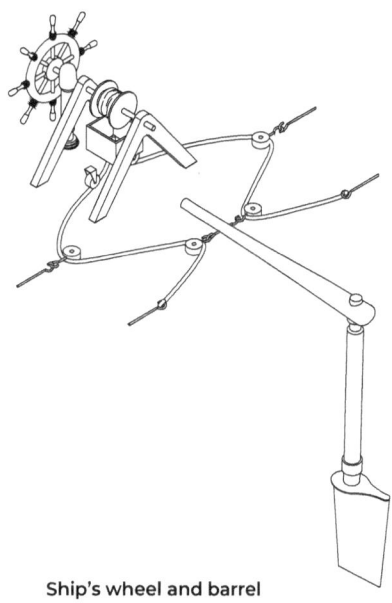

Ship's wheel and barrel

- **Double ship's wheel:** an additional ship's wheel can be added to the axle before the barrel so four people can operate the steering assembly, one on either side of each wheel.

- **Ship's wheel and screw:** one half of the screw has a left-handed thread and the other half has a right-handed thread. Nuts on each half of the screw are connected by chain through the quadrant and move in opposite directions when the screw is turned. One nut moves to pull the chain while the other nut moves to relax the chain, turning the quadrant and rudder. Alternatively the nuts may be linked by connecting rods to a cross-head to the same effect.
- **Steering engine:** the earliest version of powered (as opposed to manual) steering gear used steam engines (see page 112 onwards). Gearing from the engine shaft drives a toothed quadrant to position the rudder.

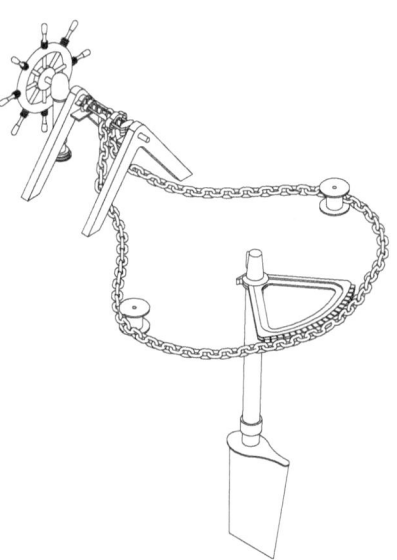

Ship's wheel and screw

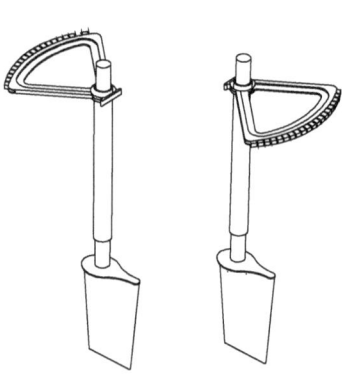

Quadrant
(for use with steering engine)

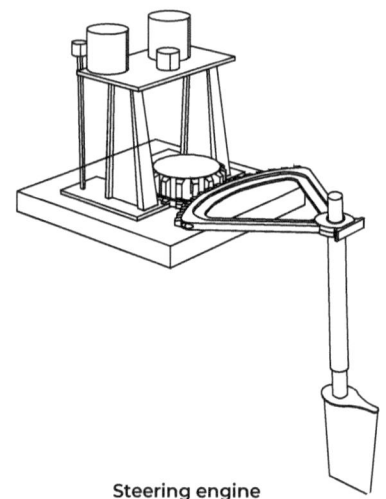

Steering engine

STERN: PROPULSION/STEERING

- **Hydraulic ram:** two or more electrically controlled hydraulic rams move the crosshead. Requires a connected pump unit.
- **Hydraulic rotary vane:** a rotor with fixed vanes attached to the rudderhead sits within a stator housing attached to the hull. Oil is pumped through the chamber to turn the rotor, turning the rudder and the vessel. Requires a connected pump unit.

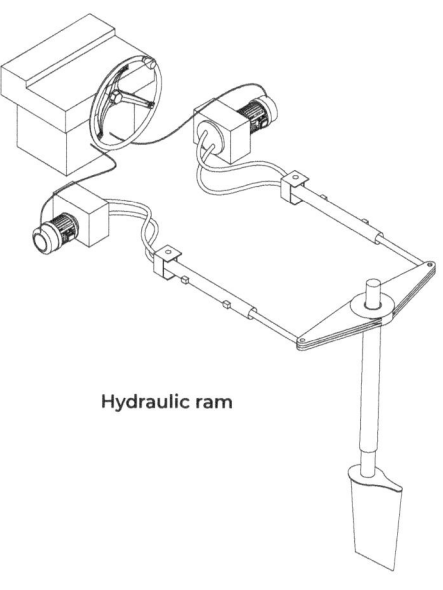

Hydraulic ram

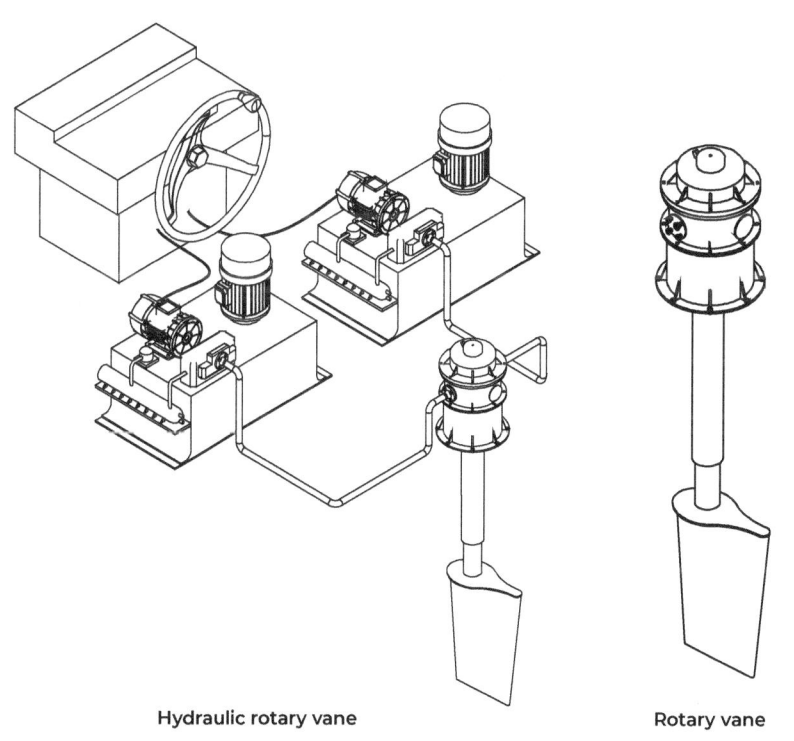

Hydraulic rotary vane

Rotary vane

THE SHIPWRECK DECODER

Leeboard

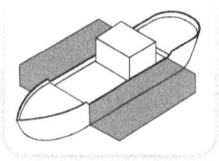

- Large and flat paddle-shaped board, disconnected from the hull or connected by only a single pivot point at the narrower end ➔ Leeboard ➔ Suggests a shallow draft vessel such as a barge

> **759** Chinese leeboard
> **1570** European leeboard

Lowerable board located midships on both sides of a shallow-draft craft without a fixed keel. The leeboard on the leeward (downwind) side of the vessel can be rotated or lowered into the water to reduce lateral drift to that side.

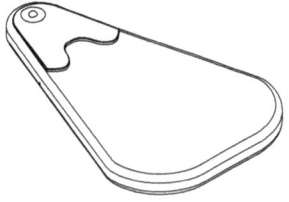

Leeboard

Reduction gearbox

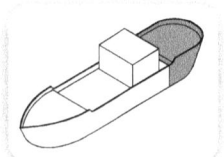

- The gearbox will be located between the engine and propeller assembly, close to the engine
- Heavy metal casing with shafts entering from opposite sides and offset to each other

> **1786, 1826 (likely)** Reduction gearbox

Marine gearboxes convert the (engine side) high-speed low-torque rotation of the thrust shaft; to the (paddle or propeller side) low-speed high-torque rotation of the tail shaft.

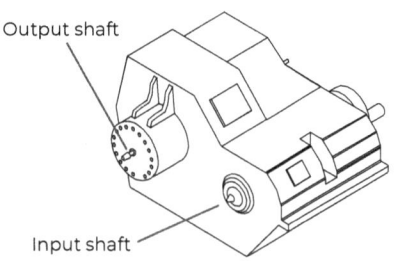

Reduction gearbox

STERN: PROPULSION/STEERING

Paddlewheel

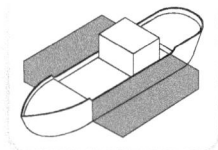 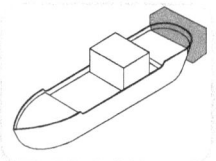

- Large spoked wheels, axles and/or bearings located on the outside of the main hull
- Side wheel coverings or guards

> **1704–1959 (likely 1802–1846)** Steam-driven paddle wheel
> **1829** Feathered paddlewheel

The paddlewheel evolved from rowed propulsion and essentially consists of a continuous series of oars. The first marine engines were used to drive paddlewheels until they were replaced by the invention of propellers.

The paddlewheels could be mounted at the stern (sternwheeler), or on either side of the hull (sidewheeler). Sternwheelers were mostly used on the Mississippi River.

There is an interesting history of manually-driven paddlewheel vessels: by teams of men in China from approximately 420 to 1900, and by teams of horses in the United States from approximately 1791 to 1925.

- **Feathered paddlewheel:** a late development where the paddles are hinged and their orientation controlled by linkages to the central hub. This keeps the paddle vertical for the whole submerged sector of the revolution, and prevents churn as the paddles leave the water.

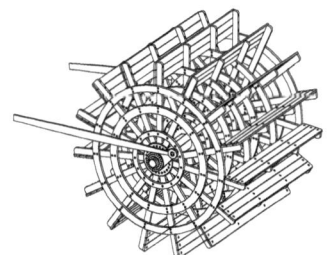 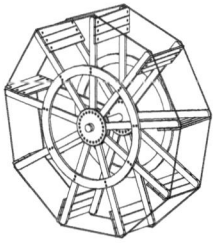 

Stern paddlewheel	Side paddlewheel	Feathered paddlewheel

Propeller

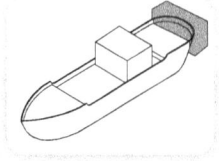

- Number of blades ➤ Vessel sensitivity to noise and vibrations
- Blade diameter, pitch and rake ➤ In combination with engine power define performance characteristics of the propulsion unit
- Blades have fixed or variable connection to the hub ➤ Suggests the range of speeds and directions at which the vessel required full power
- Cavitation damage

> **1776** Archimedes screw (experimental)
> **1826** Bladed propeller

The propeller is a rotating blade angled to move in a spiral through water like a screw in wood. The force of water pushed behind the propeller generates propulsive force in the opposite direction, driving the vessel forward.

- **Propeller hub:** the core of a propeller with blades attached around the outside edge, and mounted over the end of the tail shaft.
- **Propeller blades:** shaped surfaces angled to create a pressure differential between the front and rear of the blade moving in a spiral path through the water.
  - **Handedness:** right-handed propellers have blades with the leading edge moving clockwise. Left-handed propellers have blades with the leading edge moving anti-clockwise.
  - **Diameter:** distance across a circle connecting the

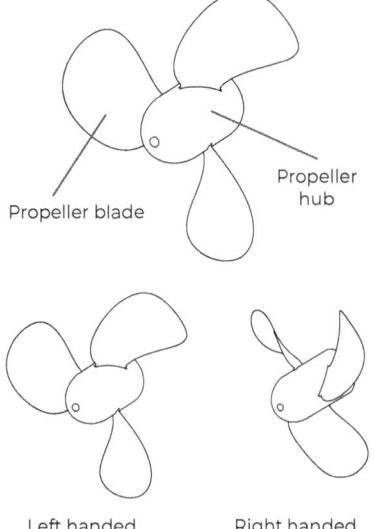

STERN: PROPULSION/STEERING

furthest edge of all blades. Larger diameter propellers move a larger volume of water but need a more powerful engine to take the load.

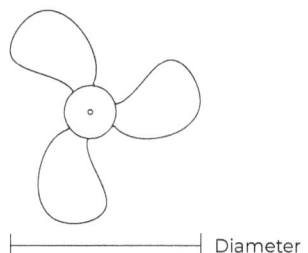

- **Pitch:** distance the propeller would move through the medium for each complete revolution. Pitch must be matched to the engine's recommended RPM at full throttle. Broadly-speaking, higher pitch gives higher speed for the same RPM.

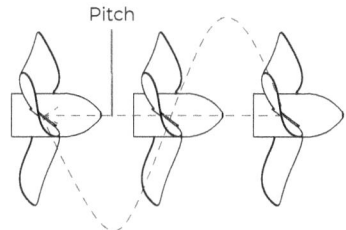

- **Rake:** the angle between the blade and the perpendicular to the propeller shaft. Negative rake offers stronger blades. Positive rake allows a larger diameter.

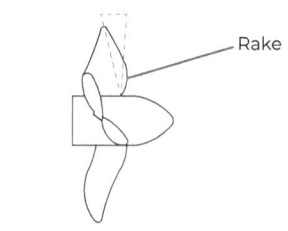

- **Cavitation:** water vaporising to gas at the trailing edge of a blade due to high-speed pressure changes.
  - **Cavitation damage:** pitting on the propeller, usually at the trailing edges, caused by cavitation gas pockets collapsing.

Propeller types

- **Archimedes screw:** an unbroken helical surface describing one or more complete rotations. The device looks like the spiral edge winding down a wood screw. Some early experimental powered vessels used Archimedes screws before bladed propellers were identified as having far greater efficiency.

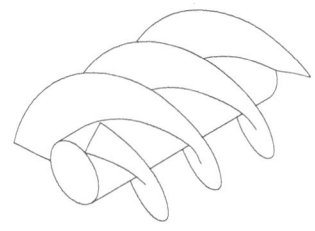

Archimedes screw

- **Bladed propeller:** blades placed at regular increments each describe a complete turn of the spiral when rotated. Some efficiency is lost due to friction as the leading edge moves through the water so that a single blade is the most efficient, but is unbalanced and therefore unstable. More blades can be added for greater stability, most commonly seen are two to five blades. More than three blades could mean vessel function is sensitive to noise and rotation (e.g. submarines for stealth, cruise liners for comfort, or technical vessels for stability, etc.).

Bladed propeller (two, three, four and five blades)

- **Fixed pitch blades:** the distance the propeller would move in one rotation through a soft solid is the "pitch". Most vessels will have fixed-pitch blades.
- **Variable pitch blades:** each blade is on a separate spindle that allows change of pitch. These systems are more complicated and expensive. This feature could mean the vessel needed full power at varying speeds, directions and resistances (e.g. tug, icebreaker, ferry, etc.).
- **Skewback propeller:** each blade curves back significantly and may overlap the base of the next blade. This shape reduces cavitation and therefore noise. The presence of skewback propellers could mean the vessel needed to reduce noise (e.g. for stealth in submarines).

Skewback propeller

STERN: PROPULSION/STEERING

Propeller assembly

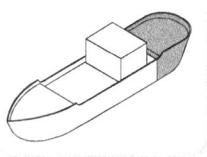

- Propeller assembly features ➔ Suggest the function and working environment of the vessel

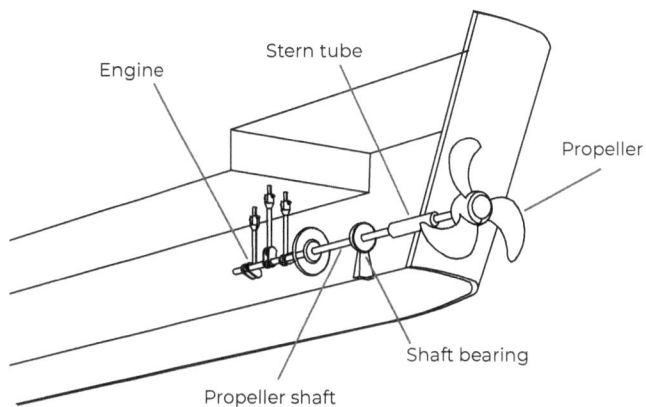

- **Stern tube:** a hollow tube containing bearings and grease around the propeller shaft, to allow the shaft to exit the hull and rotate at speed without flooding the hull.
- **Shaft bossing:** the propeller hub is positioned immediately at the opening of the propeller shaft tube, so that no part of the propeller shaft is exposed between the tube and the hub.
- **Bracket holder:** a bracket mounted at the end of a pillar or frame holds a length of propeller shaft that extends externally beyond the hull.

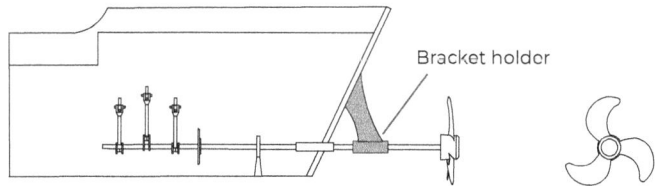

- **Propeller shaft:** rod transmitting mechanical rotational power from the engine to the propeller hub. Consists of three parts: (1) the thrust shaft emerging from the engine and receiving rotational motion from the crankshaft; (2) the tail shaft connecting the propeller hub to the gearbox and passing through the stern tube; and (3) intermediate

shaft(s) which bridge the distance between the thrust and tail shafts. Coupled bearings connect adjacent sections of shaft.
- **Shaft bearings:** run the length of the propeller shaft internal to the hull to support the weight of the shaft.
- **Ducted propeller:** a non-rotating tube surrounds the propeller to provide protection from damage and entanglement. This feature could mean the vessel needed to operate in shallow water or other environments where the propeller needed protection.

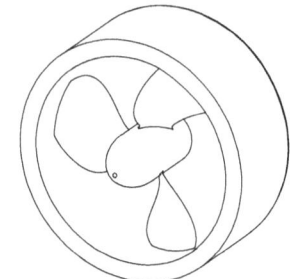

Ducted propeller

- **Azimuth propeller:** the propeller and end of the shaft assembly can be rotated for greater directional control. The propeller hub can be rotated horizontally as in an outboard motor. This feature suggests the propeller may be a thruster or the vessel needed greater directional control (e.g. harbour tugs).

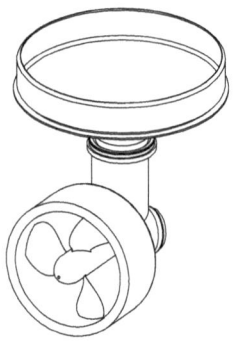

Azimuth propeller

Propeller configurations
- **Single, twin, or multiple propeller:** configurations with one or more propellers are used, each with a separate propeller shaft assembly and usually a dedicated engine system. Adding more engines and propellers to the same size vessel increases power and speed.

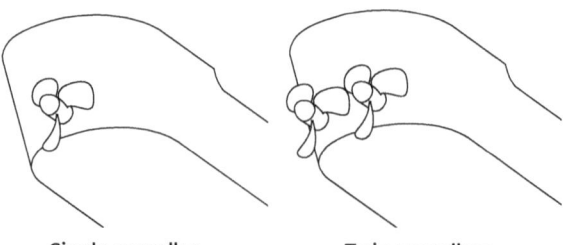

Single propeller   Twin propellers

STERN: PROPULSION/STEERING

- **Overlapping propellers:** two propellers rotating in the same direction, with shafts less than propeller diameter apart. There may be efficiency gains from the concentrated wake.
- **Tandem (co-rotating) propellers:** two propellers on a single shaft and turning in the same direction. Normally both propellers would have the same diameter and number of blades. The blades are angled in the same direction on both propellers. This layout suggests the vessel needed high power relative to its size.
- **Contra-rotating propellers:** two propellers on a single shaft or axis and turning in different directions. Normally the rearmost propeller will have a smaller diameter and fewer blades. The blades are angled in opposite directions on each propeller. This layout is useful to counter torque that would otherwise cause the hull of the vessel to drift sideways when turning. This layout suggests the vessel may have needed to travel with particular accuracy (e.g. torpedoes).

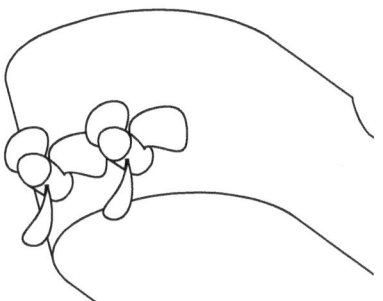

Overlapping propellers

Tandem propellers

Contra-rotating propellers

Voith Schneider propeller

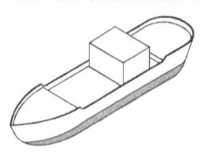

This propeller technology uses a horizontal rotating disk, with perpendicular and controllable hydrofoil blades mounted around the disk's circumference. Rotational speed of the disk determines the magnitude, and the blade angle determines the direction (of thrust). This propeller type is complex and expensive, but allows for very precise manoeuvring as well as primary propulsion.

- **Thrust plate:** a guard that acts as a nozzle at low speed, and protects the blades.

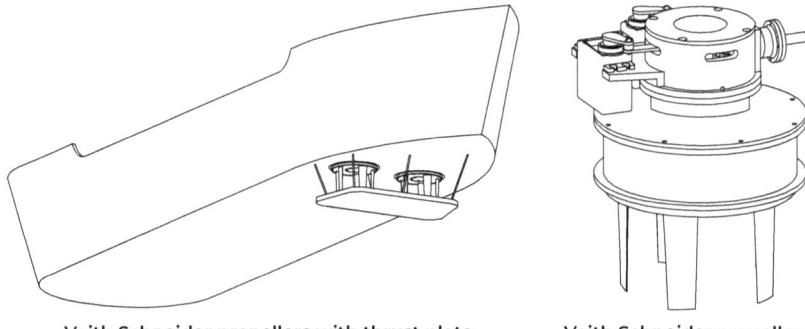

Voith Schneider propellers with thrust plate   Voith Schneider propeller

Propeller guards

- Propeller guards are located on the side of the hull above a propeller.

Propeller guards are reinforced frames to hold the stern off adjacent hard surfaces that might damage the propeller, e.g. a dock, ships coming alongside, or manoeuvring tugs.

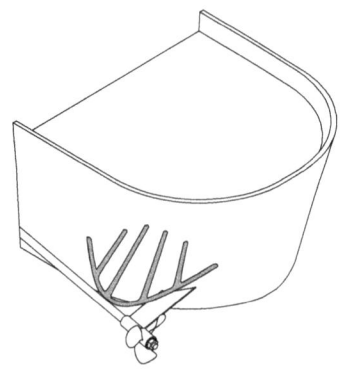

Propeller guard

STERN: PROPULSION/STEERING

Lifting screw

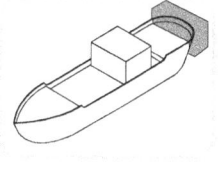

Some early warships powered by both steam and sail had propellers housed in a cradle that could be raised when the ship was under sail to reduce drag. Usually paired with a funnel that could be lowered. The reason for this system was partly lack of trust in the new steam engines, the relative efficiency of sail over underpowered steam engines for long voyages, and the unavailability of coal along distant patrol routes.

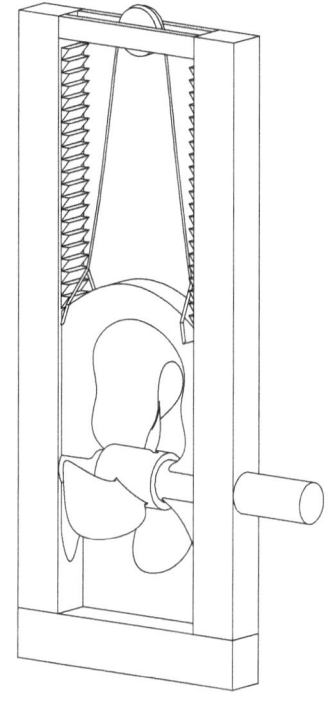

Lifting screw

Stern (kedge) anchor

An additional anchor and associated mechanisms located at the stern are usually for situations where the vessel needs to remain stationary, or manoeuvre in a restricted space (kedging). Using a stern anchor can prevent the vessel from swinging or drifting on the bow anchor.

CHAPTER 5
BRIDGE AREAS

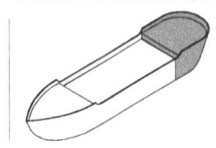

This chapter focuses on a generalised understanding of vessel command and control functions and their technological advancement. The chapter is divided into sections for instruments and gauges, navigation, and communications. Bridge equip-

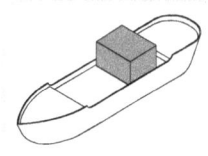

ment can carry an extra cache of symbolic value as part of the nerve-centre or brain of the vessel.

- **1855** Aluminium
- **1907** Plastic
- **1926** Circular CRT
- **1938** Rectangular CRT
- **1968** LCD; LED

Command, steering and navigation

Sailing vessels were typically commanded from the stern end of the main deck, from the quarterdeck if there was one. The helmsman would be located at the stern to operate the tiller. As the number of decks increased the helmsman would be located below the quarterdeck to operate the whipstaff, then on the quarterdeck to operate the ship's wheel. The ship's wheel may have been enclosed by a pilothouse.

When paddlewheels were added to the sides of the hull, their housings rose above the main deck and obstructed the view from the quarterdeck. To solve this problem, command was moved to a platform linking the top of the wheel housings as a 'bridge' over the main deck. The concept of a vessel's command area being located in the superstructure has been retained in modern ship design.

For vessels commanded from the quarterdeck, instruments would usually be housed in a box to be stored safely and taken out when needed. For vessels commanded from a bridge, larger instruments would usually be individually mounted in their housings and smaller instruments would usually be mounted on a panel.

BRIDGE AREAS

- **Pilothouse:** an enclosed space containing the ship's wheel and navigation equipment.
- **Compass platform:** on metal-hulled ships, a binnacle can be located on a platform raised above the deck or on the top surface of the superstructure. This prevents a magnetic compass being surrounded by metal walls, reducing the influence of the metal hull as much as possible.
- **Flying bridge:** an open platform located on top of the superstructure with duplicate bridge equipment.

Measurements from the various instruments consulted in command, steering and navigation will appear on a gauge or electronic display screen (unless read directly from the instrument). Instruments and gauges were traditionally made from brass and glass for salt tolerance, with later versions also made from aluminium and plastic. Electronic screens may be either cathode ray tube (CRT), light emitting diode (LED), or liquid crystal display (LCD). Expensive instruments and displays are often marked with the manufacturer's name, city, and sometimes year of production. The purpose of a gauge and display will usually be marked or labelled. The purpose of unlabelled gauges may be determined from the face markings (if readable). Autopilot, GPS, radar, sonar and echo sounder devices would be operated and read on electronic screens.

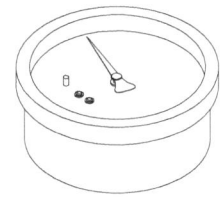
Mechanical gauge

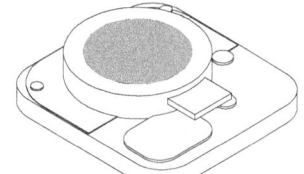
CRT screen (circular)

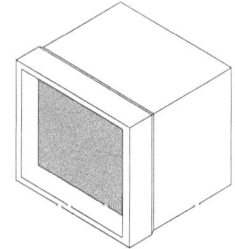
CRT screen (rectangular)

LCD screen

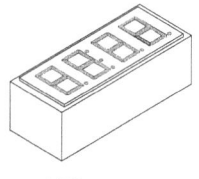
LED screen

THE SHIPWRECK DECODER

Instruments and gauges

- **1608** Telescope
- **1644** Mercury barometer
- **1661** Spirit level
- **1688** Taffrail log with directly mounted dial
- **1714** Mercury thermometer
- **1761** Marine chronometer
- **1825** Binoculars
- **1844** Aneroid barometer
- **1845** Four cup anemometer
- **1887** Taffrail log with separated dial
- **1899** Pitometer log
- **1913** Echo sounder
- **1926** Three cup anemometer
- **1991** Anemometer with directional vane

- **Mercury barometer (air pressure):** an instrument to measure atmospheric pressure by the rise and fall of mercury within a vertical tube. The vertical tube is closed at the top, submerged and open at the bottom to an atmosphere exposed reservoir of mercury. Higher atmospheric pressure on the reservoir forces mercury higher in the tube.
- **Aneroid barometer (air pressure):** an instrument to measure atmospheric pressure by the expansion of a flexible metal box, translated mechanically by springs to needle position on a gauge face marked with a sequential numerical range beginning from zero and possibly a secondary range at a greater level of sensitivity. There may also be words indicating weather conditions, and/or a secondary needle adjustable by a knob.

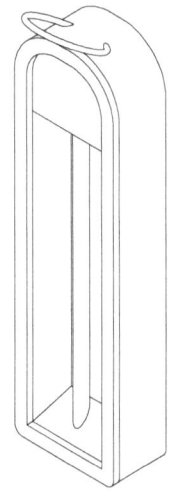

Mercury barometer

BRIDGE AREAS

- **Anemometer (wind speed/direction):** an instrument to measure wind speed by the rotation of evenly placed cups. May also measure wind direction via the orientation of a vane. An associated gauge would have a unidirectional needle, and a gauge face marked with a sequential numerical range beginning from zero.

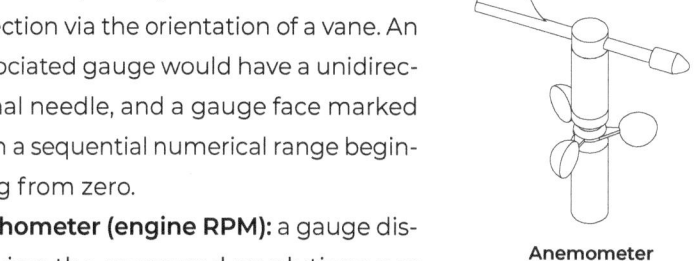

Anemometer

- **Tachometer (engine RPM):** a gauge displaying the measured revolutions per minute of the propeller shaft. The gauge would have a needle, and the face would be marked from zero.
- **Rudder angle indicator:** a gauge displaying the rudder's position relative to its neutral (zero degree) position. It would have a bidirectional needle, and the face would be marked with a zero position flanked by mirrored ranges of port and starboard angles, usually from zero to fifty.
- **Thermometer (temperature):** an instrument to measure temperature by the expansion of liquid mercury within an enclosed glass tube.
- **Temperature gauge:** a gauge displaying temperature measured in one of several temperature sensor locations, e.g. internal or external air, surrounding water, engine oil, etc. The gauge would have a unidirectional or bidirectional needle, and the gauge face would be marked with a zero position at the beginning or within a sequential numerical range.
- **Plumb bob (incline):** an instrument to establish vertical orientation relative to the line through the Earth's centre of gravity, from which pitch (longitudinal) and/or yaw (latitudinal) deviations can be measured. A weight suspended on string, usually with a pointed bottom tip.

Plumb bob

- **Inclinometer (incline):** an instrument incorporating a plumb bob with a scale to measure the degree of deviation. The scale would be marked with a zero position at its lower point, flanked by mirrored ranges of angles along an arc.

Inclinometer

73

- **Sounding/lead line (depth):** an instrument for measuring depth under a vessel consisting of a thin rope with a heavy weight at the end. The weight is called a lead even if made from some other material. Depth under a stationary vessel can be measured by dropping the lead into the water and measuring the line between the surface and the lead at the bottom. Depth under a moving vessel can be measured by swinging the lead forward before it is dropped into the water and measuring the line between the surface and the lead at the bottom when the movement of the vessel brings the line as close to perfectly vertical as possible.

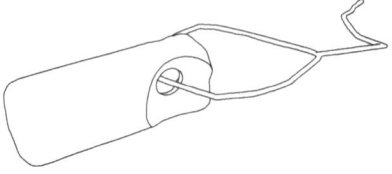

Sounding line

- **Echo sounder (depth):** an instrument for measuring depth using sonar by emitting a burst of sound under the hull and measuring the time taken for the sound to echo back from the bottom.
- **Taffrail log (speed):** an instrument to measure speed through water using a vaned rotator connected to a dial. When dragged behind a moving vessel the vanes cause the rotator to turn and its revolutions are registered on the dial as distance. Early versions needed to be pulled in to read the dial. Later versions separated the rotator from the dial by a stiff braided line that would communicate the torque so that the dial could be mounted at the stern and read in real time.

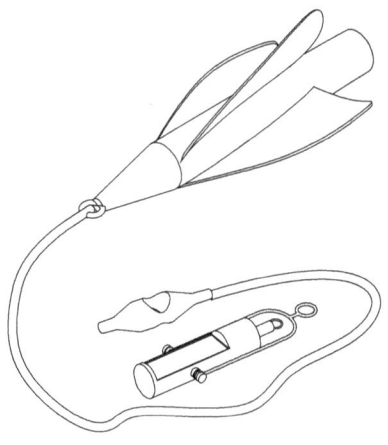

Taffrail log

- **Pitometer log (speed):** an instrument to measure speed through water by measuring the difference between water pressure longitudinally facing the direction of travel, and the static water pressure

of water latitudinally. An associated gauge would have a unidirectional needle and a face marked with a sequential numerical range beginning from zero.
- **Marine chronometer (time):** a spring clock capable of keeping accurate time under sea conditions. Longitude can be estimated by comparing time in a known location to local time estimated from celestial objects. An analogue face would have two or more unidirectional needles and associated sequential numerical markings (i.e. hours, minutes, seconds, milliseconds).
- **Telescope/monocular (observation):** an instrument to optically magnify distant objects. In maritime use taking the form of a narrow cone with a large diameter glass lens at one end and a smaller diameter glass lens at the other.
- **Binoculars (observation):** an instrument to optically magnify distant objects through twinned and aligned telescopes.

Navigation and steering (direction)

1470 Astrolabe
1705 Ship's wheel
1731 Sextant
1876 Binnacle with adjustable correcting magnets
1993 GPS

- **Ship's wheel:** controls the rudder position to steer the vessel. When mechanically linked to the rudder—as in earlier versions of the technology and in smaller vessels—the ship's wheel must be in proximity to the rudder and so is likely to be located at the stern. Later, with the advent of pneumatic and electronic rudder control, the ship's wheel could be located further away in a bow or midships superstructure.

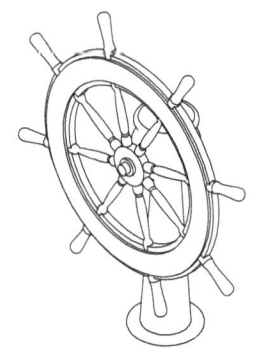

Ship's wheel and pedestal

- **Compass:** magnetic compass that can pivot to align itself with magnetic north, within a non-ferrous housing.

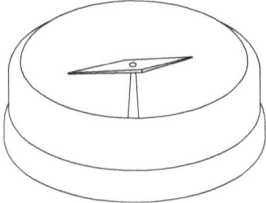

Magnetic compass (old style)

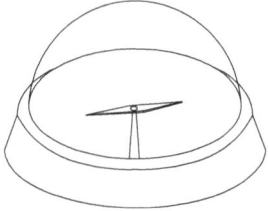

Magnetic compass (modern)

- **Binnacle:** magnetic compass housed in a non-ferrous material and bracketed by port and starboard magnets whose position can be adjusted to compensate for the magnetic influence of a metal hull.
- **Mariners astrolabe:** an instrument for measuring the height of the sun during the day, or of Polaris (North Star) at night. Consists of a graduated disk with a pivoting rule, and two vanes with pinholes mounted at either end of the rule. During the day the rule is adjusted so that a beam of light passes through the first pinhole onto the second pinhole. During the night Polaris is sighted directly through the two pinholes. The altitude of the target is read off the outer edge of the instrument.

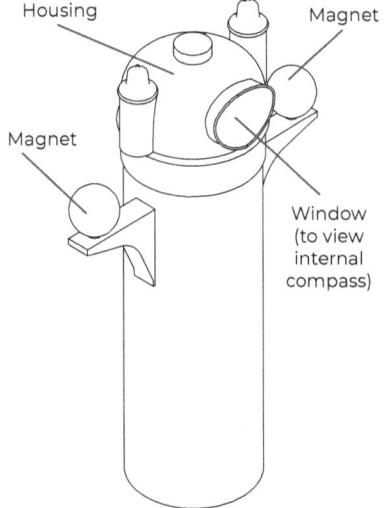

Binnacle

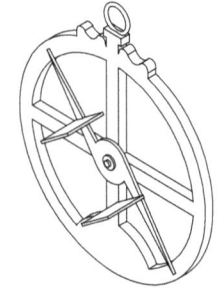

Astrolabe

BRIDGE AREAS

- **Sextant:** in maritime use, an instrument to measure the angular distance between the sun (or other celestial body) above the horizon. This angle, together with the time and date of the measurement, can be used to determine the observer's latitude. The user looks through a monocular sight to a view split between a non-refracting lens and a fixed mirror. The fixed mirror shows the view through a second variable mirror controlled by a handle that moves through a graduated arc. The sextant is aimed to centre the first object (e.g. the horizon) in both the lens and the variable mirror. The variable mirror is then adjusted to bring the second object (e.g. the sun) as seen on the fixed mirror into visual alignment with the first object as seen through the monocular sight, noting the angle on the graduated arc that achieved such alignment.

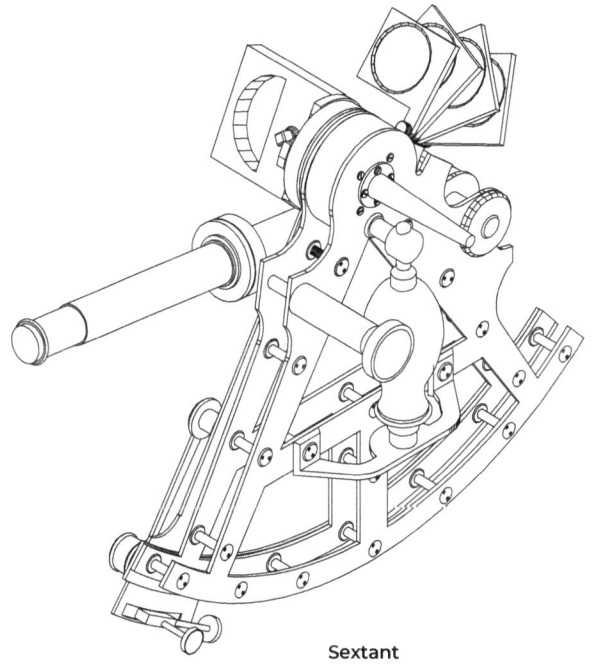
Sextant

- **GPS:** computerised system that determines position by triangulation of signals received from satellites with known positions. Direction and speed can be estimated from sequential location readings. Results are displayed on a screen.

Engine speed control

- Engine order telegraph ➙ Steam engine
- Telegraph connection ➙ Manual speed control
- Cable connection ➙ Mechanical speed control
- Hose connection ➙ Pneumatic speed control
- Wire connection ➙ Electronic speed control
- Mechanical control head ➙ Combustion engine located in close proximity (within 15 m cable length)
- Pneumatic control head ➙ Combustion engine located further away (beyond 15 m cable length)
- Electronic control ➙ Electric engine or relatively recent combustion engine

1872 Engine order telegraph
1948 Electronic control

- **Engine order telegraph:** aka Chadburn, after the manufacturer Chadburn of Liverpool, was installed as a set on steam-powered vessels: one unit on the bridge and the other in the engine room. Likely to have a plate or dial marking that identifies the manufacturer by name and city. They were connected by telegraph wire, with signals transmitted electronically. Each unit had speeds marked on a dial, a handle that could be moved around the dial, and a pointer. Moving the handle on one unit moved the pointer on the other to the corresponding position and caused a bell to sound from both. The bridge gave the order to change speed and/or direction by moving the bridge

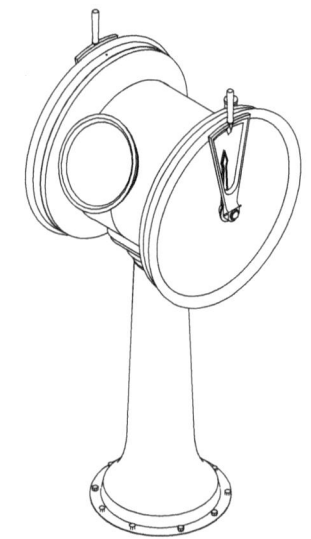

Engine order telegraph (aka Chadburn)

unit handle, causing the bell to ring and the pointer to move on the engine room unit.

- **Engine room telegraph:** The engine room acknowledged the order by moving the handle on the engine room unit handle, causing the bell to ring and the pointer to move on the bridge unit. Crew in the engine room could then set the communicated engine speed.

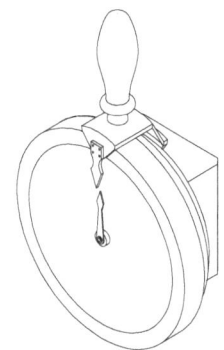

Engine room telegraph

- **Push-pull control head:** the control head on a bridge is connected by a system of cables and pulleys to the clutch and throttle on the engine. Signals are transmitted mechanically through tensioning the cables.
- **Pneumatic control head and actuator:** the control head on the bridge is connected by gas hoses to an actuator which controls the clutch and throttle on the engine. Signals are transmitted through the hoses by pressurised air.

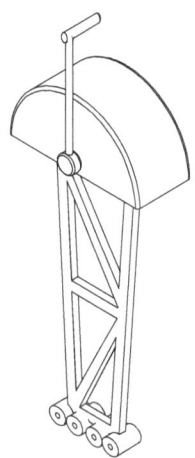

Push-pull control head

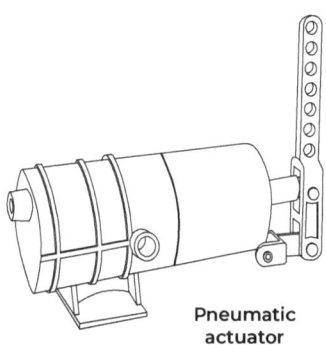

Pneumatic actuator

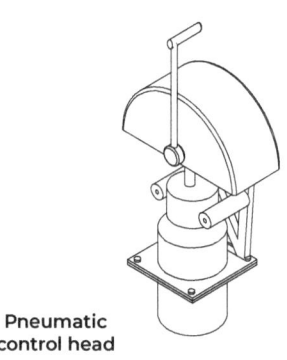

Pneumatic control head

- **Electronic control head and actuator:** the control head on the bridge is connected by a data cable to an actuator which controls the clutch and throttle on the engine. Signals are transmitted digitally and interpreted by processors at each end.

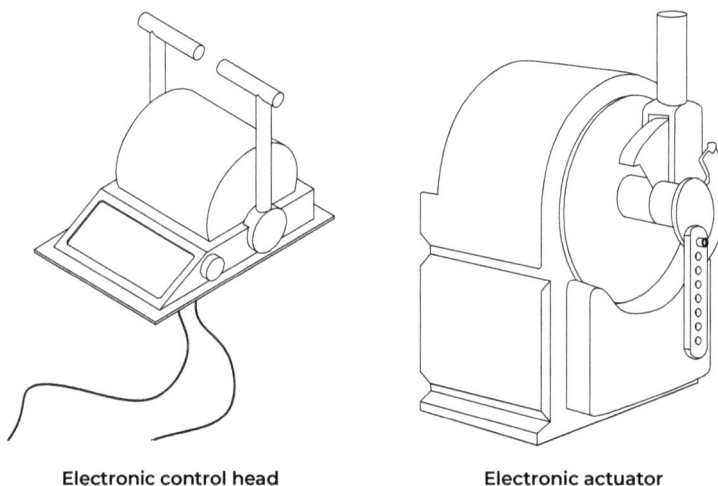

Electronic control head   Electronic actuator

Communications

1876 Microphone
1894 Wireless telegraph
1910 Radio headphones

- **Signal lamp:** a shuttered lamp used for visual transmission of coded signals from a vessel to external recipients at night.
- **Signal flags:** a system of flags used for visual transmission of coded signals from a vessel to external recipients in daylight.
- **Wireless telegraph:** the earliest means of radio communication

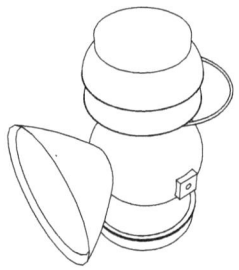

Signal lamp

by coded on/off sequences. Larger vessels may have had dedicated spaces for radio equipment.

- **Radio communications:** vessels with the capability to transmit and receive audio by radio transmission will have had a device to tune the operating frequency, as well as a microphone and speaker set either as a headset or handset. Larger vessels may have had dedicated spaces for radio communications.
- **Internal public address system:** larger vessels may have had a system of loudspeakers for the bridge to communicate with the crew.
- **Internal telephone system:** larger vessels may have had a system for voice communication between rooms/spaces. Older systems may have had a dedicated manual switchboard.

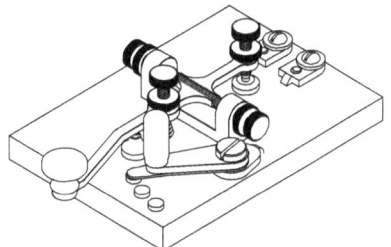
Wireless telegraph key

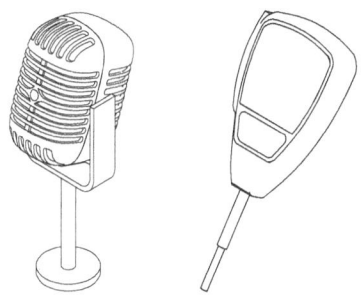
Radio microphones

Headset

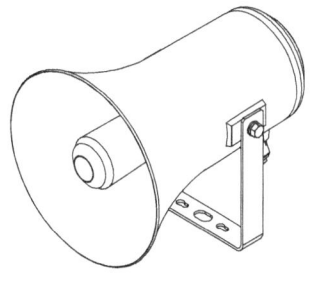
Loudspeaker

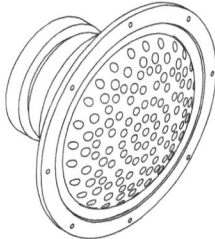 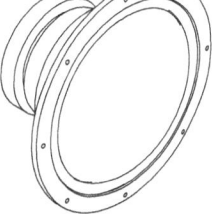
Modern speakers

CHAPTER 6
FITTINGS AND EQUIPMENT

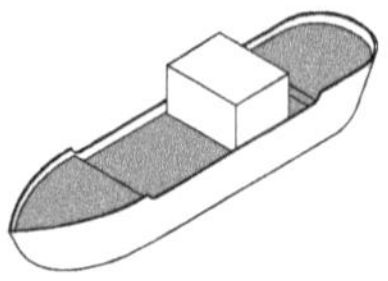

Fittings and equipment installed on vessels address key operational functions. These include keeping hulls dry and ventilated, maintaining liveable crew spaces, and other standard gear vital for onboard operations, such as winches and portholes.

Ship's bell

- Ship's bell ➔ Engraved with the ship's name and year of launch

1485 Ship's bell

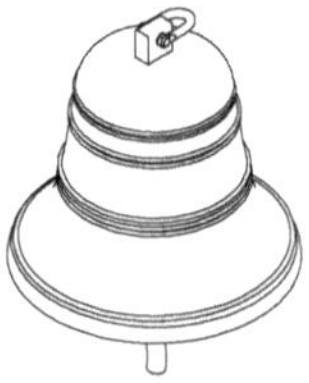

Ship's bell

The tradition of a ship's bell developed in post-medieval Europe. There is no prescribed location, although for functional reasons it will typically be located externally but under shelter. Cast from brass or bronze as a single piece, the bell will have the ship's name and year of launch on the surface.

- **Bell uses:** as a warning signal in poor visibility; to keep time (traditionally struck every half hour); as an alarm (e.g. to warn of a fire on board); and for ceremonial purposes (e.g. arrival or departure of senior officers in the US Navy, baptisms in the British Royal Navy).

Winches

- Vertical spool ➔ Capstan
- Horizontal spool ➔ Windlass

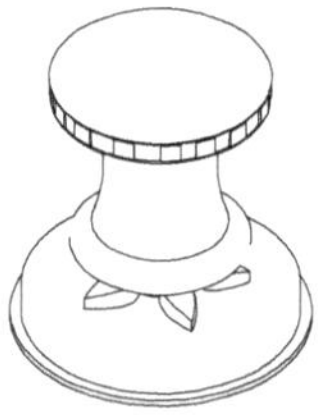

Capstan (manual, wood)

Winches are mechanisms for moving heavy weights using a cylinder which is rotated to wind a cable in or out. Depending on the relevant technological era, the cylinder may have been rotated manually with handles (small manual winch) or levers (large manual winch), driven by steam piped

FITTINGS AND EQUIPMENT

in from the main boilers, or motorised.

Winches are distributed around vessels for various purposes, they may be present: at the bow to raise an anchor (pre-motorisation this will usually be a capstan with levers operated by multiple people, post-motorisation it will be a windlass); on the main decks in proximity to sailing masts to raise and lower sails; a windlass centred on the main deck beside cargo holds to raise and lower cargo; windlasses at the stern for towing; windlasses with fishing rigging to pull in nets; motorised capstans located by bitts to pull in mooring lines; and in the engine room as part of the crane mechanism to move large engine parts.

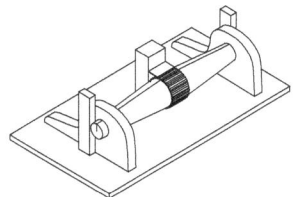
Windlass (manual, wood)

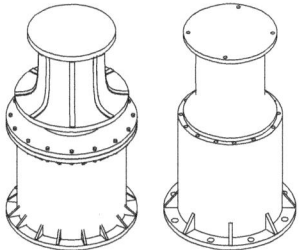
Capstans (automatic, metal)

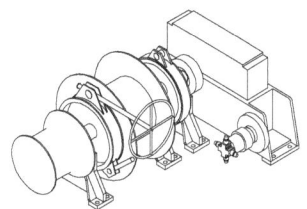
Windlass (automatic, metal)

- **Capstan:** winch with the cylinder mounted vertically.
- **Windlass:** winch with the cylinder mounted horizontally.

Deck fittings for mooring

Common fittings used to route and secure mooring lines between a vessel and fixed structures (e.g. wharf, pier, dock) include:

- **Cleat:** light pair of horns connected by a base plate. Cleats allow the mooring lines for smaller vessels to be secured with figure-of-eight turns to control tension.
- **Bollard:** stout vertical post fixed to the deck, may be flared or include horns towards the top to prevent the line slipping off. Bollards provide a secure attachment point for mooring lines.
- **Bitt:** double bollards connected by a sturdy base plate. Bitts allow the mooring lines for large vessels to be secured with figure-of-eight turns to control tension.

Bollard

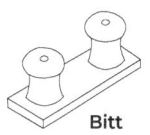
Bitt

- **Chock:** smooth and reinforced aperture for routing lines or to pass lines through the hull. May have an open or closed top.
- **Roller chock:** chock fitted with rollers to reduce friction on the lines.

Open chock

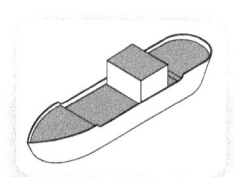
Roller chock

Ventilation

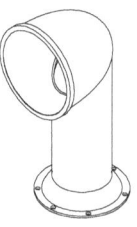

- Number and placement of vents ➜ Suggests the layout of living spaces and scale of the onboard population, e.g. you would expect to see many more vents for a passenger ferry than a general cargo vessel

Ventilators can be mounted at various locations around the highest decks to provide ventilation to the decks below.

- **Cowl vent:** a vertical pipe topped at a right angle by a flared opening. Cowl vents are passive systems and require wind to drive airflow. They can be weatherproofed to exclude water by covering the opening with baffles and/or installing a dorade box at the base. Dorade boxes create a u-bend passable by airflow while heavier water is expelled out the bottom.
- **Mushroom vent:** a vertical pipe topped by a cowling cover for weatherproofing. The cover is raised above the lip of the vertical pipe to open a u-bend passable by airflow but leaving an overlap to exclude water.

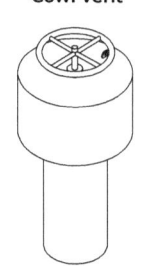
Cowl vent

Mushroom vent

Bilge pumps

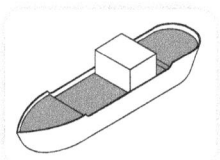
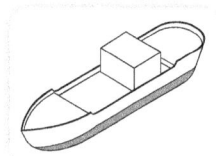

Wooden hulls leak despite the best attempts at sealing them. A scoop or bailing bucket is sufficient for primitive and small open vessels. For larger vessels with decks, some form of hand operated or motorised pumping mechanism is needed to remove water.

FITTINGS AND EQUIPMENT

Hand-operated pumps

- **Burr pump:** the base of the mechanism is an input with a one-way valve through which water can be drawn into a wooden pipe leading to the pump head. The pump head has a lever used to move a rod up and down within the pipe. Suction is provided by a leather cone on the lower end of the rod. The diameter of the open end of the cone is the same as the diameter of the pipe. In the upward motion water fills the cone and is lifted; in the downward motion the cone closes to pass down through the water column.

- **Common/suction pump:** the base of this mechanism is the open end of a pipe made from wood, and later metals (lead in the early 18th century, copper and bronze in the later 18th century, and iron in the 19th century). The lower valve is a stationary seal with a one-way valve, and it is located towards the middle of the pipe. The upper valve is one-way, with a plunging seal. The pump head has a lever used to move a rod up and down within the pipe. The rod is attached to the upper valve. When the upper valve is forced down the water pressure below closes the lower valve and water flows through the upper valve. When the upper valve is drawn up, the water pressure above closes it and lifts the water above. Meanwhile, the vacuum created between the two valves draws more water from below the lower valve.

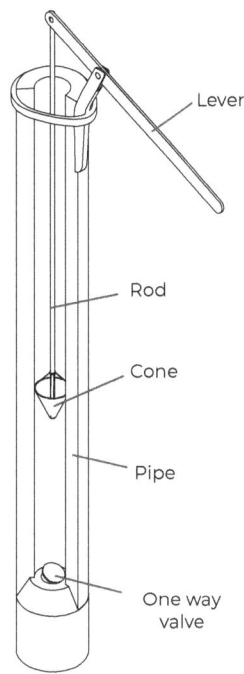

Burr pump

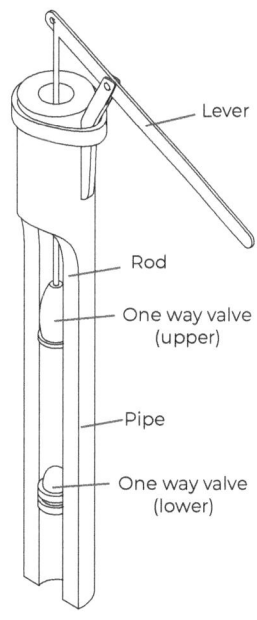

Common/suction pump

- **Chain pump:** this mechanism has a continuous chain moving in a loop from the bottom of the bilge, to the pump head, and back. The chain runs within a pipe, with incrementally-spaced disk-shaped seals that match the diameter of the pipe bore. The chain is driven by a winch that can be turned by one or more people working together for additional force. The chain turns on rollers at the base and top. As each seal rises within the pipe it carries water upwards.

Motorised pumps
- **Centrifugal pump:** this mechanism uses a motor-driven impeller. When the impeller is rotated, centrifugal force sends water outwards along the impeller blades creating flow through the volute and out of the discharge port, and suction to draw more water into the impeller eye.
- **Piston pump:** this mechanism uses a piston to change the volume of a chamber between two one-way (check) valves. A downward piston stroke increases chamber pressure, forcing water out through the outlet check valve. An upward stroke decreases internal pressure, drawing water in through the inlet check valve.

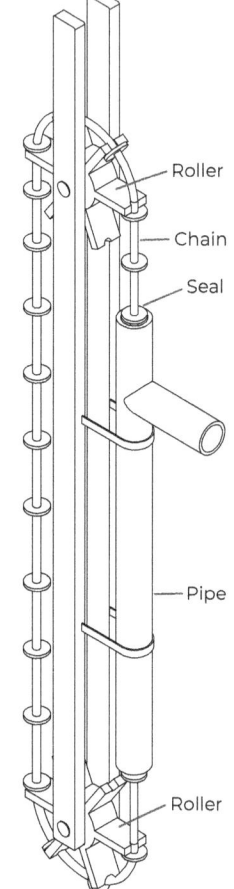

Chain pump

Centrifugal pump

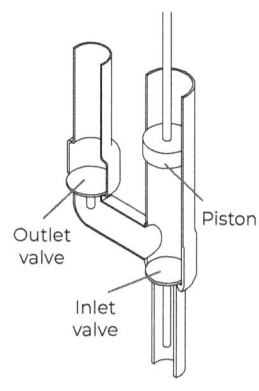

Piston pump

FITTINGS AND EQUIPMENT

Sensor and communication masts

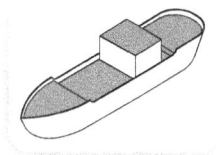

- Volume and diversity of communications equipment ➔ Suggests the level of communication with external parties
- Volume and diversity of sensors ➔ Proportionate to the possible threats to the vessel, e.g. warships would have far more sensor types than simple collision avoidance and weather radar sensors

1896 Radio
1900 Metal pole mast
1906–1922 Hyperboloid lattice mast
1910 Tripod mast
1935 Radar
1957 Satellite communications
1975 Electro-optical sensors

For a transitional period between sail and steam, motorised vessels continued to be built with masts for signal flags and cargo handling. From the beginning of the 20th century, vessels were designed with metal masts to raise communication antennas and sensors as high as possible above other structures.

The three mainmast designs are pole, tripod and lattice. The US Navy commissioned warships with a signature hyperboloid lattice mast design from 1906 to 1922. Masts may also include a crow's nest for lookouts and range spotters. On a military vessel this may be an armoured compartment.

Antennas and sensors mounted on a mast include:
- Radio communications
- Radar sensors
- Satellite communications, and/or
- Electro-optical sensors

Rotating parabolic antennas are often enclosed by a round or spherical weatherproof cover (radome).

THE SHIPWRECK DECODER

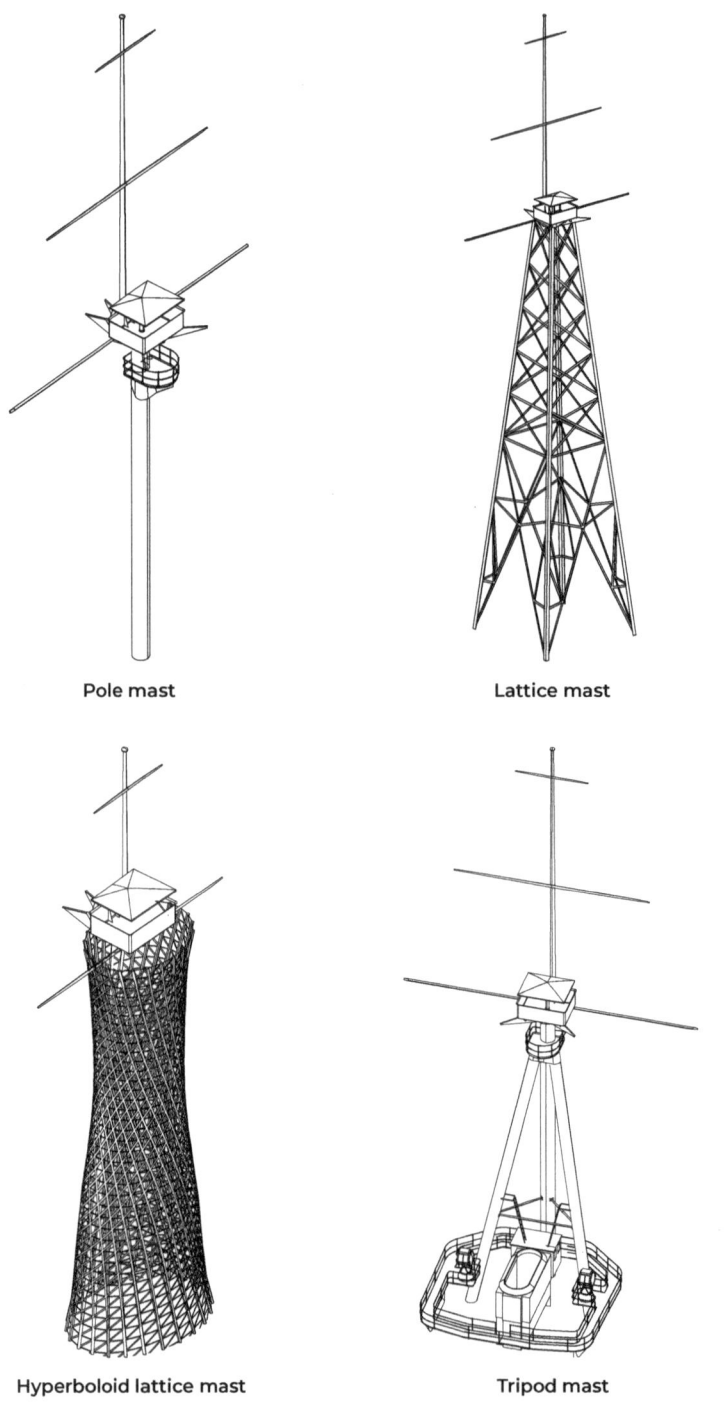

Pole mast

Lattice mast

Hyperboloid lattice mast

Tripod mast

FITTINGS AND EQUIPMENT

Fishing rigs

- **Outrigger:** outrigger trawlers have a boom projecting from each side to tow their fishing gear. The working deck can be located at the bow with aft superstructure, or aft with bow superstructure. The gear winch is located on the working deck. If the working deck is aft, the winch will usually be oriented parallel to the centreline. If the working deck is forward then the winch will usually be oriented perpendicular to the centreline.

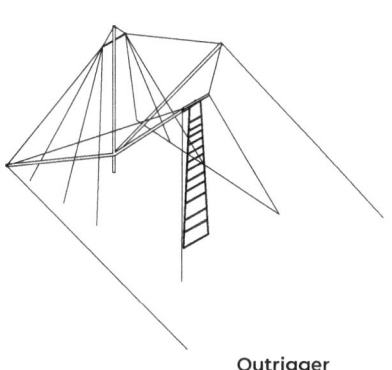

Outrigger

- **Stern:** stern trawlers tow their fishing gear directly behind the vessel. The working deck is located aft, with bow superstructure. The gear winch is located on the working deck oriented perpendicular to the centreline. The stern may have a derrick or a ramp to recover the fishing gear.

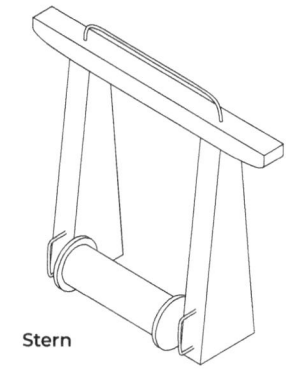

Stern

- **Sidewinder:** the fishing gear is set over the side from frames mounted forward and aft. Usually the working deck is located at the bow with aft superstructure. The gear winch is located at the front of the superstructure and oriented perpendicular to the centreline.

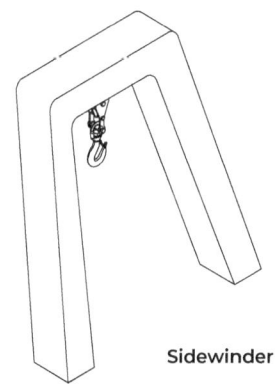

Sidewinder

THE SHIPWRECK DECODER

Maintenance

- Adjacent to the engine room

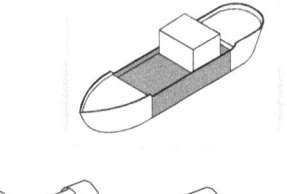

Larger wooden-hulled vessels expecting to be away from their home port for extended periods would include a carpenter among the crew and carry his woodworking tools. Warships may have had a weaponsmith (to maintain hand weapons) and carried his small brick forge and anvil.

The introduction of motors increased the need to carry tools and spares for maintenance and repairs. A vessel's workshop will usually include a lathe, drill press, grinder, welding gear and hand tools. There may also be a supply of spare parts that cannot be manufactured on board such as propeller blades, propeller shaft sections, and engine pistons.

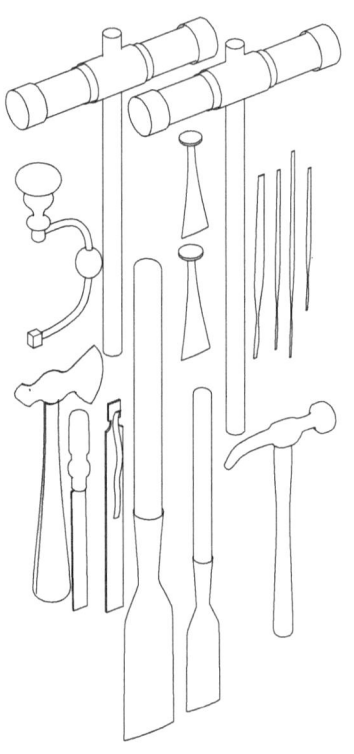

Shipwright tools

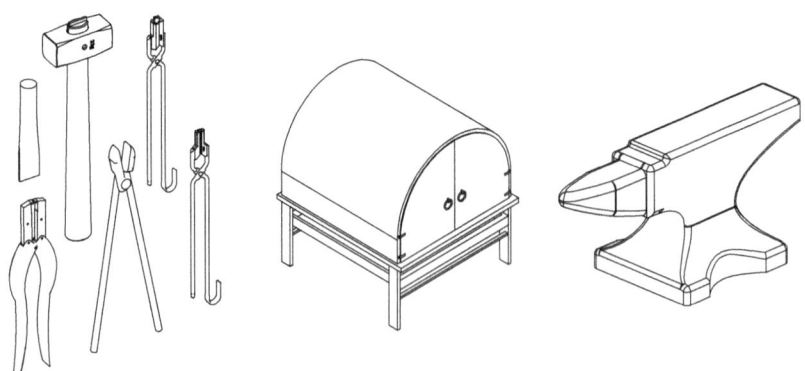

Weaponsmith tools, forge and anvil

FITTINGS AND EQUIPMENT

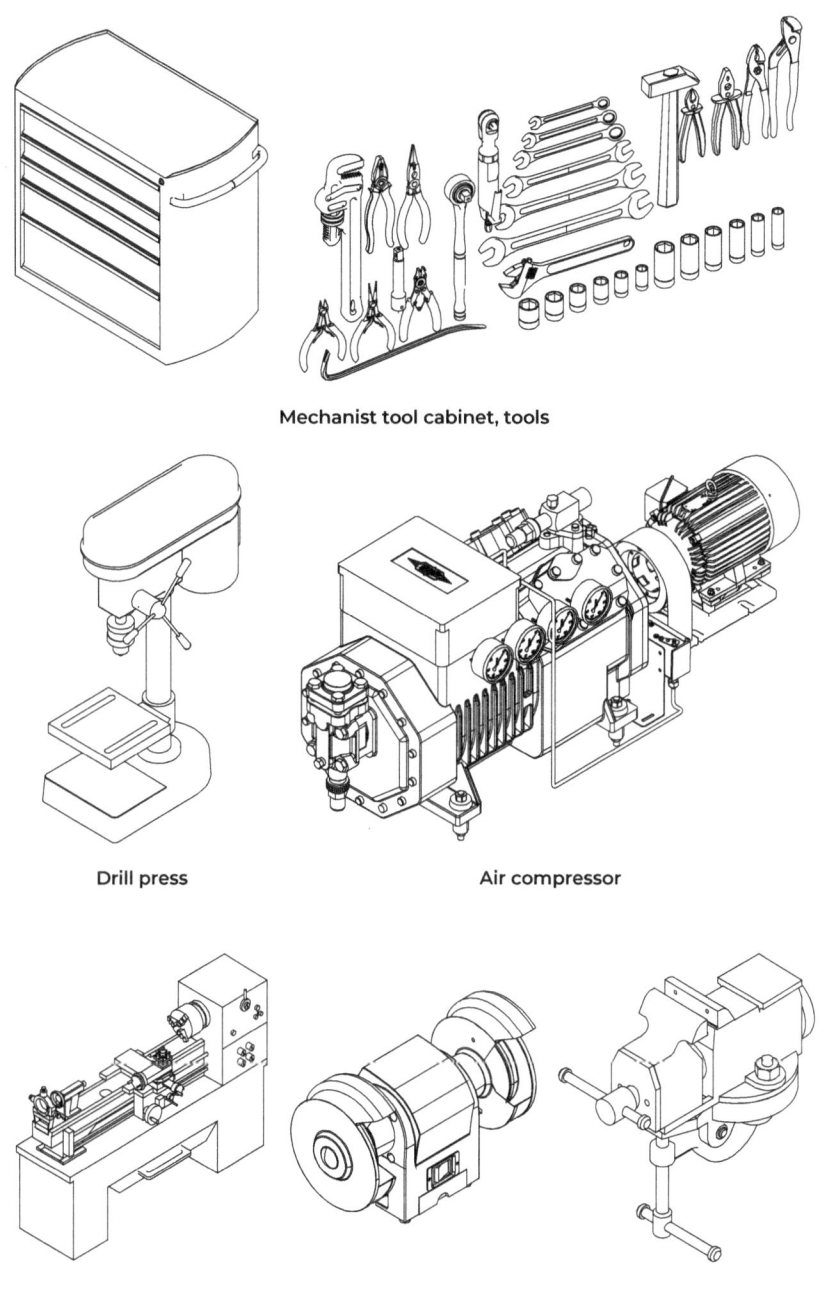

Mechanist tool cabinet, tools

Drill press

Air compressor

Lathe

Grinder

Vice

Galley (kitchen)

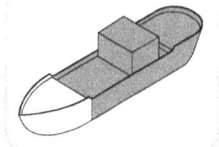

- Bricks ➜ Open fire or fire chamber
- Flat base pots ➜ Simple cookfire, cooktop
- Round base pots ➜ Fire chamber

Pre-history Open fire stove, cut stone
4400 BCE Fired brick (China)
400 BCE Fired brick (Mediterranean)
1642 Cast iron
1735 Enclosed fire chamber
1826 Cooktop only, gas stove
1833 Coal stove
1882 Electricity
1913 Stainless steel

- **Simple cookfire:** the most basic cooking arrangement for a wooden vessel is a cut stone or brick base below an open-topped sand box for a wood fire. The base is necessary to insulate wooden hull materials from the fire. Locating small quantities of cut stone or brick suggests you have located the galley (large quantities suggest cargo). Simple cookfires can use tripod pots and lengths of firewood stored nearby.

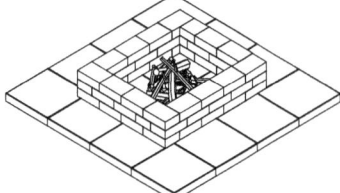
Simple cookfire

- **Open fire chamber:** the next design stage entailed building up brick walls to create a fire chamber. This design required a cauldron of the same width as the chamber, and a lip on the top edges of the walls to rest it on (to suspend it above the fire). An enclosed chamber requires firewood cut to fit the size of the chamber.

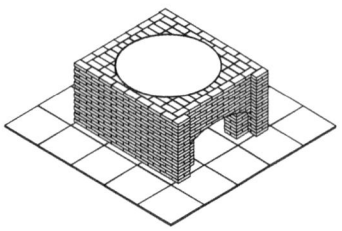
Open fire chamber

FITTINGS AND EQUIPMENT

- **Cast iron:** stoves made from cast iron were first invented in 1642 and would be installed on a fired brick base to insulate them from wooden decks. Cast iron stoves have a cooktop so require pots with a flat base.
- **Enclosed fire chamber:** stoves that fully enclose the fire were first invented in 1735. They may be constructed from fired brick or iron. Fully enclosed fire chambers require pots with a flat base for the cooktop, and firewood cut to fit the size of the chamber, or coal (from 1833).
- **Cooktop only:** new technologies enabled cooking with gas from 1826 and electricity from 1892. These stoves do not require a fire chamber but may have an oven chamber instead. Unless gas-fired, cooktop-only stoves require pots with a flat base.

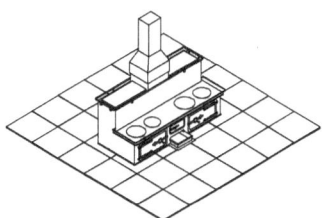

Cast iron stove

Modern stove

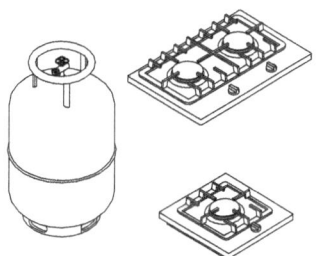

Gas burner

Pots and pans

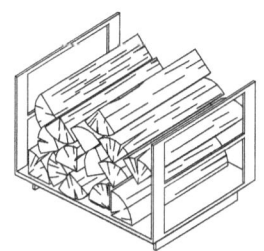

Firewood

Head (bathroom)

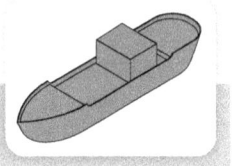

- **1851** Flush toilet
- **1866** Urinal
- **1890** Solid porcelain bathtub

Pre-1850, toilet facilities were located at the bow of the vessel (on the beakhead if present). The toilet was a wooden seat over a vent opening at the other end, near water level, where it could be cleaned by normal wave action. The captain may have had a private toilet in quarters at the stern with similar design, and chamber pots may also have been present in quarters. Bathing facilities were wood, ceramic, or metal basins and portable metal tubs.

Indoor plumbing was invented in 1850 so modern-style bathroom facilities started appearing on vessels after that date. The timeline for developments in bathroom technology can help refine a vessel's age: the flush toilet was invented in 1851, the urinal in 1866, and solid porcelain bathtubs in 1890. Porcelain survives a long time in marine environments and will often include maker's marks and other useful information.

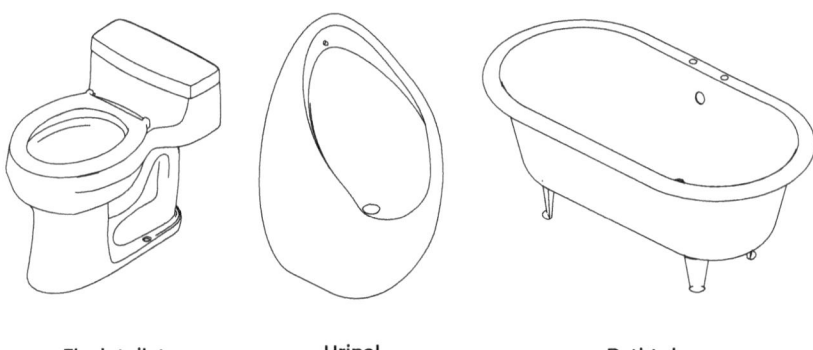

Flush toilet   Urinal   Bathtub

FITTINGS AND EQUIPMENT

Deck lighting

1880 Electric lights

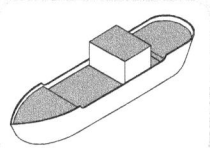

Pre-1880, lighting within a vessel was provided by deck gratings, skylights, deck prisms and portholes to let in daylight. At night, lighting was from candles or oil lamps, usually within a lantern housing for fire safety.

- **Deck prism:** glass prism embedded within the top deck or superstructure surface, with a flat face flush with the upper surrounding surface. The prism dispersed sunlight sideways below.
- **Skylight:** usually a box at knee height above the deck, topped with a triangular (apex) roof mounting hatches with glass portholes. Skylights allow fresh air and natural light into spaces below deck. Steam-powered vessels will have a large skylight located on the main deck above the boiler and engine rooms.
- **Electric lights:** electric light bulbs with associated power cables usually mounted high on walls or the ceiling of internal spaces.

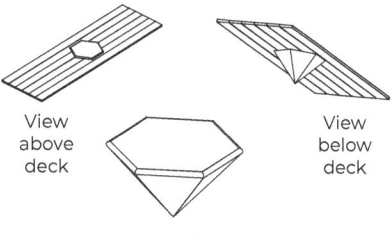

Deck prism

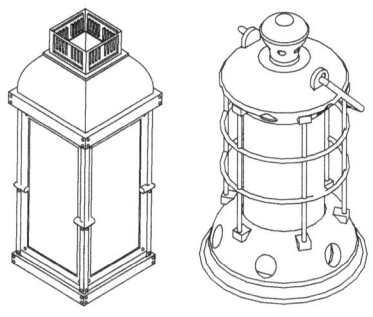

Oil lamps

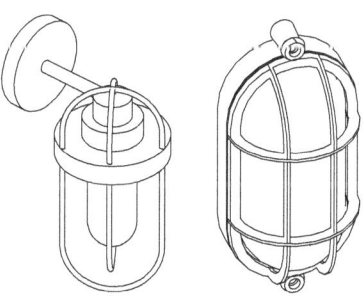

Electric lights

Navigation and anchor lights

The United States in 1838 was the first country to mandate the use of navigation lights, and the United Kingdom in 1848 was the first to specify the colour and location. International rules were first agreed in 1889. The basic scheme for navigation lights is white lights on the foremast, mainmast and stern; white lights on the mainmast or bow for a vessel at anchor; red light on the port side; and green light on the starboard side. Navigation lights were oil lamps until the 19th century, afterwards electric lights.

Gunports and portholes

1490 Gunport
1569 Porthole

- **Gunport:** opening cut into the side of the hull with an associated cover of wood or iron that could be sealed shut in bad weather. Gunports were introduced to allow higher calibre cannon to be mounted on lower, more stable decks. Originally designed for wooden-hulled vessels, the concept survived into the period of iron-hulled ships at least until the dreadnought class of battleships, where they were used for secondary guns. Gun ports also proved useful for allowing light and air through the lower decks in fair weather. The ongoing need for dedicated light and ventilation in all parts of a ship eventually led to the development of the side scuttle, aka porthole.

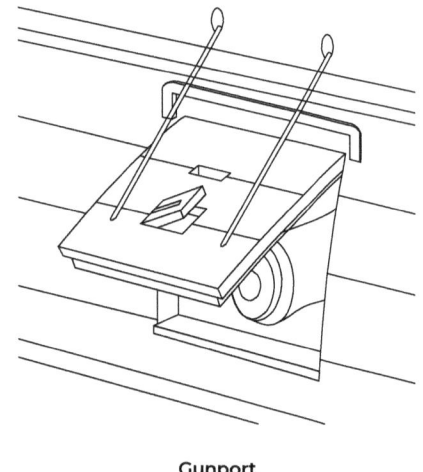

Gunport

FITTINGS AND EQUIPMENT

- **Fixed porthole:** a rounded glass disk in a fixed metal frame mounted within a gap in the hull to allow the passage of light. The circular shape minimises the impact of the opening on the structural integrity of the surrounding hull.
- **Hinged porthole:** a fixed metal frame is mounted within a gap in the hull to allow the passage of light and air. The opening can be covered by a metal plate or glass disk within a metal frame attached by a hinge and secured with bolts.
- **Storm cover:** metal cover mounted on a hinge to reinforce and backup the porthole glass in bad weather, or to avoid compromising the armour on a warship.

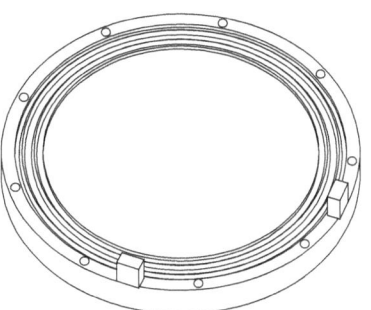

Fixed porthole

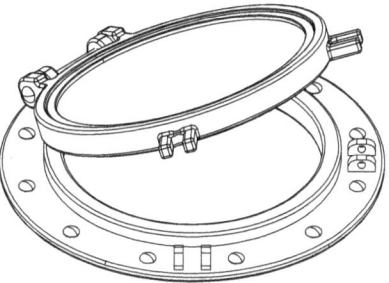

Hinged porthole

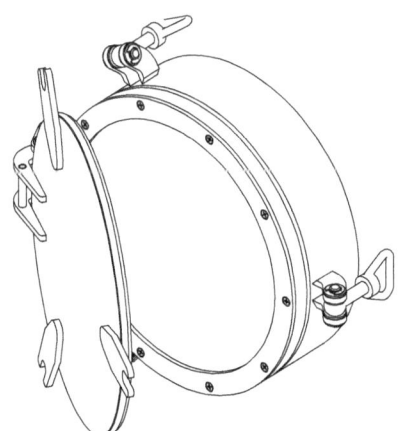

Porthole with storm cover

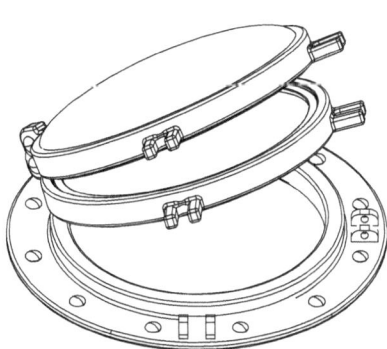

Hinged porthole with storm cover

Searchlights

- Shutter plates ➜ Used for signalling
- Iris shutter ➜ Militarised vessel

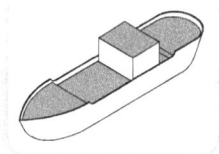

1872 Searchlight

Searchlights generate a narrow beam of high intensity light for signalling or tracking targets. In search and rescue operations, they can illuminate objects or people, while in military contexts they are used to identify other vessels and aircraft at night. The main housing contains a powerful electric bulb and a parabolic mirror reflector to focus the light into a concentrated beam. For signalling purposes, searchlights may be fitted with a signalling shutter consisting of hinged parallel plates that can rapidly cover and uncover the aperture. On military vessels searchlights are often fitted with an iris shutter to enable light emission to be instantly stopped without turning off the bulb or waiting for it to cool.

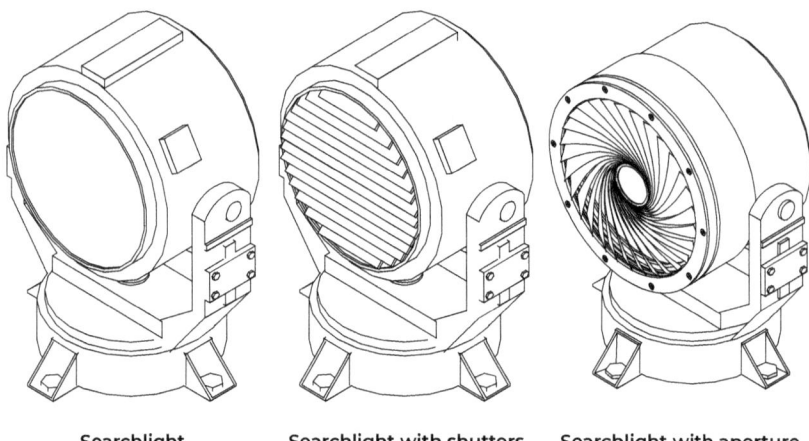

Searchlight   Searchlight with shutters   Searchlight with aperture

FITTINGS AND EQUIPMENT

Safety devices

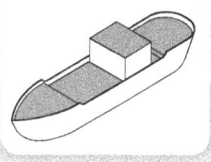

1855 Ring buoy
1882 Life raft

- **Ring buoy:** a positively buoyant ring designed to be thrown to a person in the water to prevent drowning.
- **Liferaft:** modern liferafts are automatically-inflating boats, with tent-like covered tops, and normally contain a small freshwater store, rations, signalling and survival equipment. They are stored on the exterior of the vessel in a case, and automatically deploy when an integrated sensor detects that the case is below a certain water depth. A liferaft will be limited to basic rowed propulsion.
- **Enclosed lifeboat:** modern lifeboats are small, rigid, covered boats capable of motorised propulsion. They are stored on davits and/or launch rails for rapid deployment if the primary vessel needs to be evacuated. Lifeboats normally contain a small fresh water store, rations, navigation, signalling and survival equipment.

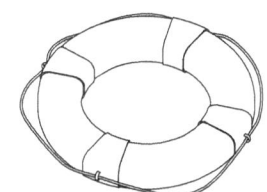

Ring buoy

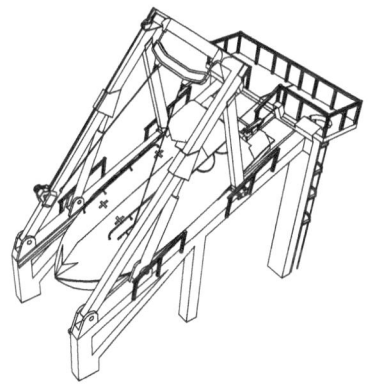

Lifeboat on free-fall rails

Davits and small boats

All but the smallest vessels usually carry smaller boats for e.g. short distance transport, separately performing fishing and hunting operations, or for safety if it is necessary to evacuate the primary vessel.

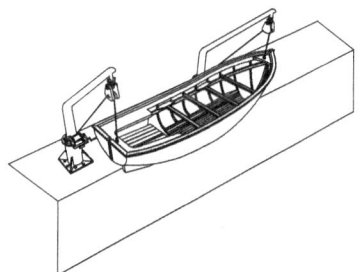

Boat on davits

- **Davit:** simple crane-like structure used for lowering and raising small boats. It consists of one or more arms with winches and pulleys, providing mechanical advantage for heavy lifting.

Computers and electronics

1890 Electrical fuse
1904 Vacuum tube
1924 Circuit breaker
1947 Transistor
1971 Microprocessor
1981 Personal computer

The rapid pace of change in electronics and computer technology can allow for precise dating of equipment observed on a vessel.

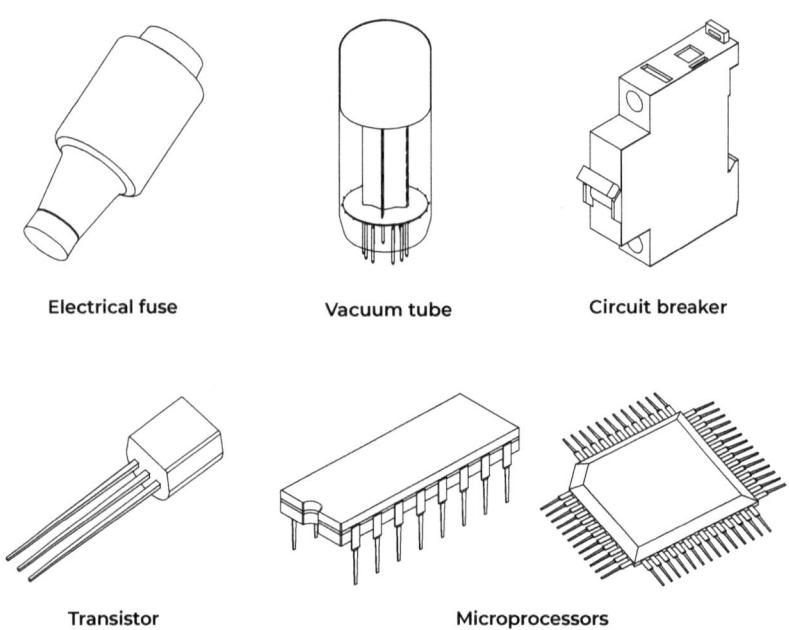

Electrical fuse   Vacuum tube   Circuit breaker

Transistor   Microprocessors

FITTINGS AND EQUIPMENT

Gangway

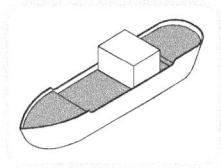

A walkable passageway that can be deployed to join the vessel to another structure for the embarkation or disembarkation of passengers and crew.
This can be, for example, a staircase, ramp, combination of the two, or just a single plank called a brow.

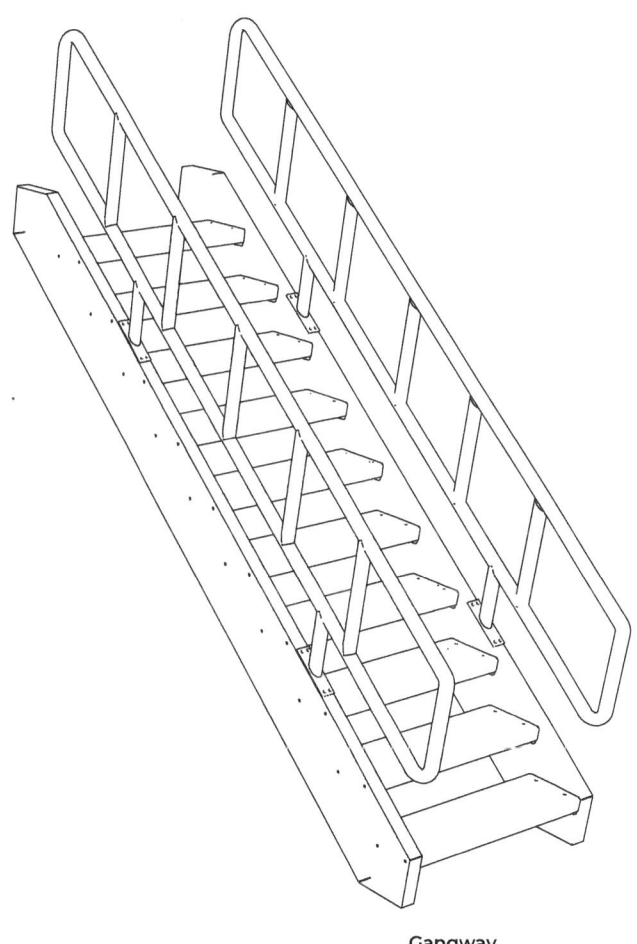

Gangway

THE SHIPWRECK DECODER

Movement between decks

- Elevators are relatively expensive equipment usually limited to passenger comfort on big ships

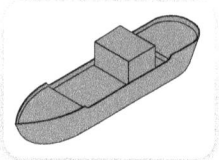

1900 Elevator

- **Ladder:** on most vessels (except cruise ships), stairs are typically referred to as ladders, and often narrow and steep to save space.
- **Staircase:** on cruise ships and ferries, staircases are often designed as architectural features for the use of passengers and may be wider, more decorative, and less steep than ladders found on other types of vessel.
- **Elevator:** platform/compartment within a shaft for moving people or freight within the vessel.
- **Escalator:** some very large vessels (e.g. aircraft carriers and cruise liners) contain moving staircases.

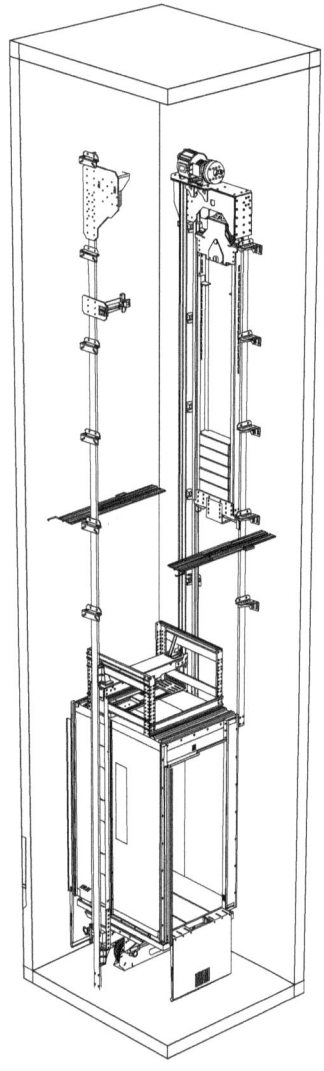

Elevator

CHAPTER 7
ROWED VESSELS

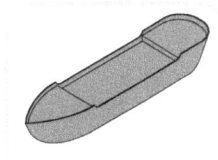

Rowing-powered vessels represent one of the earliest, simplest, and most enduring forms of maritime propulsion. While the fixtures and fittings for rowing are individually simple, increasing a vessel's size and efficiency demands sophisticated hull designs and complex, overlapped banks of rowers and oars.

Types of rowing

- **Sculling:** each rower works two oars, one on either side of the hull. Only feasible on small boats.
- **Sweep rowing:** each rower works one oar, on one side of the hull. The form of rowing seen on ships.
- *Alla sensile*: sweep rowing with one rower per oar, and two or more rowers per bench.
- *A scaloccio*: sweep rowing with two or more rowers per oar, sharing the same bench.

Rowing positions

Aside from the easy to understand seated and standing positions, there is:
- **Stand and sit:** stand up to push the oar forward, sit down to pull the oar back.
- **Sliding:** pad slides over a wide bench, or bench itself slides back and forth, so that leg strength can be used to push the oar forward.

Rowing equipment

- Number of oars, oarlocks, oar ports ➜ Number of rowers
- Oar size and length ➜ Single or multiple rowers

  - **Oar:** pole with a flat blade. From the perspective of the rower, the oar is a first-class lever with the load at the

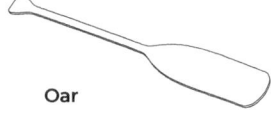
Oar

flat blade, the pivot point at the oarlock or oar port, and the effort at the end of the pole worked by the rower. As the number of rowers per oar increases, the oar must become longer to reach additional rowers, and wider diameter or stronger material to survive the increased force applied.

- **Bow sweeps:** extra-long oars located at the bow, used for manoeuvring.
- **Oarlock:** pivot point for an oar fixed to the railing or outrigger. To enable efficient rowing the railing cannot be too high above the water surface.
- **Oar port:** an opening in the hull through which an oar is rowed, reinforced to serve as a pivot point.
- **Bench:** a seat for one or more rowers. The length indicates the number of rowers: longer benches may have seated more rowers. Wider benches may indicate sliding rowing (where rowers slide back and forth on pads) rather than fixed positions. Bench layout correlates to rower positions and may be side-by-side or staggered.
- **Sliding seat/slip thwart:** the bench itself slides back and forth in sliding rowing.
- **Outrigger:** a pivot point or rail extended out from the deck and braced by a framework to support oars pivoting further from the hull. In ancient times outriggers were used to add additional levels of rowers. In modern times outriggers are used to extend the pivot point of the oar to trade increased resistance for a shorter stroke.

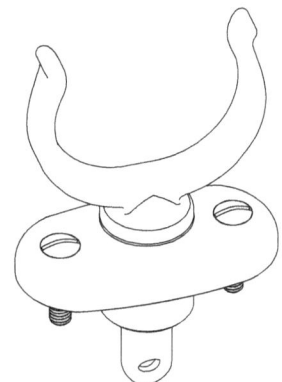

Oarlock (metal)

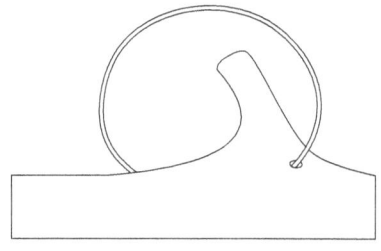

Oarlock (wood and rope)

CHAPTER 8
WIND-POWERED VESSELS

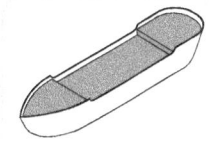

Sail stands as one of the earliest and most enduring forms of maritime propulsion. The immense variety in the form, detail, and terminology for erecting and securing sail area is further complicated by significant regional and temporal differences, which are beyond the scope of this guide. This text primarily focuses on the basic design of generic sailing rigs at their peak scale and complexity in the late Age of Sail (c.1850–1910). This approach aids in understanding the underlying logic of a sail-powered vessel, and it is not a guide to modern sailing or yacht architecture.

- Coin in mast step
- Sail cloth rarely survives but groupings of brailing rings can identify their previous location
- Number of masts, and mast sections
- Number and type of sail

> **Pre-1500** Mast stack with multiple sections
> **1783** Wire rigging and metal components
> **c.1850** Steel tube mast

Mast structure

The proliferation of poles and ropes on a tall ship can seem unfathomable at first glance but the underlying logic is usually based on a single mast section and its supports, repeated horizontally for multiple masts and stacked vertically for multi-section mast stacks. Each individual section is a pole; braced to the front, rear and sides; from which a sail can be suspended at height to capture wind; and with a low attachment point to translate following wind force to forward hull momentum.

Masts are single poles of wood, or (on ships from the mid-19th century) steel tubes, from which the sails are set to provide forward momentum to the hull. The mast is secured to the keel and stabilised laterally and longitudinally.

- **Mast step:** angular slot cut in the keel into which the matching shaped bottom (heel) of the mast is seated, and which ensures a stable connection. If the masts are missing you can determine their number by counting the mast steps. Traditionally a coin is placed in the mast step before the mast is seated, which can help with dating the vessel.

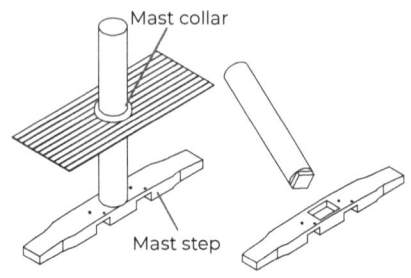

Mast step and collar

- **Mast collar:** waterproof ring where the mast passes through a deck.
- **Shrouds:** standing rigging used to stabilise a mast section laterally. Ropes or wires that run from the masthead or crosstrees to the sides of the vessel. Lower shrouds connect to chainplates on the side of the hull, while upper shrouds connect the masthead to crosstrees mounted on the mast section immediately below.

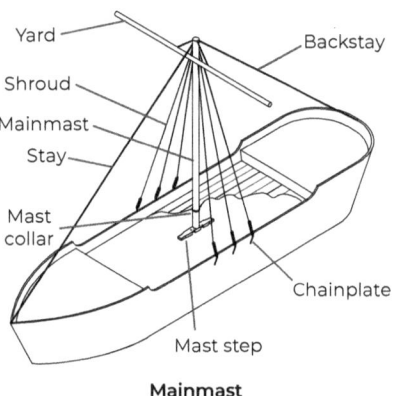

Mainmast

- **Chainplate:** metal plate mounted on the hull to create connection points that distribute the load from the shrouds and other rigging.
- **Stay:** standing rigging to stabilise a mast section from the fore (so that it does not fall backwards).
- **Backstay:** standing rigging to stabilise a mast section from the aft (so that it does not fall forwards or bend under pressure from the sails).
- **Spar:** horizontal pole hung from the mast used to hang and/or shape sails.
- **Yard:** horizontal spar mounted across the mast, from which a square sail is hung. Traditionally, the yard is evenly bisected by the mast.
- **Boom:** horizontal or angled spar mounted behind the mast, from which an aft-mounted sail is hung.

WIND-POWERED VESSELS

Multiple masts

There is a limit to the sail area that can be suspended from a single mast. To provide more area to larger vessels it is necessary to use multiple masts. Each has its own name:

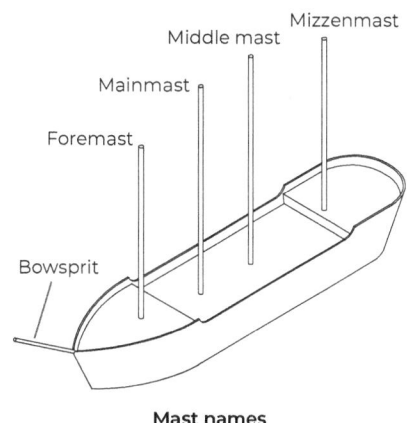

Mast names

- **Mainmast:** the primary mast. If a vessel has two or more masts the mainmast will be second from the bow.
- **Foremast:** the mast closest to the bow.
- **Mizzenmast:** the rearmost mast.
- **Middle mast:** located between the mainmast and mizzenmast.

Vessels with five or more masts have different naming conventions for masts behind the mainmast, but these are rare.

Mast stack

To increase the sail area that could be suspended from a single mast it was necessary to increase its height. The limit was the height of available trees. To provide more sail area a mast could be constructed from multiple (stacked) sections.

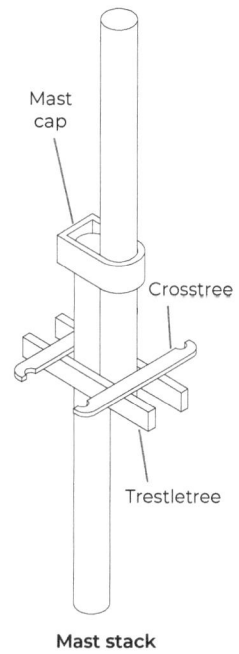

- The **lower mast** is the bottom section mounted directly to the keel. Additional mast sections from the bottom are the **topmast**, **topgallant mast**, and **royal mast** (upper masts). The logic of a single mast mounted on a fixed base and stabilised laterally and longitudinally by rigging is repeated for each section of mast.
- **Mast cap:** a metal collar fitted to lock the top of the lower section to the heel of the higher section with some overlap so that both sections function as a single vertical unit. The

Mast stack

higher section is mounted forward of the lower section and the overlap acts as a cantilever for the force on the higher section under sail.
- **Trestletrees:** longitudinal beams mounted each side of the masthead of the lower section. A square bar passing through the foot of the higher section rests the weight of the higher section on the trestletrees.
- **Crosstrees:** lateral beams mounted on the trestletrees to spread the shrouds of the higher section and hold it upright.
- **Futtock shrouds:** connect the higher section shrouds at the crosstrees to chainplates or eyes on the lower section head. This converts lateral pull on the shrouds into vertical tension on the mast, preventing the crosstrees from being subjected to immense crushing forces and helping to maintain the overall stability of the mast structure.

Rigging

Rigging is the system of ropes or cables used to stabilise the masts and set the sails. Common components may include:

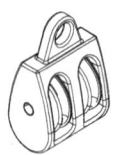

Pulley block

- **Block:** pulley with one to four runners.
- **Belaying pin/pin rail:** a belaying pin is a short cylindrical peg that sits in the pin rail with ends projecting on either side to secure running rigging using a figure of eight knot. The belaying pin can be withdrawn to release the line without undoing the figure of eight.

Bullseye

- **Bullseye:** round wooden disk with a single hole to guide a line or change its direction.
- **Deadeye:** round wooden disk with three holes for tensioning lines.
- **Cleat:** fitting with overhung arms for securing lines with a figure of eight.

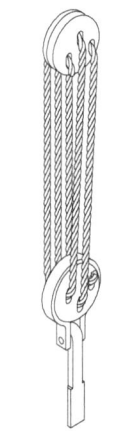

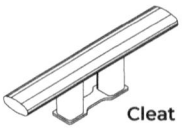

Cleat

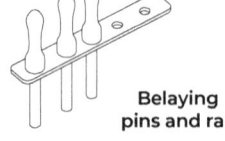

Belaying pins and rail

Deadeye (top), and deadeye fixed to chainplate (bottom)

WIND-POWERED VESSELS

Sails

Divers are very unlikely to find sails on a shipwreck. This section is included to help understand the logic of associated equipment and structures. Sails have their own names deriving from their shape, the mast and mast section from which they are set. Square rigging presents the largest possible surface area to the wind so is the most efficient for sailing downwind; but has a large angle of attack which requires more tacking to sail upwind. Schooner-rigged vessels have a smaller angle of attack so are more manoeuvrable and require less tacking to sail upwind.

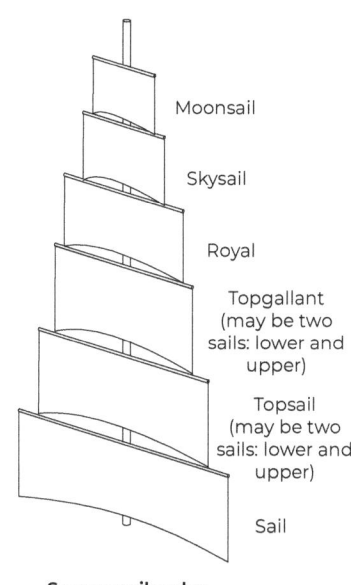

Square sail order

Larger sails require a lot of manual labour, and each additional sailor adds costs in wages, living space, and sustenance. Breaking the sail area into smaller units allows the vessel to operate with a smaller crew. Later sailing vessels made use of steam donkeys and motorised winches so that the largest sailing ships ever built operated with very small crews.

- **Brailing rings:** hard rings fitted along the edges of a sail as attachment points for the lines used to gather or furl it.

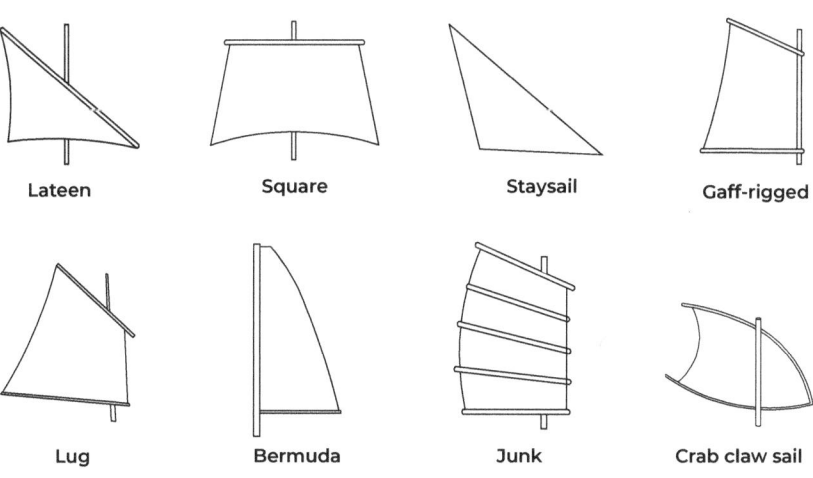

THE SHIPWRECK DECODER

Types of sailing vessel

Age of Sail vessels can be categorized by their mast configuration and sail rigging. The types outlined below are not exhaustive, but demonstrate the progression of common vessel categories based on square and schooner-rigged combinations from this era:

- **Sloop:** a single-masted ship with fore-and-aft (schooner) rigging.
- **Cutter:** a single-masted ship with schooner rigging and a bowsprit.
- **Schooner:** a multi-masted vessel (most commonly two-masted) with all masts primarily rigged with fore-and-aft ails.
- **Brig:** a two-masted ship with square rigged foremast and mainmast.
- **Brigantine:** a two-masted vessel with a square rigged foremast and a schooner-rigged mainmast.
- **Barquentine:** a three-masted vessel with a square rigged foremast, schooner-rigged mainmast and mizzenmast.
- **Bark:** a three-masted ship with square rigged foremast and mainmast, schooner-rigged mizzenmast.
- **Full-rigged:** three (or more) masts, all square rigged.
- **Three-mast schooner:** three masts, all schooner-rigged.

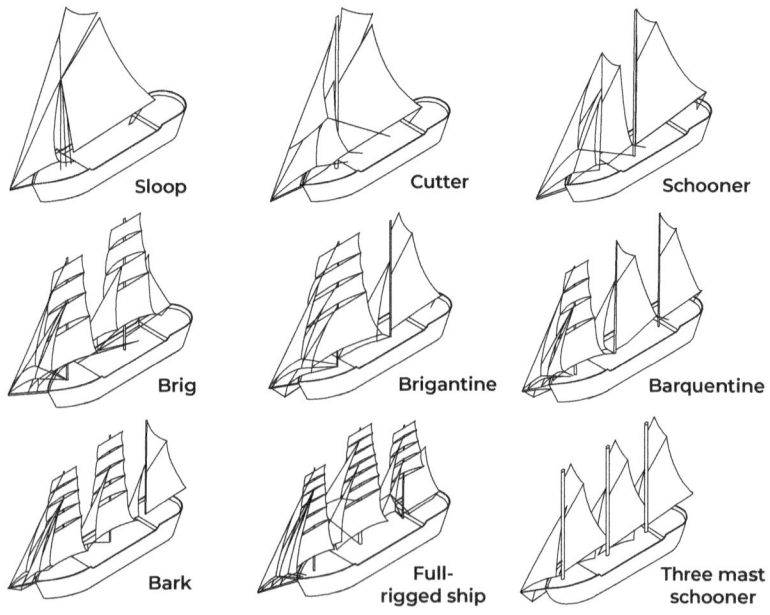

Bipod and tripod masts

There is evidence of bipod and tripod masts from the earliest recorded days of seafaring and across continents, including traditional boat building in ancient Egypt, China, Pakistan and South America, and continuing to the present day in Indonesia. Many more occurrences of this technology in other cultures likely await identification in the literature. The presence of this mast type could mean hull design or materials without sufficient strength to support a pole mast, or the continued use of traditional boat building techniques originally developed under such conditions.

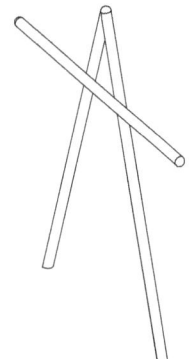

Bipod mast

- **Bipod mast:** two poles arranged in a triangle with the bottom of each pole fixed to a side of the hull and joined together at the top. Often seen in vessels lacking a sufficiently strong keel to support a single-pole mast.
- **Tripod mast:** similar to a bipod mast but with a third forward pole to take the longitudinal force from the sails, replacing or reducing the pressure on backstays.

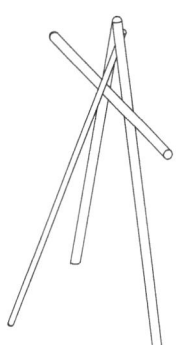

Tripod mast

Mast/boom crutch

- **Mast/boom crutch:** pole topped with a U or V-shape forked support to hold a lowered/disassembled mast pole, boom and/or spars when they are not required, e.g. during transport. Mast crutches can be seen in early Egyptian depictions of sailing vessels and are in use today on sail boats and smaller yachts.

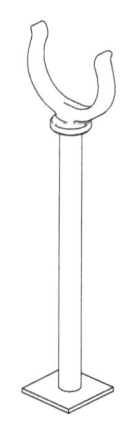

Mast/boom crutch

CHAPTER 9
STEAM-POWERED VESSELS

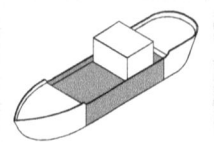

Steam engines revolutionized maritime propulsion, offering consistent, reliable power, independent of weather or human endurance. This steady travel vastly improved efficiency for commerce, military operations, and long-distance voyages.

This chapter explores the evolution of steam-powered vessels, detailing their construction, key equipment, and the innovations that made them the backbone of industrial-era maritime progress. Sections follow the steam cycle: from feedwater and fuel inputs, to heating water into high-pressure steam within a boiler, then steam expansion for work in an engine, and finally, heat and pressure extraction in a condenser before returning to the boiler for the next cycle.

Feedwater system

- **1765** Condenser
- **1865** Evaporator
- **1931** Deaerator

Water from the outside environment, whether fresh or salt, contains impurities that will damage the boiler system through corrosion or scale build-up. To minimise these effects, vessels needed the ability to store distilled water, generate new distilled water to make up losses, and to recycle steam generated by the boilers back into usable feedwater.

- **Feedwater tank:** used to store distilled water for boilers. Usually identifiable as a horizontal closed cylinder with separate input and output pipe fittings and located in proximity to the boiler at the flue end. May be fitted with a deaerator for additional purification of feedwater.
- **Deaerator:** often integrated with the feedwater tank to remove dissolved gases (primarily oxygen and carbon

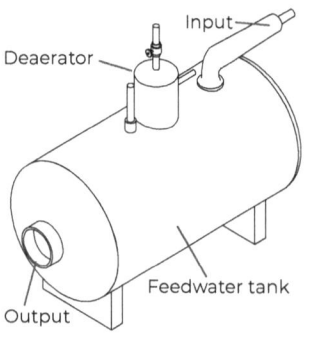

Feedwater tank with deaerator

STEAM-POWERED VESSELS

dioxide) from the feedwater to minimise boiler corrosion. Often appears as a vertical dome or turret on top of the tank. A deaerator works by heating feedwater within its tank. Internal baffles maximize the water surface area, promoting mixing and preventing water carryover for efficient gas removal. A vent then releases the gases.

- **Evaporator:** produces distilled feedwater from the external marine environment. Typically a vertical closed cylinder with two chambers. Raw water enters the lower chamber and is heated by steam coils from the main boilers. The resulting vapour rises through the upper chamber to a condenser. Generally found near the boilers.
- **Condenser:** recycles exhaust steam from the engine circuit back into feedwater. Usually a horizontal closed cylinder, it works like a reverse of a fire-tube boiler, with cool water fed through a circuit of internal tubes as a coolant. Hot steam is fed into the tank, the coolant circuit removes heat, and the resulting condensate is collected in a sump then pumped back into the boiler or feedwater tanks. The cooling process creates a vacuum effect to draw remaining steam from the final pot.

Coal or oil fuel supply

- Black rocks (coal) located in an otherwise bare room close to boilers ➜ Coal-fired boilers
- Boiler with a brick-lined combustion chamber ➜ Originally coal-fired boiler converted to oil-fired
- Boiler with piping input to the combustion chamber ➜ Oil-fired boilers

1881 (likely c.1950) Oil burner

Loading coal bunkers involved most of the crew carrying sacks of coal through the vessel to bunkers, or the vessel may have had coal chutes accessible via hatches on the outside hull or main deck. Once on board, it was necessary to maintain an even distribution of coal across the beam to prevent weight imbalance. Sailors working in the bunkers (trimmers) also had to break the coal into fist-sized chunks ready to be fed into the boilers and shovel coal from the bunkers into carts for transport to the boilers.

Meanwhile, stokers shovelled coal into the boiler combustion chamber.

- **Coal bunkers:** rooms laid out laterally across the hull (cross-bunker) forward of the boilers they were intended to feed, with doors opening into the engine room. Warships had additional protective bunkers around and above the engine room to absorb the energy of incoming projectiles. Locating coal around the engine room helps resolve whether the vessel was coal or oil-fired.

Oil became a cost-efficient alternative to coal by the 1950s. In an oil-fired boiler, fuel injects via a spray nozzle. Unlike coal's labour-intensive loading and handling, oil is continuously loaded, balanced, and transmitted through pipes. As it burns hotter, oil-fired boilers are more compact.

- **Oil tanks:** storage tanks for oil occupy the same spaces previously used for cross-bunkers. A bunker door will not be present, instead there will be pipe fittings.

Converting coal-fired boilers to burn oil is possible. Such conversions are distinguished by a brick lining in the combustion chamber. This brickwork both protects the lining from excessive temperatures and reignites the oil spray if the flame blows out.

Marine boilers

- **1812–c.1850** Cornish boiler
- **1820–c.1875** Box boiler
- **1830–c.1850** Lancashire boiler
- **1843–c.1955** Scotch boiler
- **1887** Yarrow boiler
- **1893–1905** Reed boiler
- **1894** Normand boiler (French)
- **1894** Schulz-Thornycroft boiler (German)
- **1895** Babcock & Wilcox boiler
- **1895** Mumford boiler
- **1906** White-Forster boiler
- **1927** Admiralty boiler
- **1933** Babcock & Wilcox Express boiler (aka M-Type)

STEAM-POWERED VESSELS

The boiler, the heart of steam power, burns coal or oil in a combustion chamber to produce superheated steam. Boiler technology advanced sequentially (in the order set out below) assisted by manufacturing and materials developments. Each stage improved efficiency by increasing the surface area of water in contact with the heat source.

- **Flued boiler:** one (see Cornish) or two (see Lancashire) large diameter flues (tubes) inside the water tank. In later versions the upper surface of the flues may have been corrugated to increase heating surface area. Flued boilers were only capable of generating low steam pressures.
- **Fire-tube boiler:** directed hot-air combustion gases into many narrow tubes immersed in a water tank (see Box, Scotch). Flat-sided box boilers were limited to low pressures, unlike the more robust cylindrical Scotch boiler, which permitted higher pressures. Scotch boilers, extensively used in maritime vessels, could feature up to five combustion chambers in single or double-ended arrangements.
- **Water-tube boiler:** inverted earlier designs by circulating water through tubes within a heated air tank (see Yarrow, Reed, Normand, Schulz-Thornycroft, Mumford, White-Forster, Admiralty, Babcock & Wilcox Express). Maritime designs tended towards small diameter water-tubes (~50 mm or less) to improve heating efficiency. The Babcock & Wilcox boiler was a bit of an oddity in that it used large diameter water tubes (75-105 mm), and a single drum for both feedwater and steam.
- **Three-drum boiler:** high-pressure small-diameter water-tube boiler. Featured two water drums at the base and a steam drum at the apex of a triangle (see Yarrow, Reed, Normand, Schulz-Thornycroft, Mumford, White-Forster, Admiralty, Babcock & Wilcox Express aka M-Type).

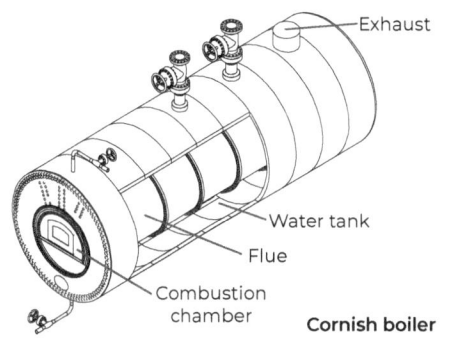

Cornish boiler

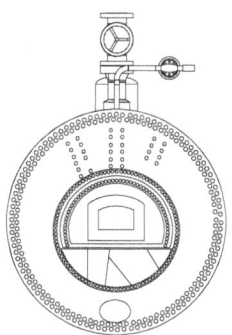

THE SHIPWRECK DECODER

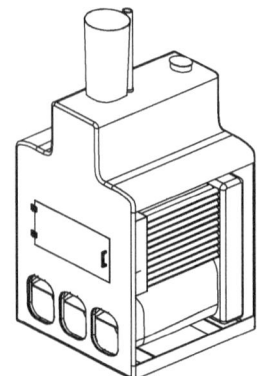
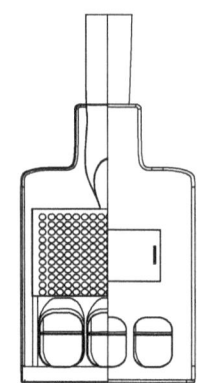

Box boiler

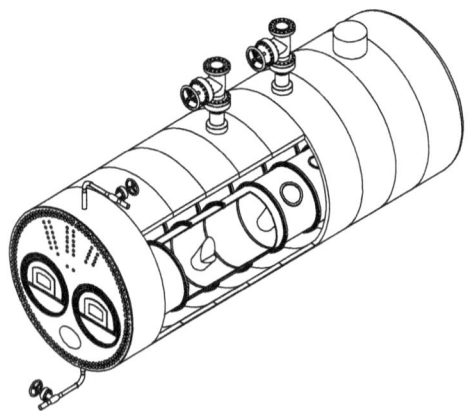
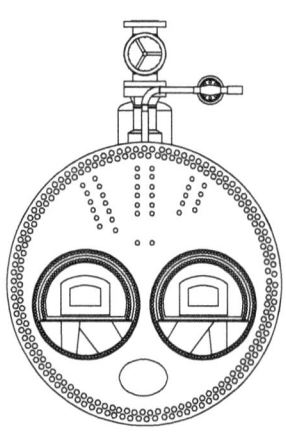

Lancashire boiler

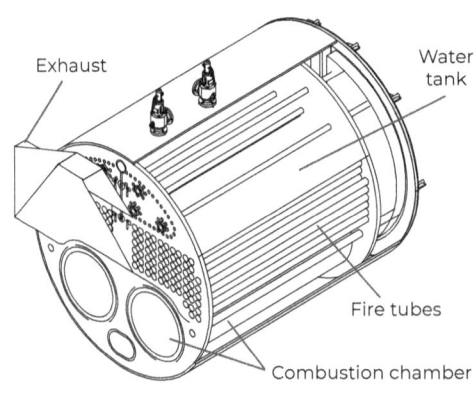

Scotch boiler

STEAM-POWERED VESSELS

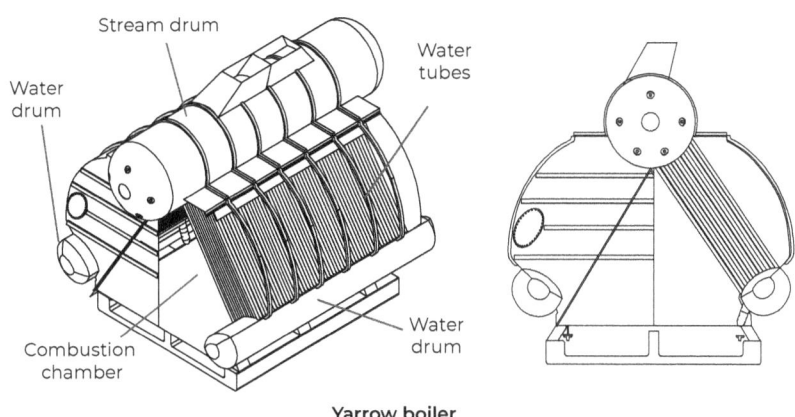

Yarrow boiler

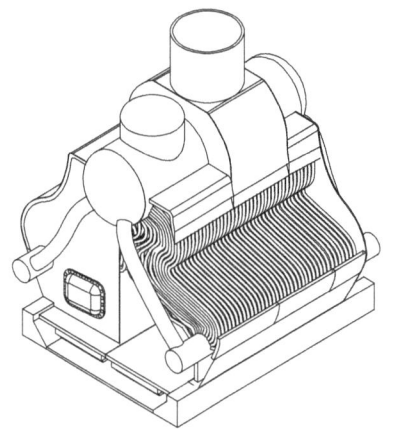
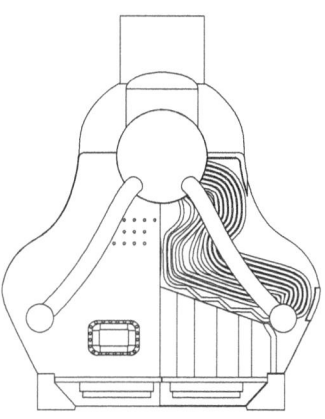

Reed boiler

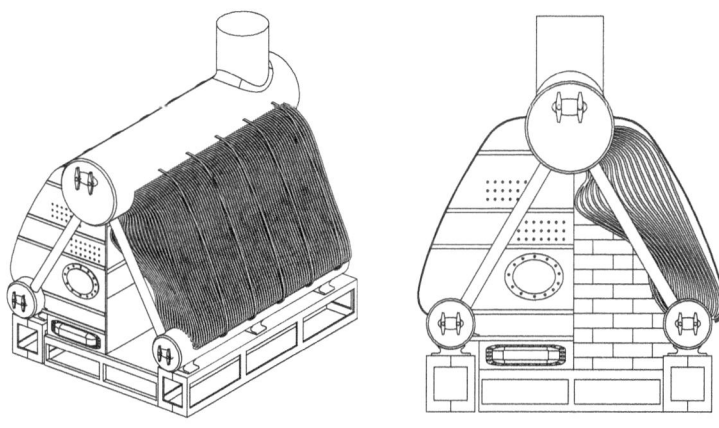

Normand boiler

THE SHIPWRECK DECODER

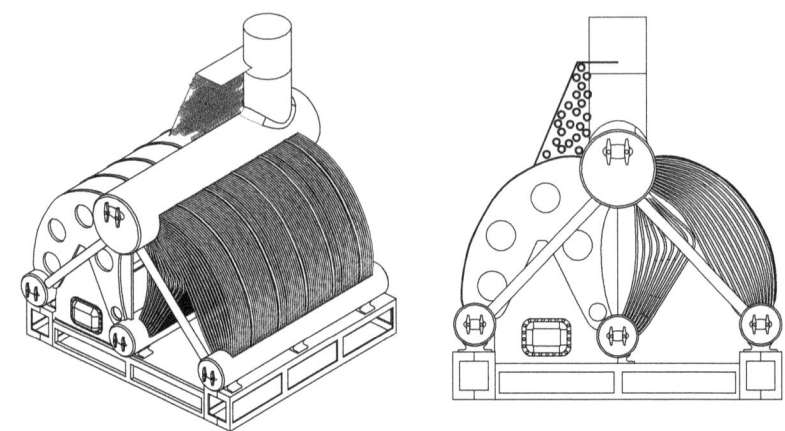

Schulz-Thornycroft boiler

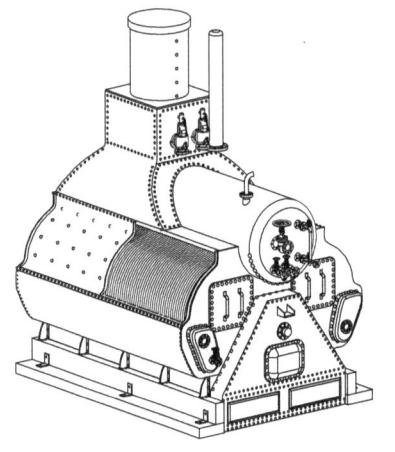
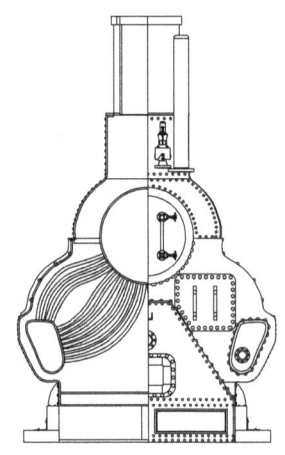

Mumford boiler

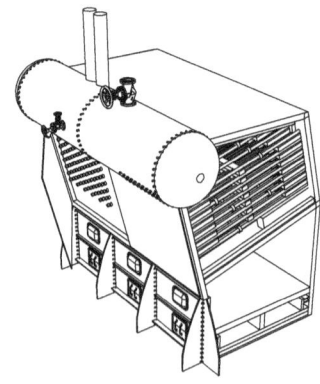

Babcock & Wilcox boiler

STEAM-POWERED VESSELS

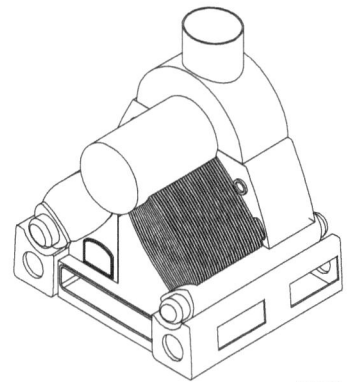
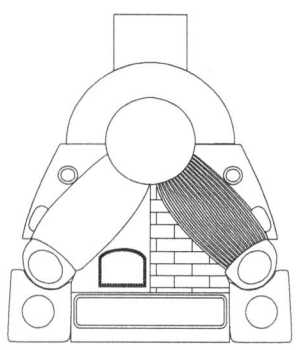

White-Forster boiler

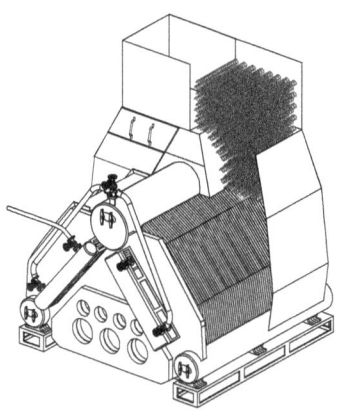
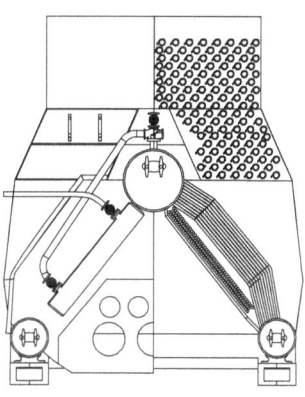

Admiralty boiler

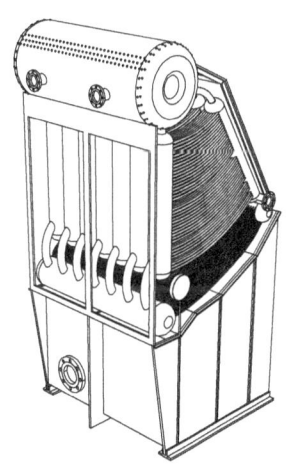
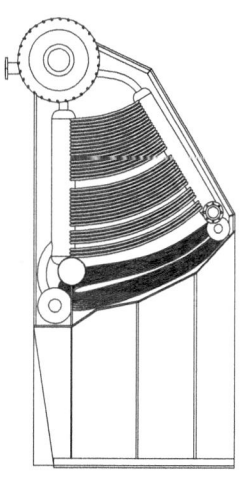

Babcock & Wilcox Express boiler (M-Type)

Donkey boiler

- A smaller, auxilliary boiler of the same or less advanced type as the main boilers, or a compact vertical boiler ➜ Donkey boiler

> **1881** Steam donkey

A small boiler used to run auxiliary equipment such as winches instead of main propulsion. The steam donkey was a common type of vertical donkey boiler.

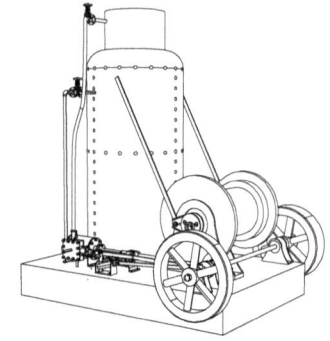

Donkey boiler

Exhaust funnel

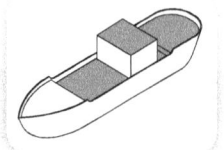

- Funnels are located to vent combustion gases from boiler rooms
- Number and size of functional funnels compared to the number and size of the vessel's boilers ➜ Combustion fuel expected by the vessel's designers

Boiler exhaust gases were lifted clear of the vessel and expelled through one or more funnels. The number and diameter of funnels depended on how cleanly and how much combustion fuel was burned to power the vessel. Older coal-burning vessels needed larger diameter funnels. Vessels with more and larger boilers generated more exhaust and may have required multiple funnels. In the early 20th century, funnels became associated with power and prestige, so they were painted in the livery (colours) of the shipping company and occasionally false funnels were installed for symbolic purposes.

STEAM-POWERED VESSELS

Steam whistle

1835 Steam whistle

A streamship typically had a whistle mounted on its leading funnel for signalling manoeuvres, warnings, and communication. Further whistles functioned as low water alarms on each boiler, preventing potential damage or explosions.

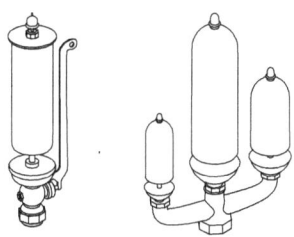

Steam whistle

Steam engine

- Two cylinders (pots) of same diameter ➔ Twin pot engine
- Two or more pots of increasing volume ➔ Compound engine (double, triple, quadruple)
- Looking down at the top of a triple expansion engine, the smallest cylinder diameter points to the boiler and bow, the largest cylinder diameter points to the propeller and stern

1712 Newcomen engine
1769 Watt engine
1781 Crankshaft
1800 Cornish engine
1856 Compound engine
1880 Triple expansion

If the boiler is the heart of a steamship then the engine is the muscle, translating the steam's energy into propulsive force. Interpreting marine engines seems daunting at first. The most commonly encountered variety is the triple expansion engine with all its complicated rods and valves, but this is the culmination of two centuries of mechanical evolution. Once you understand that evolution the parts become clear.

This section will outline the evolution of steam engines by explaining the innovative changes between milestone models. There were many variations and exotic dead ends but we will stick to the main line of evolution that produced the triple expansion engine. It will be helpful to keep in mind that each innovation worked towards the objective of generating more torque (rotational force) as smoothly as possible.

To understand the concept of torque smoothness, it is useful to consider the manually powered crankshaft on a bicycle. The rider generates torque by pushing down on each pedal in sequence. The two pedals are positioned directly opposite each other and joined by connecting rods to the shaft (connecting rods at 180 degrees). For a single pedal from the top of the arc, the torque generated starts at zero, reaches its maximum at the forward midpoint and drops to zero at the bottom. The pedal will not return to the top because no torque is generated on the rear arc—another force is needed. This is provided by the second pedal which also generates torque on the forward part of *its* arc. In this system torque is not smooth because it drops to zero twice in each rotation, each time the pedals are in the vertical position. Torque smoothness could be improved by adding a third, evenly-spaced pedal (connecting rods at 120 degrees), or by adding a flywheel. The latter is used in stationary exercise bikes, which is why the spin continues for a time after pedalling ceases.

Steam engine concepts
- **Beam engine:** an engine that uses a large, central rocking beam (e.g. Newcomen, Watt, Cornish), and where the piston connects via a beam and connecting rod to the crankshaft.
- **Single-action pot:** a cylinder and piston assembly where only one chamber of the cylinder exerts force to move the piston to the power position and an external force is needed to restore the piston to the rest position (e.g. Newcomen, Watt, Cornish, Side-lever, Grasshopper).
- **Dual/double-action pot:** a cylinder and piston assembly where both chambers of the pot exert alternating force and no external force is needed. In a dual-action pot there are two power positions.
- **Simple engine:** a reciprocating engine with one or more pots of equal volume arranged in parallel so that each can receive steam directly

STEAM-POWERED VESSELS

from the boiler. Usually seen in single pot and twin pot configurations.
- **Compound engine:** a type of reciprocating steam engine with two or more pots of progressively increasing volume, arranged in parallel from smallest to largest (see Triple expansion).
- **Steam turbine:** a rotary engine that uses the flow of steam against angled blades fixed to a rotor to generate rotational energy.

Basic steam engine assembly
- **Boiler:** the boiler generates steam at the input pressure. The input steam pressure is higher than the exhaust steam pressure, the difference measured represents the potential work that can be done.
- **Cylinder and piston assembly ("pot"):** the cylinder houses a piston that divides it into two chambers: the steam chamber (C1) and the atmosphere side chamber (C2). The piston seals the chambers C1 and C2 from each other and can move (reciprocate) within the cylinder. The total volume of the cylinder stays the same but as the piston moves it changes the distribution of volume between C1 and C2 (e.g. if the piston moves towards the C2 end, the volume of C1 will get larger as the volume of C2 gets smaller). The piston is fitted with a connecting rod on the C2 side.
- **Steam input assembly:** the boiler is connected to the steam chamber (C1) by an input pipe (IS) regulated by an input valve (V(IS)). Steam pressure is highest at the input stage.
- **Exhaust assembly:** after expanding and performing work, steam is released from C1 by an exhaust pipe (ES) regulated by an exhaust valve (V(ES)). Steam pressure is lowest in the exhaust stage.

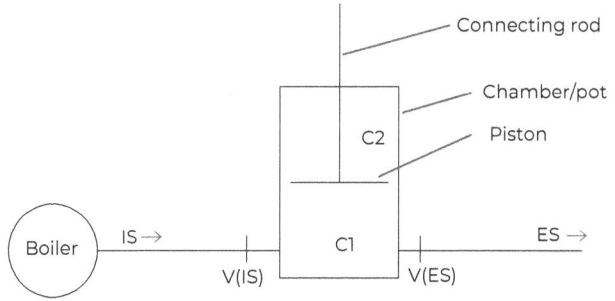

Basic steam engine schematic

Newcomen engine

The Newcomen engine operated from very low-pressure steam and was primarily used in mining. It was not suitable for marine use but understanding the components and operation provides a good foundation for understanding later steam engines.

In this setup, C2 is open to the force of atmospheric pressure (ATM) which at sea level has partial pressure of 1 bar, and the following components are added to the basic assembly:

- **Water tank:** provides cool water input to the spray nozzle.
- **Spray nozzle:** located towards the C2 end of the cylinder so that when the piston is fully moved towards C1 the spray nozzle will open into C1. The spray nozzle converts water flow into water mist.
- **Water input assembly:** the water tank is connected to the spray nozzle by a pipe (IW) regulated by an open/close valve (V(IW)).
- **Rocking beam and weighted rod assembly:** the rocking beam is a lever acting over a fulcrum at the pivot point. It is joined by chains to the connecting rod at one end and the weighted rod (WG) at the other. Lever action transmits the downward force of gravity on the weighted rod to apply equal upward force on the connecting rod.
- **Exhaust assembly:** instead of steam, water condensate is released from C1 by a pipe (EW) regulated by an open/close valve (V(EW))

The resting position of the Newcomen engine is with the weighted rod fully down. In this position, C2 is fully contracted and C1 is fully expanded. The opposite, the power position, has C1 fully contracted and C2 fully expanded. To transition from rest to power position:

1. Steam admission: C1 is filled with steam from the boiler at slightly above ATM pressure (V(IS) open, V(EW) closed, V(IW) closed);
2. Condensation: Cool water from the water tank is injected through the spray nozzle into C1. This causes the steam in C1 to cool and condense back to liquid water, creating a partial vacuum in C1 (i.e. partial pressure less than ATM). The resulting water condensate is then drained away through EW (V(IS) closed, V(EW) open, V(IW) open);
3. Power stroke: The higher partial pressure of ATM in C2 pushes the piston towards the lower partial pressure in C1 (vacuum effect). The

STEAM-POWERED VESSELS

force of the vacuum effect overcomes the weight of the weighted rod to lift it towards the power position.

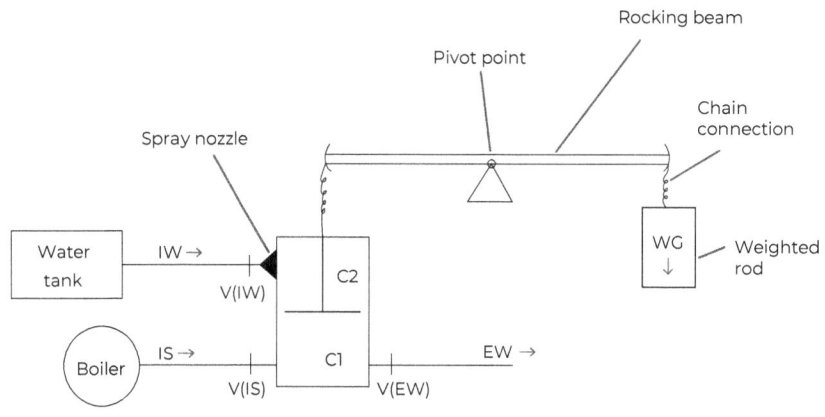

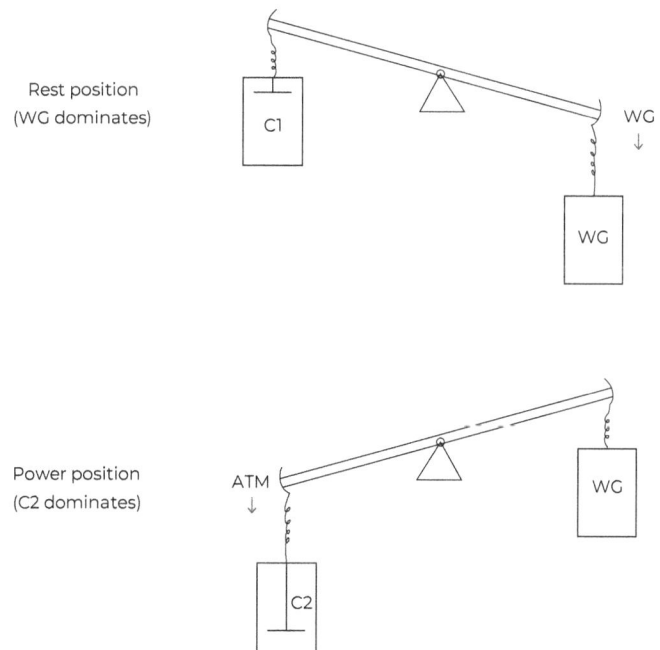

Newcomen engine schematic

Watt engine

The Newcomen engine was inefficient because the injected spray of water into C1 cooled the whole cylinder. In the Watt engine, the water input assembly was removed, and instead cooling occurred in a separate condenser added to the exhaust assembly. Around this time we also start to see the addition of a crankshaft to convert linear motion into torque, and a flywheel to improve torque smoothness.

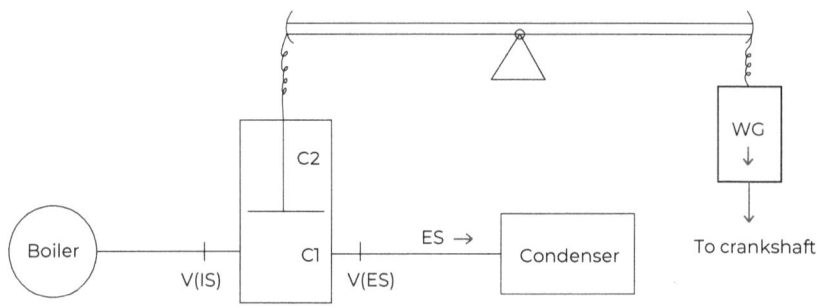

Watt engine schematic

- **Crankshaft:** rotating shaft to convert the reciprocating motion of pistons into rotary motion.
- **Flywheel:** rotating mass to smooth uneven torque from the crankshaft. The crankshaft generates torque with peaks and troughs as each piston moves though its power position and rest position cycle. The flywheel's rotational inertia stores kinetic energy during torque peaks and releases it during troughs, resulting in a more consistent spinning speed.

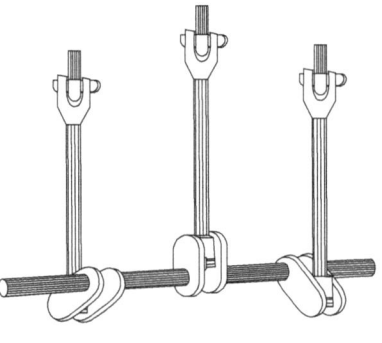

Crankshaft

Cornish (walking beam) engine

The development of boilers able to generate high pressure steam meant that engines could use it to push the piston downwards rather than relying on the vacuum effect. In this setup the steam input assembly now connects to C2.

- **Linking assembly:** C1 and C2 are now connected by a pipe (L) regulated by an open/close valve (V(L)). V(IS) and V(L) are connected so that when one is open the other must be closed.

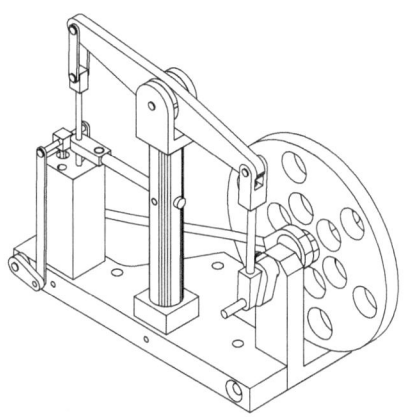

Cornish (walking beam) engine

In this setup to move from the rest position to the power position:
1. C2 is filled with high pressure steam from the boiler and steam is vented from C1 (V(IS) open/V(L) closed, V(ES) closed); and
2. The increase in pressure in C2 pushes the piston towards C1, lifting the weighted rod to the power position.

To return to the rest position from the power position, the high-pressure steam in C2 is released through L to C1 (to avoid creating a vacuum in C1) and then to the condenser through V(ES) (V(IS) closed/V(L) open, V(ES) open).

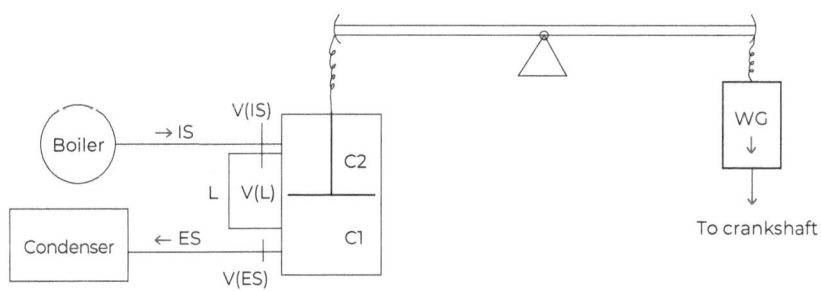

Cornish engine schematic

THE SHIPWRECK DECODER

Side-lever and grasshopper engine

The side-lever engine is a variation on the Cornish engine where the rocking beam is replaced by a low lever connected to the piston rod by a cross head and side rod assembly (side-lever). The fulcrum is in the centre of the side-lever, or in the grasshopper engine variant at the far end of the lever in order to use the lever's own weight to return the piston to the rest position.

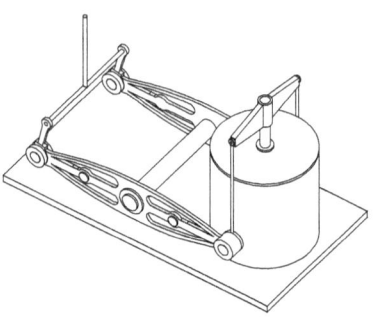

Side-lever engine

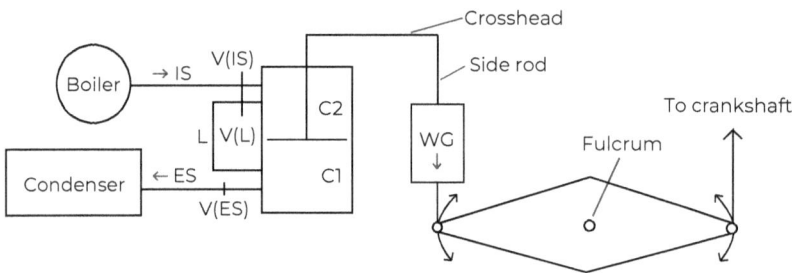

Side-lever engine schematic

Side-lever engines had a lower centre of gravity than beam engines so were more suitable for marine applications and found use on paddleboats.

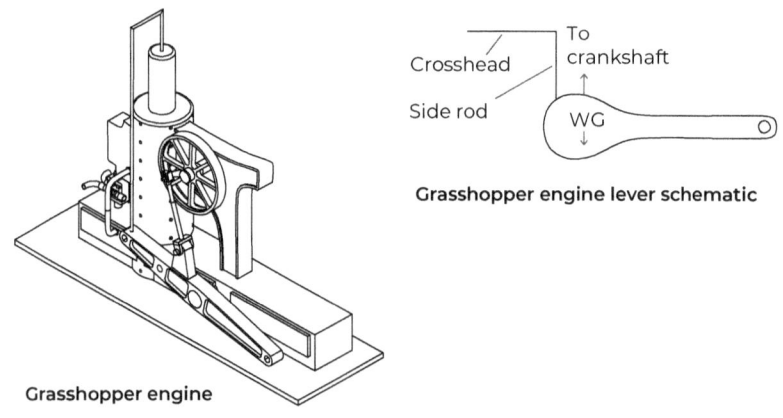

Grasshopper engine

Grasshopper engine lever schematic

STEAM-POWERED VESSELS

Dual-action pot

In this design the rocking beam (or side-lever) and weight assembly is redundant. There is no longer a defined rest position, instead the cylinder (pot) alternates between power positions for each chamber (C1-Power and C2-Power). Since the pot does not rely on an external force to return to the rest position, it can be set up in any orientation. For locomotives and some early marine vessels the pot was laid horizontally. For most marine vessels the pot was vertical but inverted from previous engine types, with C2 and the piston rod orientated downwards so that the crankshaft was directly in line with the propeller shaft.

- **Piston valve (or sliding valve):** a piston valve is added to co-ordinate the input steam and exhaust steam from each chamber, controlling four ports. Steam input (IS) from C1 is V(IS-1), exhaust (ES) from C1 is V(ES-1), IS from C2 is V(IS-2), and ES from C2 is V(ES-2). The piston valve is driven by a separate control rod, riding on a crankshaft.

In C1-Power: the piston valve completes the input circuit to C1 (so C1 becomes high pressure) and completes the exhaust circuit from C2 (so C2 becomes low pressure). The pressure differential (C1 > C2) causes the piston to move towards C2. Valve states: V(IS-1) open, V(ES-1) closed, V(IS-2) closed, V(ES-2) open.

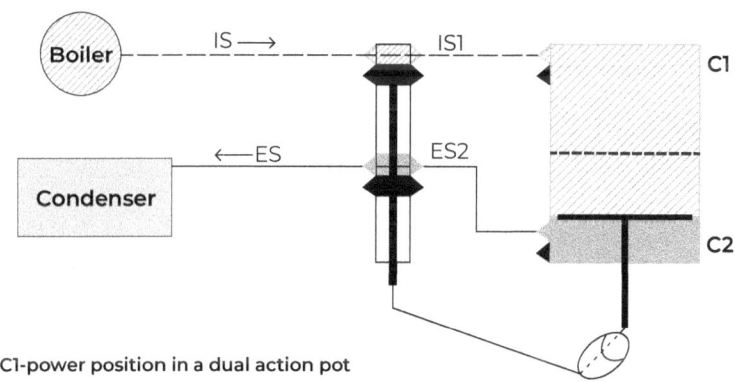

C1-power position in a dual action pot

In C2-Power: the circuits are reversed. The piston valve completes the exhaust circuit from C1 (so C1 becomes low pressure) and completes the input circuit to C2 (so C2 becomes high pressure). The pressure difference (C1 < C2) causes the Piston to move towards C1. Valve states: V(IS-1) closed, V(ES-1) open, V(IS-2) open, V(ES-2) closed.

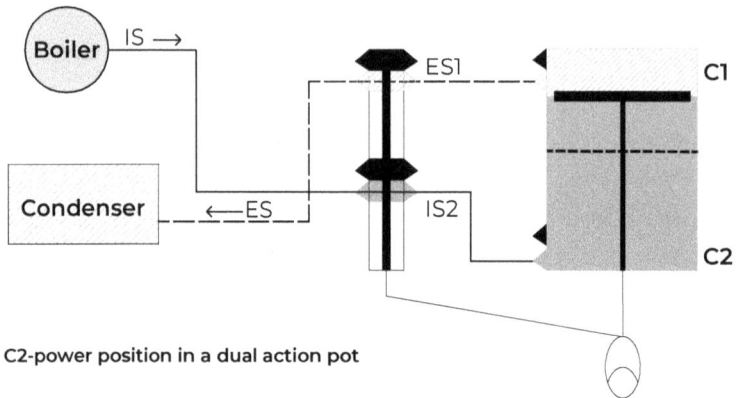

C2-power position in a dual action pot

Compound engine

In a compound engine the exhaust steam from one pot becomes the input steam to the next pot in the sequence. As previously noted, that exhaust steam has a lower pressure than input steam, with the difference representing the work done in moving the piston. Consequently, each pot in the sequence will receive progressively lower pressure steam. To generate the same force with lower pressure steam it is necessary for the piston to have a larger surface area, in turn requiring a larger cylinder volume.

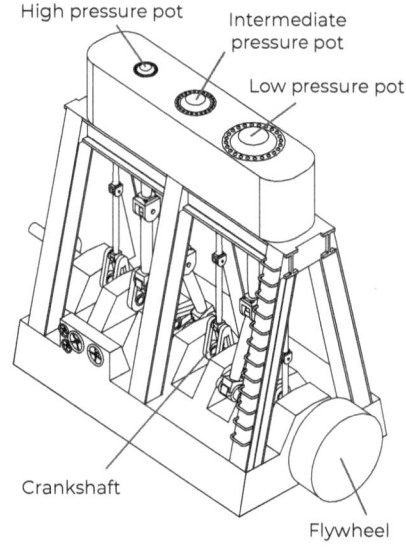

Triple expansion engine

Therefore, the cylinders (pots) must be of different sizes arranged from smallest to largest. The smallest pot receives the highest pressure steam directly from the boiler, and the final, largest pot receives the lowest pressure steam that has already done work in each preceding pot.

While 'compound engine' usually refers to an engine with two cylinders, the most common marine steam engine was the triple expansion engine with three cylinders. Much rarer, but there were even some quadruple expansion engines with four pots.

Engine configurations

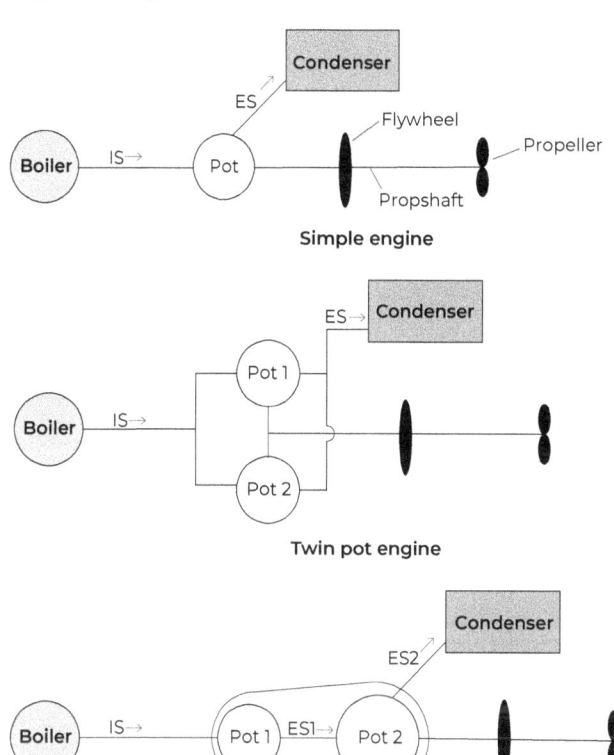

Simple engine

Twin pot engine

Compound engine (double expansion)

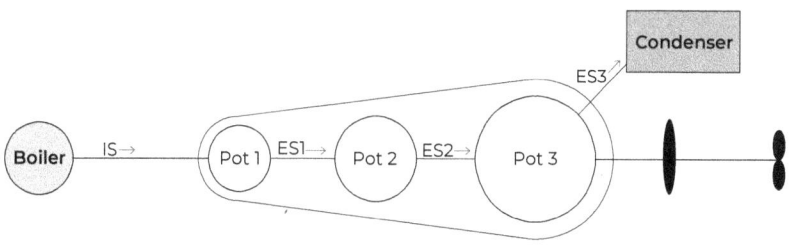

Triple expansion (compound) engine

Steam turbine engine

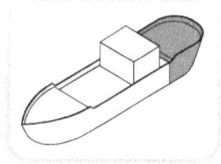

- Bucket-shaped blades ➔ Impulse turbine
- Wing-shaped blades ➔ Reaction turbine

1894 Steam turbine

- **Impulse turbines:** the steam is accelerated by expansion through stationary nozzles and directed onto rotors shaped like miniature buckets. May be pressure-compounded with sequentially larger rotors, or velocity-compounded with sets of equally sized rotors that move at progressively slower speeds absorbing the steam's velocity in stages.
- **Reaction turbines:** the steam is directed across rotor blades shaped similarly to airplane wings so that the flow off the edge of the blade generates a reaction force pushing the blade in the opposite direction. May be pressure-compounded through sequentially larger rotors.

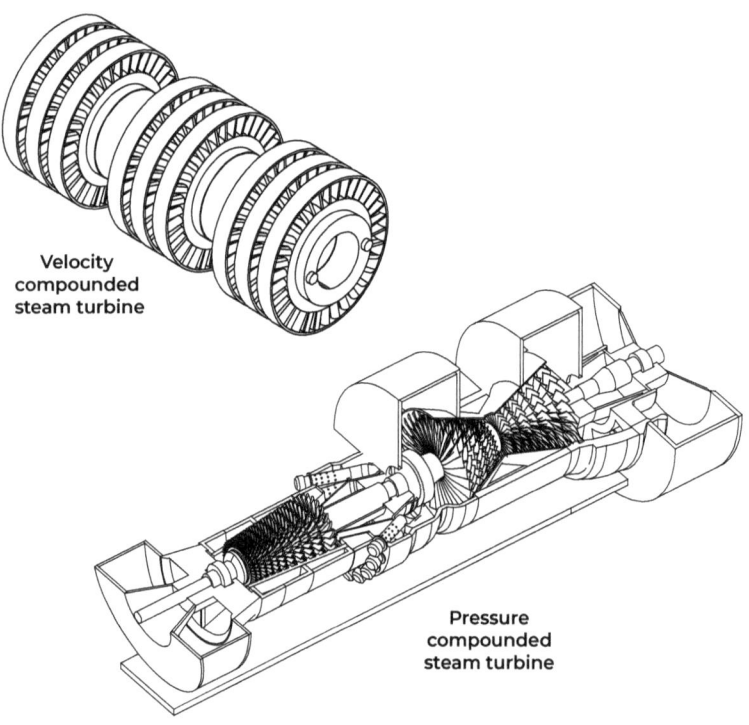

Velocity compounded steam turbine

Pressure compounded steam turbine

CHAPTER 10
COMBUSTION-POWERED VESSELS

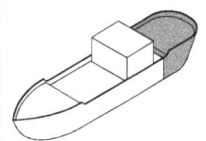

Combustion engines significantly improved maritime propulsion over steam power, offering enhanced efficiency, reliability, and operational flexibility. Unlike steam engines, which demanded extensive fuel, large boilers, and continuous water replenishment, combustion engines were more fuel-efficient and compact, allowing for greater autonomy and reduced maintenance. Diesel engines especially provided superior durability and lower operating costs.

This chapter explains engine types and cycles in simple terms to aid identification. It introduces petrol and diesel engines, along with the stages of four-stroke, two-stroke, and gas turbine engine cycles.

- Electrical wires to spark plugs ➜ Petrol engine
- Fuel lines to injectors ➜ Diesel engine

1862 Four stroke engine
1879 Two stroke engine
1885 Petrol engine
1897 Diesel engine
1947 Gas turbine

Combustion engine

- **Petrol engine:** In a petrol engine the air-fuel mixture is ignited by an electrical spark generated by a spark plug. Older petrol engines did not have the now almost universal fuel injection systems, instead using a carburettor to mix fuel and air.
- **Diesel engine:** In a diesel engine the air-fuel mixture is compressed to the point of spontaneous combustion. Two stroke diesel engines are taller than comparable four stroke diesel engines. Diesel engines have a fuel injector, and do not have spark plugs and a carburettor.

THE SHIPWRECK DECODER

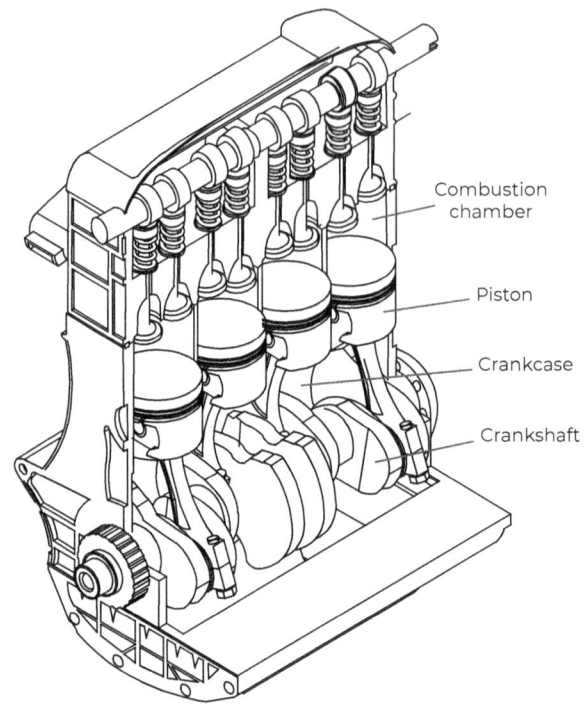

Combustion engine

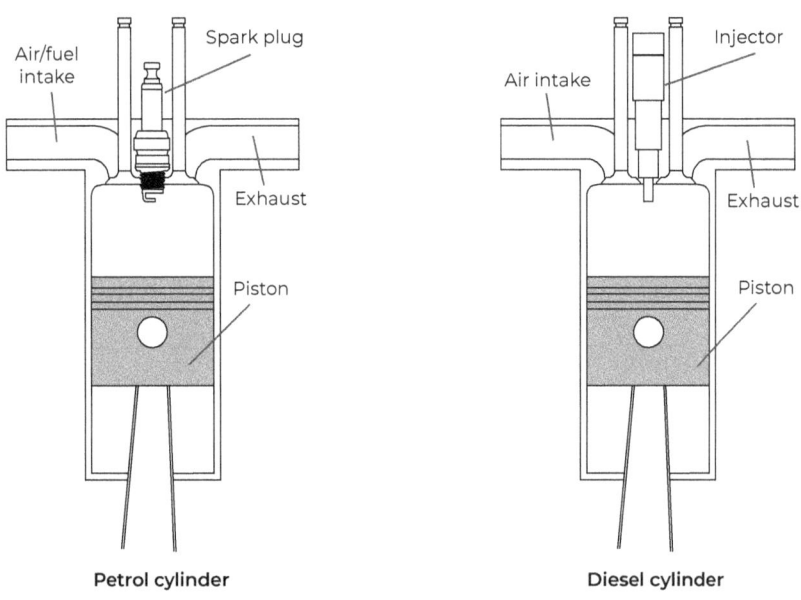

Petrol cylinder **Diesel cylinder**

Four stroke engine cycle

The four-stroke engine cycle consists of four distinct piston strokes:
1. **Intake stroke:** intake valve is open; exhaust valve is closed; outward movement of the piston creates a partial vacuum to draw new (a) air-fuel mixture (petrol), or (b) air (diesel), into the combustion chamber through the intake valve.
2. **Compression stroke:** both the intake and exhaust valves are closed; inward movement of the piston compresses the (a) air-fuel mixture (petrol), or (b) air (diesel) (significantly increasing its temperature), in the combustion chamber.
3. **Power (combustion) stroke:** both valves remain closed; (a) the compressed air-fuel mixture is ignited by a spark plug (petrol); or (b) fuel is injected into the combustion chamber and mixes with the hot compressed air causing spontaneous (compression) ignition (diesel); the energy released by the rapid combustion moves the piston outward, turning the crankshaft.
4. **Exhaust stroke:** intake valve is closed; exhaust valve is open; inward movement of the piston forces waste gas out of the compression chamber through the exhaust valve.

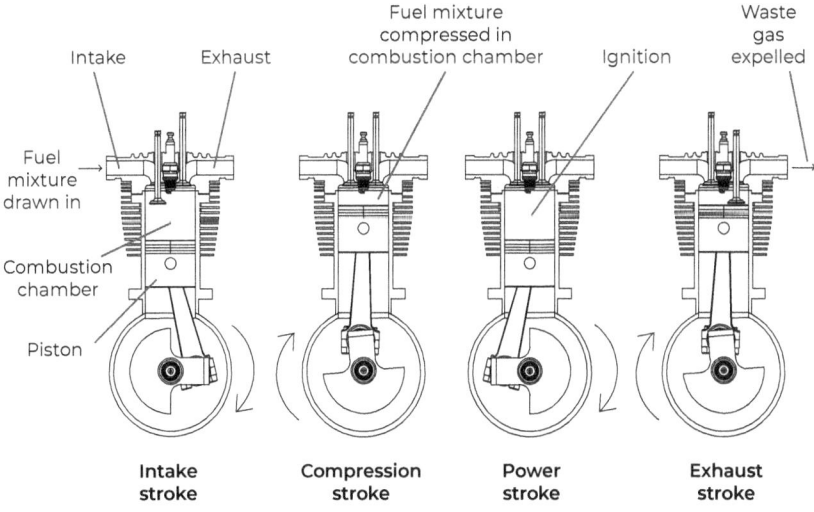

Two stroke engine cycle

The two-stroke engine cycle completes a power stroke with every revolution of the crankshaft, combining intake/compression and power/exhaust into two piston movements:

1. **Intake and compression stroke:** inward movement of the piston opens the intake port and creates a vacuum to draw in new (a) air-fuel mixture from the carburettor (petrol), or (b) air (diesel), into the crankcase (air-fuel chamber); closes the transfer port and exhaust port to isolate the combustion chamber; and compresses the (a) air-fuel mixture (petrol), or (b) air (diesel), in the combustion chamber.
2. **Ignition:** (a) the compressed air-fuel mixture in the combustion chamber is ignited by a spark plug (petrol), or (b) fuel is injected into the combustion chamber and mixes with the hot compressed air causing spontaneous ignition (diesel); the energy released by the rapid combustion moves the piston outward, driving the crankshaft.
3. **Power and exhaust stroke:** expanding gases from combustion cause outward movement of the piston, which closes the intake port; opens the transfer port and creates over-pressure in the air-fuel chamber to force (a) air-fuel mixture (petrol), or (b) air (diesel), into the combustion chamber, scavenging the remaining exhaust gases; and opens the exhaust port to allow escape of waste gas in the combustion chamber that is displaced by the incoming air-fuel mixture (petrol), or air (diesel).

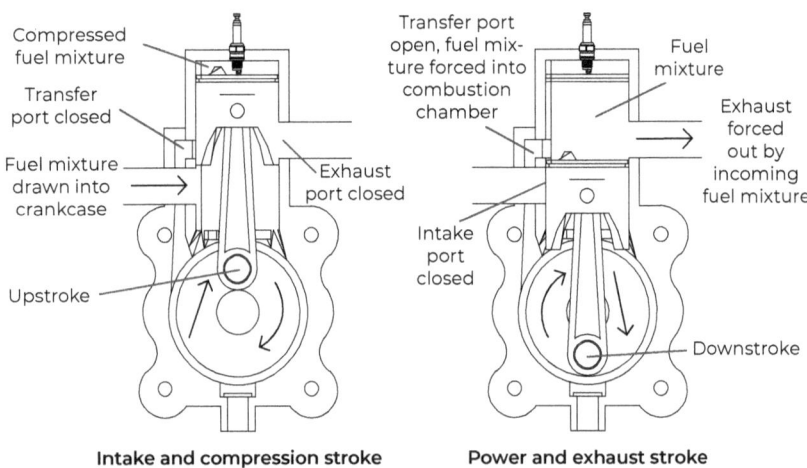

Intake and compression stroke   Power and exhaust stroke

COMBUSTION-POWERED VESSELS

Gas turbine engine cycle

There are four phases to the gas turbine engine cycle, known as the Brayton cycle:

1. **Isentropic compression phase:** air is drawn into the compressor and pressurised. Increasing air temperature and pressure.
2. **Isobaric heating phase:** compressed air flows into the combustion chamber. Fuel is injected into the combustion chamber and ignited to further heat the air. The air pressure does not change. Heated compressed air exits the combustion chamber.
3. **Isentropic expansion phase:** heated compressed air expands through a turbine turning the rotor. The air loses pressure and temperature. Some of the energy produced is re-used to power the compressor for the next isentropic phase.
4. **Isobaric heat rejection (cooling) phase:** air is cooled further, e.g. through a heat exchanger, before entering the compressor for the next isentropic phase.

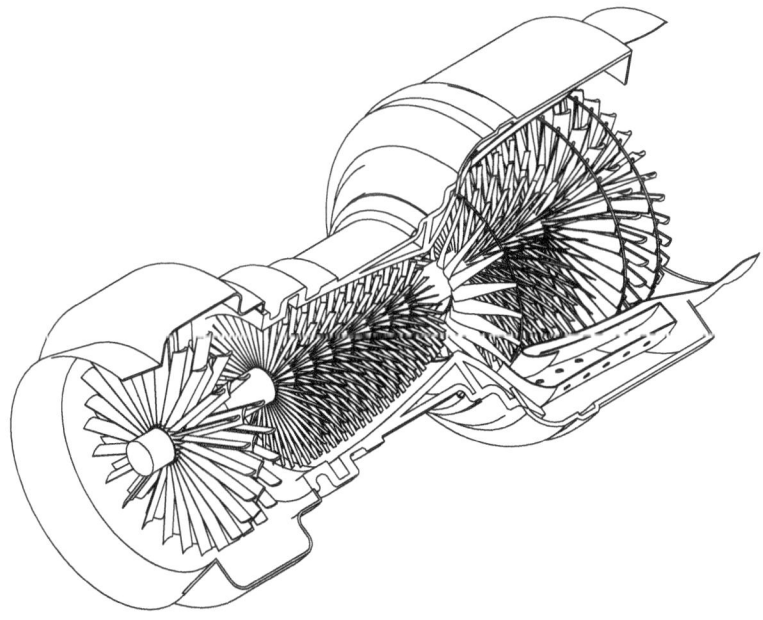

Gas turbine

CHAPTER 11
ELECTRIC-POWERED VESSELS

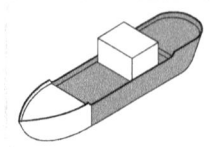

Electric engine

- Tightly wrapped coils of copper wire within a cylindrical housing ➔ Electric engine

1880 Electric engine

Electric engines work by converting electrical energy into mechanical energy. They do this by passing electricity through conductive coils to create opposing magnetic fields between a stationary part (stator) and a rotating part (rotor). The magnetic fields in opposition cause the rotor to turn. The process creates heat as a by-product so electric engines will have either a water-cooling system or be fitted with heat radiating fins.
- **Rotor:** the moving part which turns the output shaft. The rotor is fitted with magnets or conductive coils that generate a magnetic field.
- **Stator**: the stationary part around the rotor. The stator is fitted with magnets or conductive coils that generate a magnetic field.

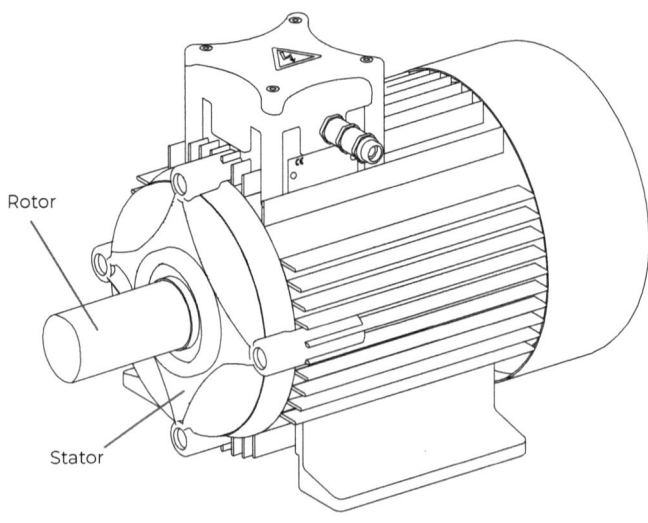

Electric engine

Electric generator

- Tightly wrapped coils of copper wire within a cylindrical housing and connected to an engine ➔ Electric generator

1875 Electric generator

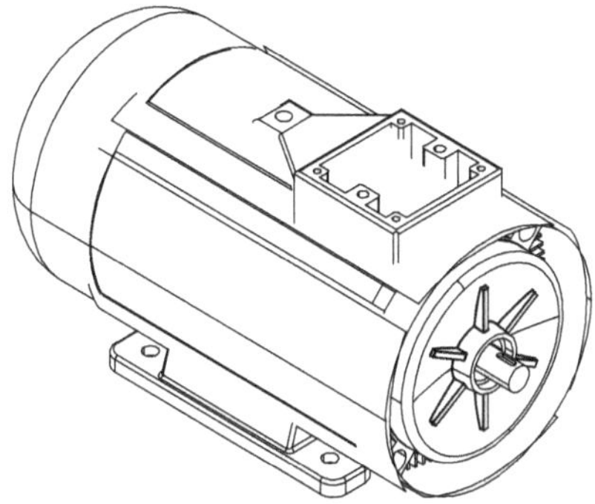
Electric generator

Electric generators are essential for powering onboard electrical systems. They must be driven by an engine and are connected by electrical cables to batteries and/or the vessel's electrical system.

Electric generators operate on the same principles as electric engines but in reverse, and both devices are similar in appearance. An electric generator converts the rotational motion of the shaft into electricity (whereas an electric engine converts electricity into rotational motion of the shaft). The main visually distinguishing feature is that an electric generator must be paired with some form of motor. Small electric generators may have an integrated diesel engine. Those on smaller vessels may be located by and connected to the main propulsion shafts. On larger vessels they may be paired with dedicated engines, as in the diesel-electric or turbo-electric configurations described in the next sections.

- **Batteries:** provide chemical storage of electrical energy. Reactive elements, e.g. stacked sheets of lead in a lead-acid battery, are contained within insulated boxes topped by metal terminals. May be present as single units or in banks of multiple units.

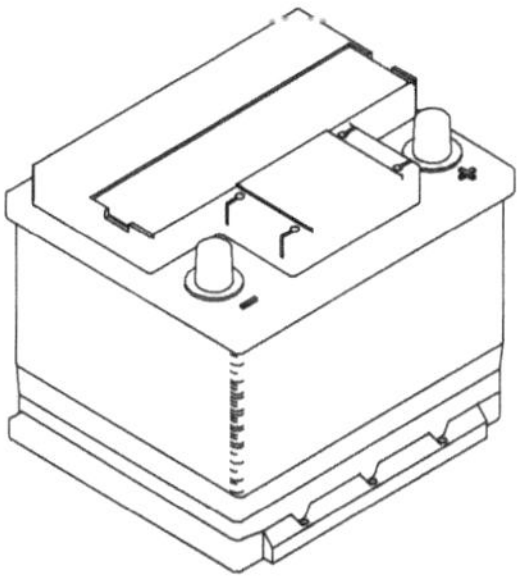
Marine battery

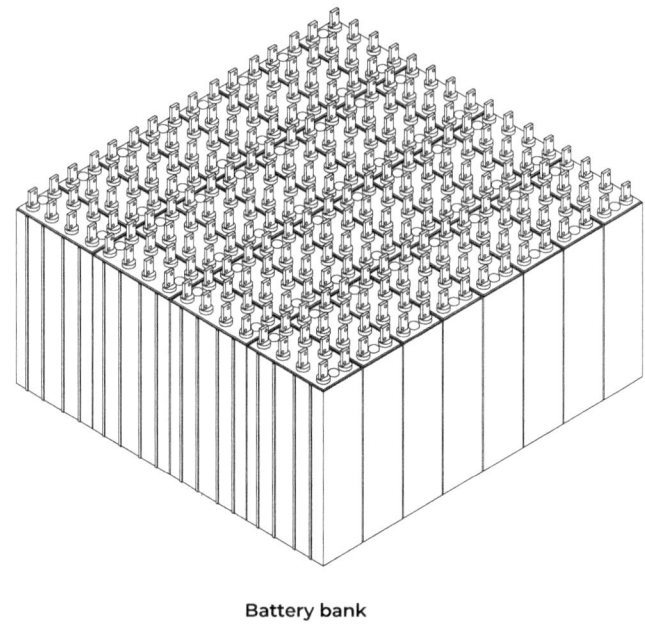

Battery bank

Diesel-electric

A diesel-electric engine replaces a direct mechanical connection to the propeller shaft with an electrical one. Mechanical rotation from the engine is converted to electricity by a generator. The electricity is transmitted by cables to an electric motor; the electric motor converts electricity back into mechanical rotation, driving the propeller shaft.

This configuration allows for more flexible engine layouts, e.g. in the confined space of a submarine; or the use of an azimuth thruster with 360 degree manoeuvrability. Propeller rotation speed is controlled by the electric engine and so a reduction gearbox is not needed to link a high-speed engine to a slow-turning propeller.

Turbo-electric

A steam or gas turbine engine is electrically connected to the propeller shaft instead of mechanically. The principle is very similar to the diesel-electric engine.

CHAPTER 12
CARGO STORAGE AND HANDLING

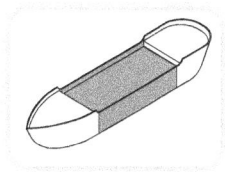

This chapter dives into the specialized structures and equipment that allowed vessels to perform their core operational functions. While previous chapters covered general ship structures like the hull, bow and stern, and universal maritime operations like anchoring and steering, here the focus is on cargo-carrying operations. Sections are organized by the type of cargo: solid, vehicles, liquid, bulk, and gaseous.

Cargo hold

> **1854** Refrigeration

- **Cargo hold:** storage space for cargo.
- **Cargo hatch cover:** closes the cargo hold, either a folding, lift-away or rolling type.
- **Refrigerated cargo hold:** enclosed and insulated storage space with cooling elements and adjacent compressors, and small openings to limit the loss of cooled air when open.

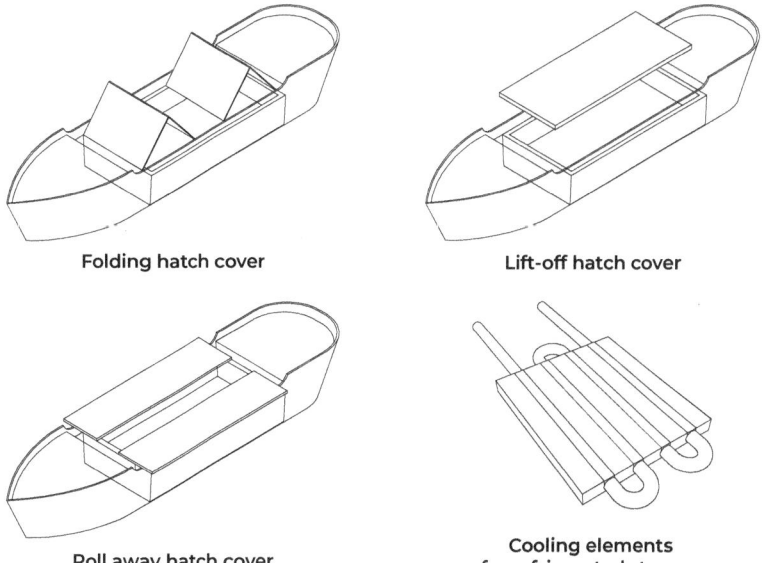

Folding hatch cover

Lift-off hatch cover

Roll away hatch cover

Cooling elements for refrigerated storage

THE SHIPWRECK DECODER

Solid cargo

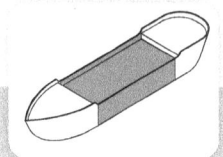

- **Pre-history** Clay pot
- **c.700 BCE–300 (likely)** Amphorae
- **1890** High pressure gas cylinder
- **1956** Shipping container

Solid cargo means discrete large objects: clay pots, amphorae, crates, barrels, gas cylinders, shipping containers, lumber, vehicles, pipes, etc. It is moved using crane-based hooks and slings. Standardising dimensions greatly improves transport efficiency, as can be seen with ancient amphorae, medieval barrels, and modern shipping containers.

- **Clay pot:** thick-walled pottery in which liquid and bulk cargo (e.g. grains) are stored.
- **Amphora:** two-handled pottery jar with a tapered base in common usage by ancient Mediterranean cultures for maritime transport of liquid and bulk cargo. The morphology of amphorae is very specific and can be used to narrow down the time and area of origin. May include markings and stamps denoting the manufacturer or owner.
- **Crate:** wood, metal or plastic box in which items are stored.
- **Barrel:** wood, metal or plastic cylinder in which liquid or items are stored.
- **Gas cylinder:** metal cylinder in which pressurised gas is stored.
- **Shipping container:** standard sized corrugated metal box used in global shipping networks.

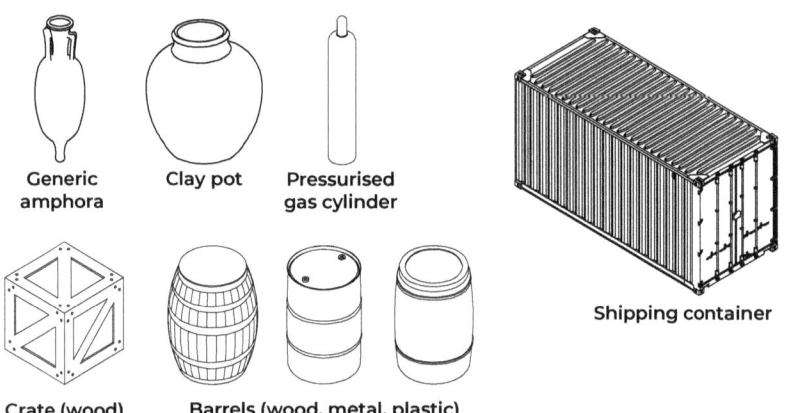

CARGO STORAGE AND HANDLING

Solid cargo handling

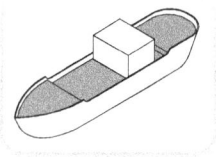

- Derrick boom or jib crane ➔ Vessel carries smaller solid cargo or used as part of bulk or liquid cargo handling gear
- Gantry crane ➔ Vessel carries containers, lumber or other large solid cargo
- Vehicle access ramps ➔ Vehicles embark/disembark under own power
- Parking deck clearance height ➔ Maximum height of receivable vehicles ➔ Broadly distinguishes whether the deck was capable of receiving passenger cars or larger freight trucks ➔ Specific dimensions can be correlated to the typical vehicle dimensions for the operating region and time period
- Railway tracks ➔ Vessel carries rolling stock
- Well deck/dock ➔ Smaller boats embark/disembark under own power ➔ Dimensions indicate maximum size of receivable boat

- **Kingpost:** a fixed vertical pole shorter than a mast.
- **Goalpost:** a pair of kingposts connected by a bridge at the top. There may be a further topmast mounted on top of the bridge.
- **Hoist:** mechanical device for raising or lowering loads using pulleys connected by rope, chain or cable. May be operated manually, pneumatically or by a small engine.
- **Derrick boom:** a hinged pole able to be (a) raised and lowered by guy lines fixed to an adjacent fixed mast or kingpost; and (b) rotated in an arc.
- **Pivoting jib crane:** Horizontal beam (jib) capable of rotating on a mast or mount. Cargo is raised and lowered by a hoist that can move along the boom.

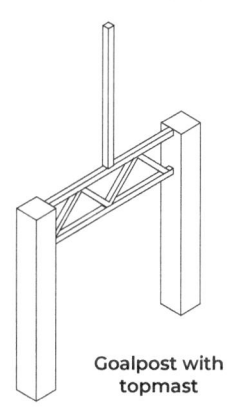

Goalpost with topmast

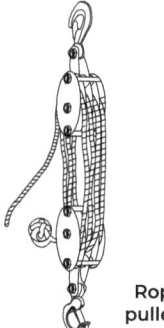

Rope and pulley hoist

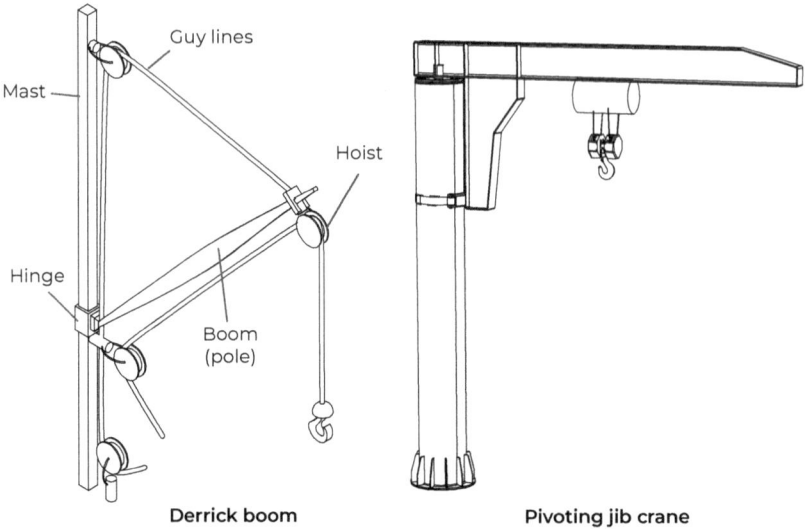

Derrick boom

Pivoting jib crane

- **Gantry crane:** two or four vertical posts connected at the top by horizontal beams to form a frame that straddles the cargo. The beams may extend outside the gantry. Hoists raise the cargo and move along the beam.

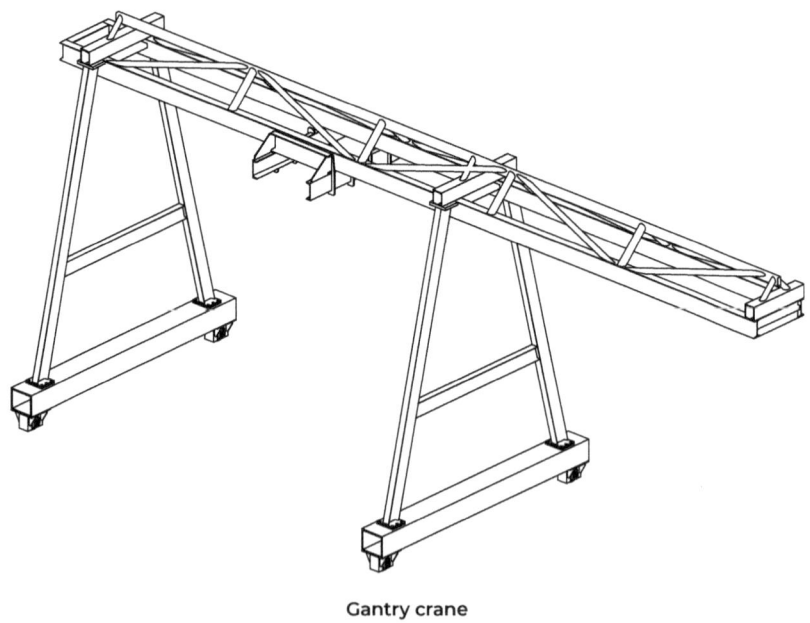

Gantry crane

CARGO STORAGE AND HANDLING

- **Luffing jib crane:** Similar to a pivoting jib crane with the additional ability to raise and lower (luff) the jib using cables or hydraulics.

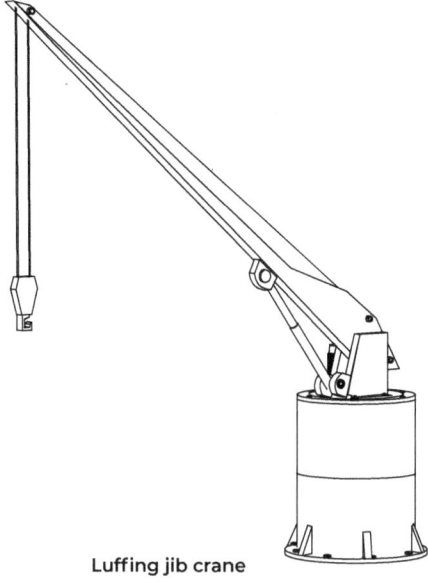

Luffing jib crane

- **Travelling gantry crane:** a gantry is capable of moving longitudinally along the main deck on rubber tyres or tracks.
- **Roll-on roll-off ramp and parking deck:** Built in ramps that allow smaller road and/or rail vehicles to embark and disembark under their own power for storage in onboard parking decks. Railway tracks would indicate that the vessel transported trains or rail cars.
- **Well deck/dock:** Enclosed deck that is partly submergible (may require taking on ballast to lower the well deck) and can be opened to allow smaller vessels to float into the deck.

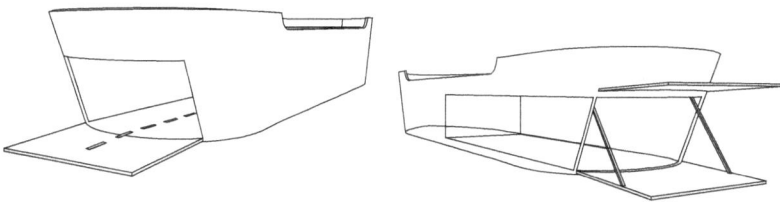

Roll-on roll-off ramp and parking deck   Well deck/dock

Landing deck and hangar

- Launch catapult ➤ Vessel has the ability to launch fixed wing aircraft
- Long rectangular area, clear of obstructions, with an arresting wire ➤ Recovery of fixed wing aircraft by landing under own power (aircraft carrier or amphibious assault ship)
- Runway length ➤ Critical factor in determining whether a specific model of fixed wing aircraft can land in the space
- Crane in proximity to launch catapult and absence of runway ➤ Fixed wing aircraft must be equipped for water landings
- Square and level area, free of obstructions, clear of surrounding vertical structures on two/three sides, and especially if next to similarly sized enclosed storage space ➤ May be a helicopter landing pad and hangar
- Areas of (a) helicopter landing pad, and (b) surrounding clear zone ➤ Maximum size class of receivable helicopter

> **1903** Aircraft
> **1910** Seaplane
> **1939** Helicopter

Clear flat spaces on upper surfaces of decks and superstructure that allow aircraft and/or helicopters to land and take-off under their own power for storage in onboard hangars.

- **Arresting gear:** wires strung laterally across the deck and attached to a breaking system to arrest the landing of fixed wing aircraft, which catch the wire with a tailhook. Secondary "barricade nets" are deployed in emergency situations when an aircraft cannot make a normal landing (e.g. if there is a problem with the tailhook).
- **Catapult launchers:** longitudinally placed tracks to assist the take-off of fixed wing aircraft.

In the period 1910 to 1945 some vessels carried seaplanes that could be lowered and raised from the water by a crane to launch and land under their own power. Some vessels were fitted with short catapult launchers on an upper surface for dry take-off.

CARGO STORAGE AND HANDLING

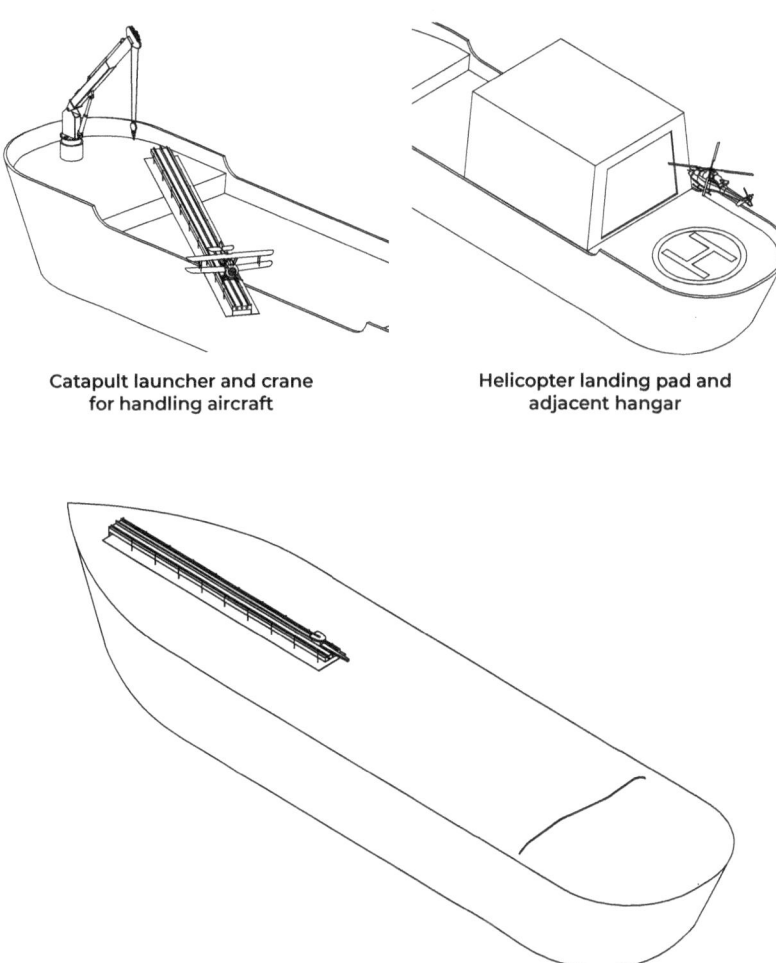

Catapult launcher and crane for handling aircraft

Helicopter landing pad and adjacent hangar

Flight deck with catapult launcher and arresting wire

Explosive cargo "magazine"

The vessel's magazine is the storage area for ammunition. In the cannon age, the magazine would typically be lined with brass plates to keep the gunpowder as dry and protected as possible. Built below the waterline for additional protection from enemy fire and so that it could be flooded in case of an emergency. In the age of modern armaments, a magazine will be heavily armoured and connected to munitions launchers by hoists.

THE SHIPWRECK DECODER

Bulk cargo handling

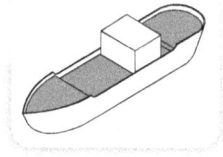

- Bulk cargo handling gear ➔ Vessel carried bulk cargo e.g. ore, coal, cement
- Gear is large enough to reach shore ➔ Self-loading/discharging capability in anticipation that at least some terminals visited by the vessel will not be capable of handling the cargo type
- Gear is not large enough to reach shore ➔ Vessel intended for use exclusively between terminals capable of handling the cargo type

> **1119** Bulkhead partitions (China)
> **1834** Bulkhead partitions (Western)

Bulk cargo means loose solids such as ore, coal, grain, sand, etc., in bulk volumes (smaller volumes would be carried in crates, barrels or shipping containers). Bulk cargo behaves like a dense liquid within the cargo hold, and is liable to shift with the pitch and roll of the vessel, but cannot be pumped through pipes or lifted with slings. Instead, bulk cargo is moved using a crane-based clamshell/bucket grab, belts, buckets, or pneumatic tubes. Conveyor systems are closer to horizontal, elevator systems are closer to vertical.

Prior to the 19th century, Western vessels were likely to have decks running the full length of the vessel, possibly with minor bulkheads to separate spaces by purpose. Loose or liquid cargo could shift with the pitch and roll of a vessel, which would change its centre of gravity and risk capsize. Flooding in one part of the hull would spread to the entire hull. In the 19th century, Western shipbuilders adopted a technology used in China since at least the 12th century and began using bulkheads to partition the hull into watertight compartments and limit the movement of cargo.

- **Bulkheads:** vertical partitions arranged laterally and/or longitudinally to divide the space into compartments to restrict the movement of cargo, particularly bulk cargo that can shift causing a vessel to roll.
- **Pneumatic systems:** use air pressure differentials to push bulk cargo through a tube.

CARGO STORAGE AND HANDLING

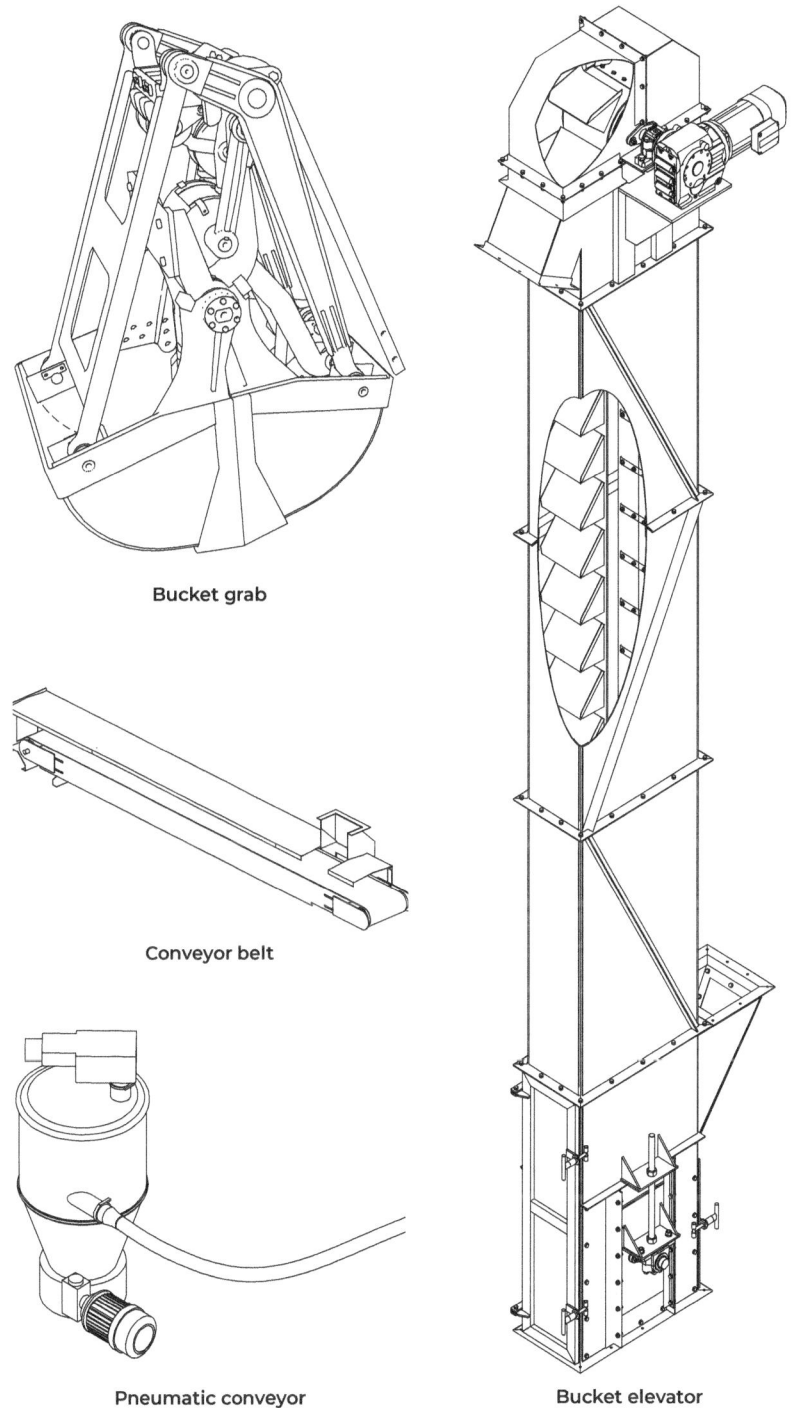

Bucket grab

Conveyor belt

Pneumatic conveyor

Bucket elevator

Liquid cargo handling

- Liquid cargo handling gear ➝ Vessel carried liquid cargo e.g. oil, water

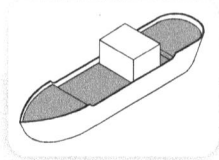

1886 Dedicated tanks for liquid cargo

- **Liquid cargo tank:** enclosed and oil-tight chamber for carrying liquid cargo in bulk volumes (smaller volumes would be carried in barrels).
- **Oil-tight hatch:** oil and gas-tight entrance to liquid cargo tanks for inspection and clearance.
- **Cargo oil pipes:** loading and discharge lines running longitudinally throughout the vessel, often both on and below the main deck (or within tanks). Different grades of oil run in separate lines, so that a vessel carrying multiple grades of oil will have many lines. In cargo tanks, lines terminate in a bellmouth.
- **Bottom lines:** pipes from the cargo tanks to the pumps.
- **Risers:** pipes from the pump to the main deck.

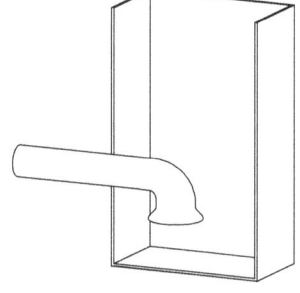

Liquid cargo tank with bell-mouth-ended cargo oil pipe

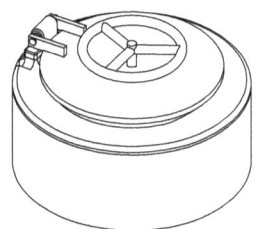

Oil tight hatch

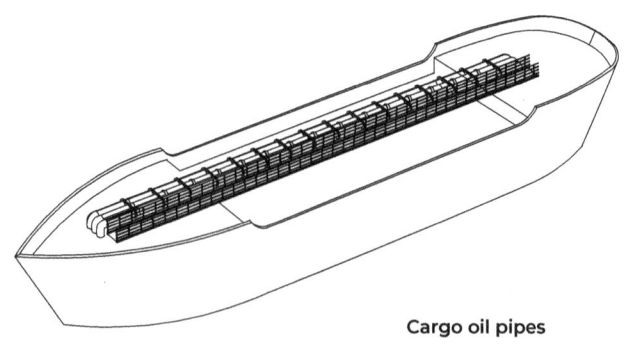

Cargo oil pipes

CARGO STORAGE AND HANDLING

- **Drop lines:** pipes from the deck to the cargo tanks.
- **Cargo oil pump:** high volume pumps for loading and discharging cargo tanks, housed in the pump room.
- **Pressure venting system:** prevents over/under pressure in cargo tanks using vapour lines and vacuum valves.
- **Vapour lines:** pipes linking cargo tanks to vacuum valves.
- **Vacuum valves:** control the release of over-pressure gas from the tank and/or the relief of under-pressure in the tank.
- **Flexible hose handling:** a flexible cargo hose on a reel handled using a small crane.
- **Ullage port:** ullage is the space between the top of the cargo tank to the upper surface of the oil. The ullage port opens to a narrow vertical pipe running down into the cargo tank to manually measure ullage.
- **Butterworth hole and cover plate:** hatch-covered service openings through the deck to cargo tanks, bolted closed.

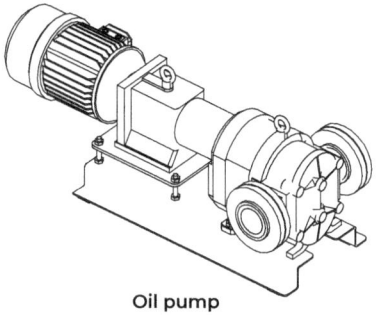
Oil pump

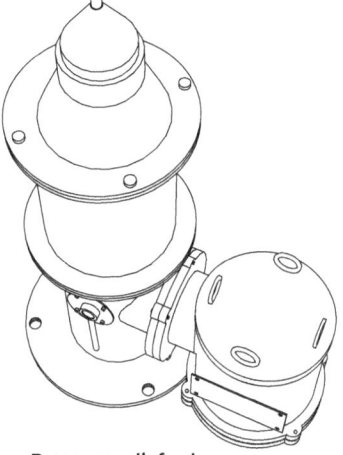
Pressure relief valve

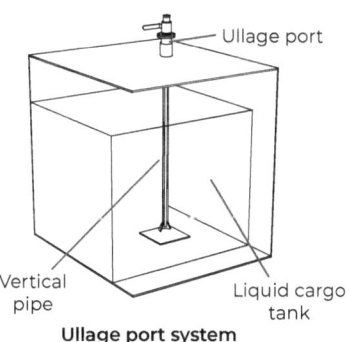
Ullage port system

Butterworth hole and cover plate

THE SHIPWRECK DECODER

Gaseous cargo handling

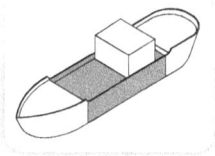

- Spherical or hemisphere-ended cylinder pressure tank ➤ Gaseous cargo

Gaseous cargo handling gear is similar in appearance to liquid cargo handling gear, and is distinguishable by the presence of gas cargo tanks.
- **Gas cargo tank:** enclosed and gas-tight chamber for carrying pressurised gas in bulk volumes (smaller volumes would be carried in gas cylinders). To evenly distribute the expansion force of pressurised gas the tank will be spherical or a cylinder with hemispherical ends.

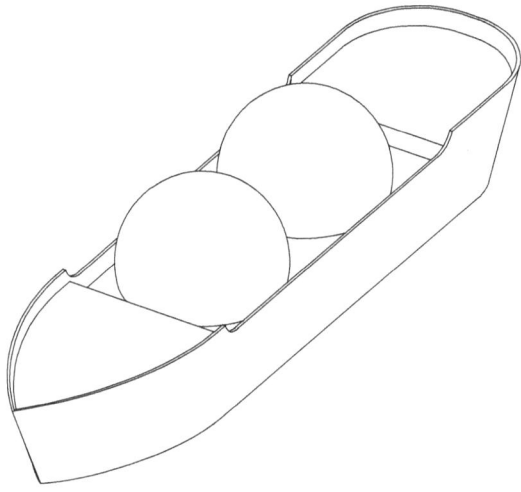

CHAPTER 13
CANNON-AGE ARMAMENT

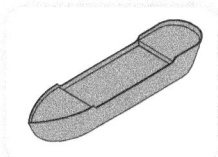

This chapter focuses on naval cannon from the earliest iterations through the Age of Cannon. The division between the Age of Cannon and modern armaments is marked by the broad and rapid obsolescence of unarmoured hulls and short-range cannon, in favour of armoured hulls, explosive shells and rifled long-range guns, at the end of the American Civil War (1861–1865).

- Where the grey interpretation boxes in this chapter suggest a national origin this should be considered only a high-level generalisation. Cannon identification is a highly specialised field and it is not feasible to attempt an exhaustive review of every expression of cannon manufacture through the ages.

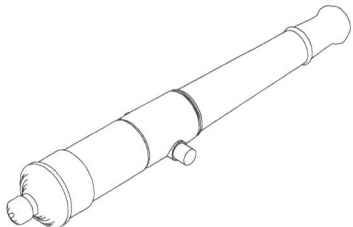
Generic cannon

Cannon are durable maritime weapons that were introduced and evolved over centuries of warfare. The costs and scarcity of advanced patterns encouraged frequent re-use, e.g. redeploying guns captured from an opponent, moving less advanced types to auxiliary or merchant vessels, or selling/donating obsolete ordnance to less wealthy allies. Care must therefore be taken to avoid conflating the context for the vessel with the context for the cannon it was carrying. While the Dahlgren Gun was the standard armament for US Navy vessels during the American Civil War, identification of a Dahlgren Gun indicates only the origin of that cannon, not that the vessel was part of the US Navy or operated during the American Civil War. Alternative explanations for the presence of a gun of this type include that it was purchased from the US Navy, captured and redeployed by the Confederates, or outfitted on a foreign vessel long after the American Civil War and after such cannon ceased to be made or used by the US Navy.

This chapter explains the features of a generic naval cannon starting with the bore and muzzle, working back through the chase, reinforces, vent field, and finally the cascabel. Later sections detail their functional evolution, construction, naval gun carriages, associated equipment, and projectiles.

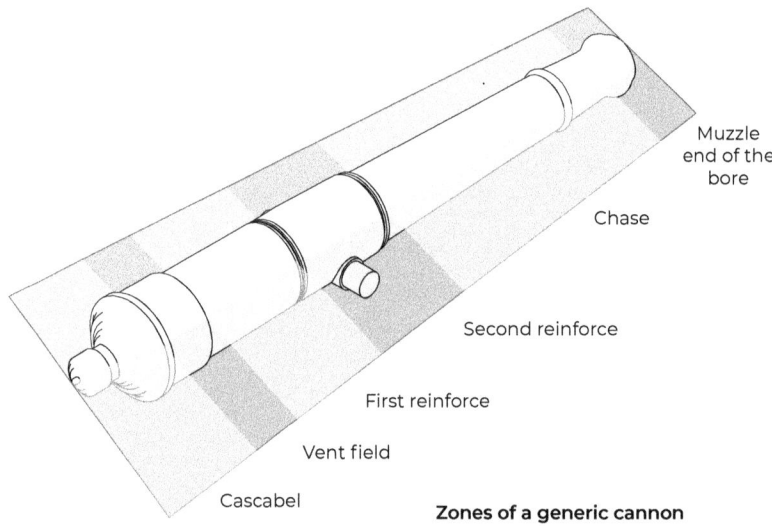

Zones of a generic cannon

- Identification is based on a combination of diagnostic features:
    - Overall length (muzzle face to button)
    - Widest point of base ring to midpoint of trunnion
    - Muzzle face to midpoint of trunnion
    - Diameter of muzzle face
    - Diameter of bore
    - Cascabel length (end of base ring to end of button)
    - Base ring diameter
    - Button diameter
    - Trunnion length and diameter
    - Reinforce diameter at midpoint of trunnions
    - Various markings, e.g. founder's marks, serial/survey numbers, disposal marks, pattern marks, nation and unit emblems

CANNON-AGE ARMAMENT

Bore

- Bore characteristics (internal shape of the barrel):
  ▷ Smooth ➜ Less advanced manufacturing process, or designed for spherical projectiles, short range munitions, higher projectile velocities, or ammunition with alternative stabilisation methods.
  ▷ Faceted ➜ Intermediate manufacturing process
  ▷ Rifled ➜ Advanced manufacturing process

1854 (likely post-1860) Naval cannon with rifled bore

Empty cylindrical space through the centre of the cannon from the muzzle to the base ring; the calibre of the cannon is the diameter of the bore; may be smooth bore or rifled.

The accuracy of a cannon can be improved by spinning the projectile as it moves through the bore. This spin improves accuracy by helping the projectile maintain its orientation and resist external forces such as wind for a straighter trajectory. Rifling imparts a spin to the projectile but requires a more technologically advanced production process. Faceting cast into the bore was sometimes used as a compromise to achieve some of the same effect but with a less advanced production process than rifling.

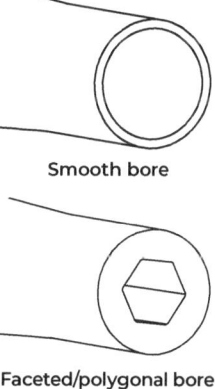

- **Smooth bore:** the bore is unrifled. Does have some advantages over a rifled bore. It is compatible with projectiles using alternative stabilisation strategies such as fins, and suffers less wear from high velocity projectiles so may be better suited to armour penetration applications.

Smooth bore

Faceted/polygonal bore

- **Faceted/polygonal bore:** the bore was cast with a spiralling polygonal cross section, which the shot or sabot (see page 171) had to match.
- **Rifled bore:** spiralling grooves cut into the bore to impart spin to the cylindro-conoidal projectile, fitted with a soft metal jacket or band to impart spin which improved accuracy.

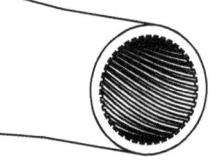

Rifled/polygroove bore

Muzzle

- Muzzle swell shape (for cast iron cannon):
  - Smooth ➔ Intended for use at sea
  - Cylindrical ➔ Intended for use on land
- Muzzle swell abruptness (for cast iron cannon):
  - Gradual ➔ English (caution: highly generalised)
  - Sharp ➔ Swedish (caution: highly generalised)
- Muzzle moulding pattern (number and pattern of rings) ➔ Place and time of manufacture

- **Muzzle:** foremost portion of the cannon.
- **Muzzle face:** flat leading surface of the cannon.
- **Muzzle swell:** the chase is thickened to reinforce against cracks developing at the tapered end of the cannon from the shock of the projectile and hot gasses transitioning from the bore to open atmosphere.

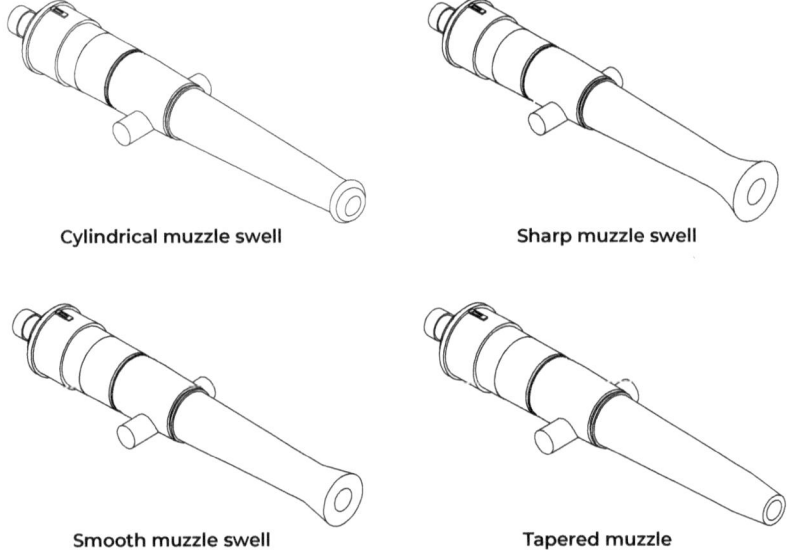

Cylindrical muzzle swell

Sharp muzzle swell

Smooth muzzle swell

Tapered muzzle

A lack of muzzle swell can indicate a 'cut', i.e. a gun that has suffered damage or loss to the muzzle and has been shortened, remaining serviceable (usually bronze guns).

CANNON-AGE ARMAMENT

Chase

The section of the barrel between muzzle and second reinforce. The chase is not exposed to as much stress as the reinforce or muzzle so can be made with thinner walls to reduce overall weight, giving the cannon its tapered look.

Reinforce

- Reinforce may have markings identifying the unit and/or statehood (e.g. royal heraldry)
- First and second reinforce may be separated by mouldings (number and pattern of rings) ➤ Place and time of manufacture
- Trunnions may have markings identifying the manufacturer, year of manufacture, and even individual serial numbers from late 18th-century
- May have decoration or embellishments to dolphins, e.g.
  ▷ Elephant head ➤ Denmark
  ▷ Fish or dolphin ➤ General form (widely used)
  ▷ Rings ➤ Portugal

c.1700 Trunnions with stepped shoulder

The reinforce section contains the explosion of the charge. With a thicker/stronger reinforce the cannon can survive higher chamber pressure from larger charges, allowing longer-range fire. Increases in calibres and ranges were limited by material science and manufacturing capability. To compensate for these limitations various alternative strategies were developed for additional reinforcement through wire wrapping, bands and sheaths until foundries could produce cannon from stronger material or with thicker reinforce walls.

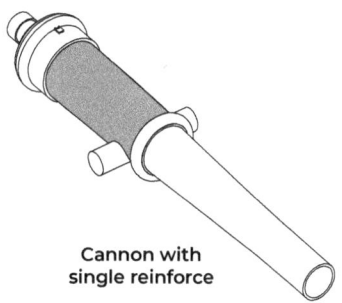

Cannon with single reinforce

- **Reinforce:** the barrel between the chase and vent field. Internally the breech area where the charge explodes, this section requires thicker walls (i.e. reinforced) because the explosive force of the charge is greatest at the breech. Includes the trunnions and dolphins.

- **Second reinforce:** for cannon with two reinforces the second reinforce is the section towards the muzzle end, and includes the trunnions and dolphins.
- **First reinforce:** for cannon with two reinforces the first reinforce is the section towards the cascabel end. As the section where the cartridge explodes, it will also have the thickest walls.

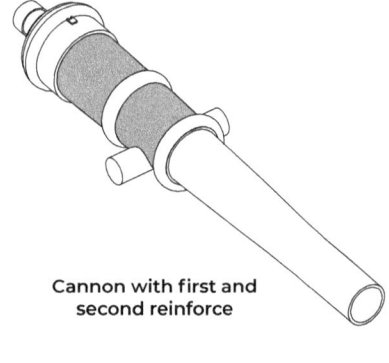

Cannon with first and second reinforce

- **Trunnions:** horizontal cylindrical projections, typically located at the forward/muzzle end of the reinforce. They are pivot points that allow the cannon to be elevated or depressed for aiming. May have markings identifying the manufacturer, serial number, and/or year of production. May be joined to the cannon with a stepped shoulder for increased stability.

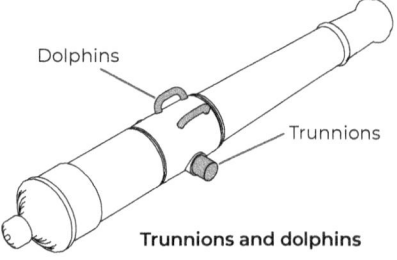

Trunnions and dolphins

- **Dolphins:** a pair of loops usually found on the upper surface of bronze guns. Dolphins are attachment points for tackle used to lift and move the cannon.

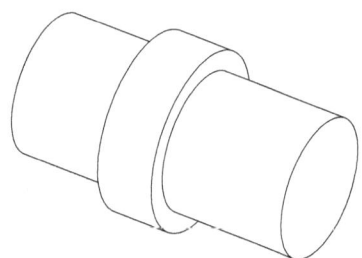

Bands as additional reinforcement to the main body of the cannon

- **Strengthening bands, hoops and tubes/jackets:** various techniques were adopted from the mid-19th century to strengthen the cast reinforce, to accept a more energetic charge without destroying the cannon.

CANNON-AGE ARMAMENT

Vent field

- Vent field marking styles ➤ Linked to place and time of manufacture
- Raised block over the vent (touch-hole) ➤ Designed for gunlock ignition

1759 Gunlock

- **Vent field:** between the first reinforce and the cascabel; includes the vent and base ring.
- **Vent/touch hole:** between the first reinforce and base ring; hole for priming powder through which the ignition is passed to the powder chamber. Presence of a raised rectangular plate drilled to mount a gunlock indicates later period of manufacture (1770s onwards).
- **Base ring:** widest part of the cannon; between the vent field and cascabel.
- **Gunlock:** trigger action apparatus (flintlock mechanism) that strikes a flint against a steel plate, to produce a spark, that is directed to ignite gunpowder in the vent. Later, a percussion lock was used with special ignition tubes.

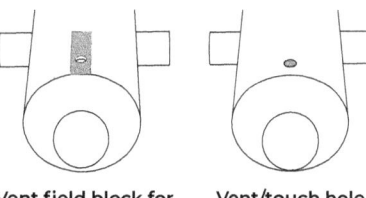

Vent field block for mounting gunlock   Vent/touch hole

Cascabel

- Button shape and decoration ➤ Place and time of manufacture
- Base plate slope (angle) and appearance (plain curve, concentric steps, decorated) ➤ Place and time of manufacture
- Cast bronze, flat base plate with simple ring to pass rope, no neck or button ➤ Portugal (1500–1650), Spain and Austria

Pre-1600 Long cascabel neck
1780 Cascabel neck loop

- **Cascabel:** rearmost portion of the cannon. Includes the base plate, neck and button.

THE SHIPWRECK DECODER

- **Base plate:** the curve connecting the base ring to the neck.
- **Neck:** the shaft between the base plate and the button. The primary hard point for securing or lifting the cannon with rope. May include a loop to secure the breaching rope in place for recoil control.
- **Button:** the flared or knob-shaped end of the neck. Stops rope looped around the neck from slipping off. May be plain or highly decorated. May have a threaded bore (oriented horizontally or vertically depending on the mechanism) for an elevation screw.
- **Elevation screw:** threaded shaft to control cannon elevation by raising or lowering the cascabel with the trunnions as the pivot point.
- **Breech:** the opening where a projectile and charge can be inserted at the rear of the cannon. This allows for faster reloading without retracting the entire length within the hull.
- **Breech mechanism:** the mechanism for closing and sealing the breech. The breech mechanism must be strong enough to survive firing the cannon without incurring damage.

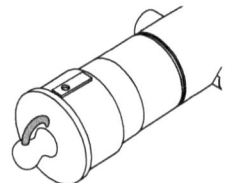

Cascabel button

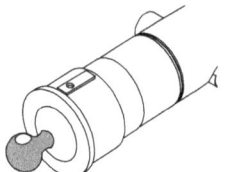

Cascabel ring

Cascabel with threaded button

Cannon types

- Cast bronze cannon were manufactured in many countries ➤ Expensive to produce but easy to decorate ➤ Likely to have elaborate decoration, heraldry, and manufacturer names and/or markings
- Cast iron cannon manufacture was dominated by England, Sweden, Holland and later the United States ➤ Mass produced ➤ Likely to have informative manufacturer markings, and light or no decoration ➤ Likely to be heavily concreted if they have been submersed in saltwater
- Cast iron with short, cylindrical muzzle ➤ Likely a naval carronade
- Cast iron with smooth or sharp thickening at the muzzle ➤ Likely intended as naval or coastal battery cannon ➤ English muzzles are typically flared or rounded; Swedish and United States designs are often angular

CANNON-AGE ARMAMENT

c.1300–c.1550 Wrought iron cannon, breech-loading, bedded
1326 Wrought iron cannon
c.1400–c.1600 Wrought iron cannon, muzzle-loading, bedded
1470–1770 Cast bronze cannon
c.1500–c.1850 Swivel gun
1543 Cast iron cannon (England)
1750 Solid bore cast bronze (France)
1770 Solid bore cast bronze/iron (England)
c.1775 Solid bore cast bronze/iron (United States)
1846 Breech-loading (Sweden/Italy)
1855 Breech-loading (England)
c.1860 Cast steel

Cannon evolved with metallurgy and production technologies. The various types of cannon each represent a compromise between the demand for larger quantities of more powerful weapons, and production costs with then current technologies. Creative innovations such as reinforcing barrels with wire or bands/jackets were methods to increase power.

Material
- **Wrought iron:** iron bars laid together around a mandrel (a shaft or rod) and bound together with iron hoops (like a barrel) to provide circumferential strength. Consequently, these cannon are undecorated and industrial in appearance.
- **Cast bronze/iron:** cannon cast as a single piece in a clay mould. The mould was oriented vertically, usually with the cascabel at the bottom. A clay core on a wooden shaft was suspended within the mould and liquid metal poured in around it. Once the molten metal had cooled and solidified, the clay mould was broken off and the wooden core broken out to form the bore. Impurities in the metal rose to the top of the mould and concentrated in the muzzle, so the end was cut off creating the muzzle face. The bore was rarely perfectly straight due to unavoidable warping of the core during the heating and cooling of the casting process. The bore was trued up as far as possible using a reamer.

- **Solid bore cast bronze/iron:** later technologies enabled cannon to be cast as single pieces and the bore drilled out later. This produced a straight bore for more accurate firing.
- **Cast steel:** much thinner and lighter weight than iron for the same resilience to the explosive force of the charge in the chamber and movement of the projectile through the bore.

Muzzle or breech-loading
- **Muzzle-loading:** single piece cannon, loaded by pushing the powder cartridge, wadding, then projectile down the bore from the muzzle with a ramrod.
- **Breech-loading:** this type of cannon has at least two pieces including a separate powder chamber and a mechanism to lock it against the breech. Loaded by inserting the projectile then the powder chamber into the bore from the breech, then locking the breech closed for firing.

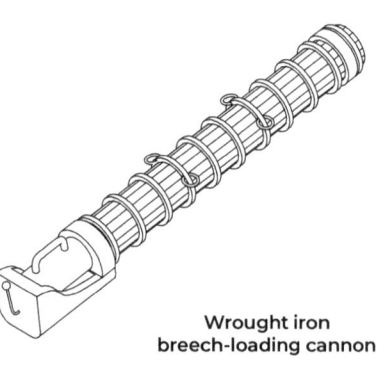

Wrought iron breech-loading cannon

Classification and trajectory
- **Cannon:** direct fire (low trajectory), small to large calibre, long barrel (for range and accuracy), mounted on a bed (rarely) or carriage.
- **Carronade:** direct fire, large calibre, short barrel, post mounted (on a slide carriage). Intended for devastating close-range fire.
- **Mortar:** indirect fire (high trajectory), large calibre, short barrel (area targeting). For attacking fortified positions and defence of towns and forts.
- **Howitzer:** mid-way between a cannon and mortar, large calibre, medium barrel, mounted on a bed or carriage. Field or siege use.
- **Swivel gun:** small-calibre, medium length barrel (short-range), breech or muzzle loaded, mounted on a swivel at the trunnions, with a distinctive tiller at the rear (for aiming). May be wrought iron, cast bronze or cast iron.

CANNON-AGE ARMAMENT

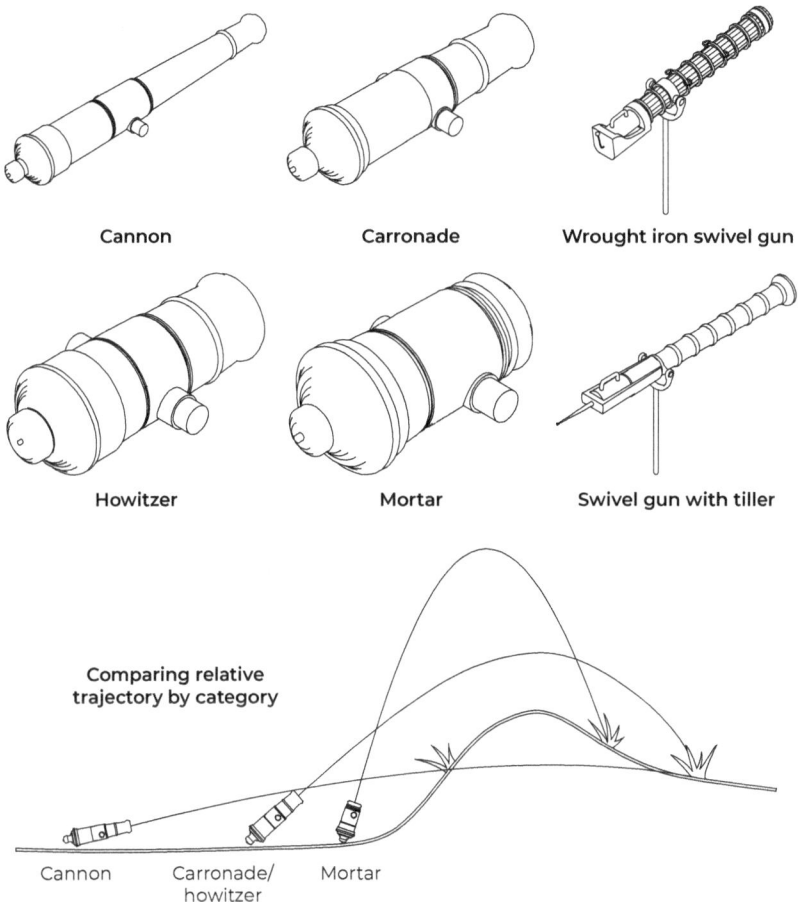

Calibre

Cannon were identified according to the weight in pounds of the standard spherical solid iron ball that fitted the bore. This convention, of naming weapons according to weight of their projectile, persisted in some services until the mid-20th-century. It was superseded by the convention of naming weapons according to their bore diameter. Different countries used different measurement systems, e.g. an English pound was not the same as a Swedish pound. English cannon c.1500–1700 were identified according to the weight of shot they fired. It could vary, but as a guide: falconet (1 lb), minion (4 lb), saker (6 lb), demi culverin (9 lb), culverin (18 lb), demi cannon (32 lb), and cannon (42 lb). After c.1600–1700 guns were identified simply by the weight of shot they fired, e.g. 24-pounder.

THE SHIPWRECK DECODER

Key types

- **1823** Paixhans gun (France)
- **1849** Dahlgren gun (United States)
- **1855** Blakely rifle (England)
- **1855–1864, 1880–1920** Armstrong gun, breech-loading (England)
- **1860** Parrott rifle (United States)
- **1861–1865** Brooke rifle (Confederate States)
- **1864–1880** Armstrong gun, rifled muzzle-loading (England)

- **Paixhans gun (France):** single reinforce of constant diameter, clearly distinguished from a tapered chase, otherwise undecorated, muzzle-loading. A revolutionary naval cannon, the first designed to fire explosive projectiles flat, direct trajectory with enough velocity to penetrate wooden hulls.

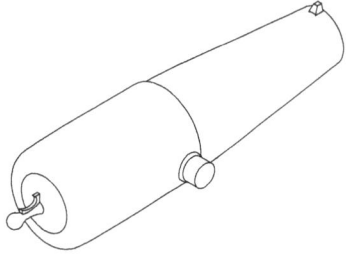

Paixhans gun

- **Dahlgren gun (United States):** tapered chase merges smoothly into a bulbous reinforce and integrated cascabel. Smooth exterior and undecorated. Muzzle-loading. Improved on the Paixhans gun for firing explosive projectiles at high velocity. Standard armament for many US naval vessels during the American Civil War and beyond.

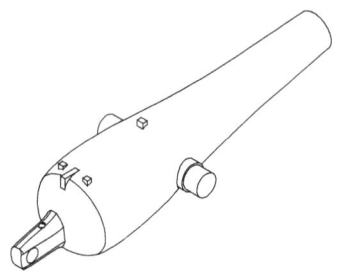

Dahlgren gun

- **Blakely rifle (England):** inner cast iron tube with additional external hoops of wrought iron

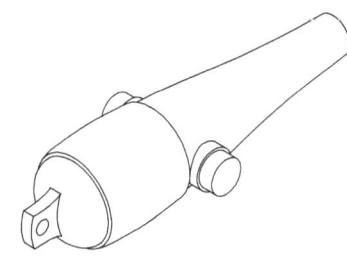

Blakely rifle

CANNON-AGE ARMAMENT

or steel to strengthen the reinforce. Muzzle- or breech-loading; cut-groove-rifled bore.

- **Parrott rifle (United States):** cast iron barrel with distinctive wrought iron band reinforce around the breech. The reinforce was heated and slipped over the barrel while water was circulated through the bore to keep the inner tube cool. The temperature gradient caused the band to constrict (onto the gun).

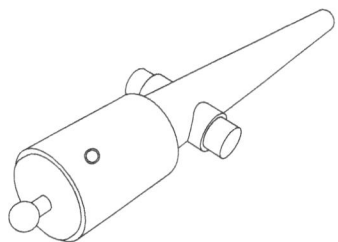
Parrott rifle

- **Armstrong gun (England):** built up design with an inner wrought iron/steel tube, overlaid with progressively shrunken concentric wrought iron coils to strengthen the reinforce. Exceptionally strong and durable cannon capable of withstanding high pressures. Breech-loading except for an intermediate period of Royal Navy return to muzzle loading; cut-groove-rifled bore.

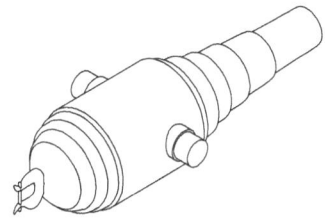
Armstrong gun (muzzle-loading)

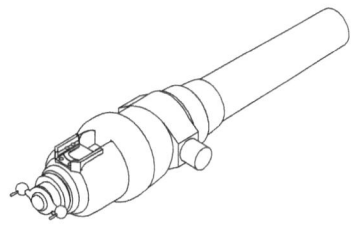
Armstrong gun (breech-loading)

- **Brooke rifle (Confederate States):** rough-finished tapering cast iron tube with at least one additional concentric band of 2 inch (51 mm) thick wrought iron to strengthen the reinforce. Muzzle-loading; mostly rifled bore but with rare smooth bores.

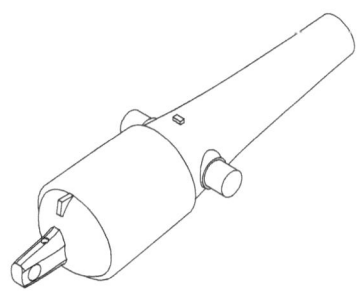
Brooke rifle

THE SHIPWRECK DECODER

Mouldings

> **1542–c.1707** Rose and Crown (England)
> **Pre-c.1700** Decorative moulding (Sweden)
> **Post-c.1700** Simple moulding (Sweden)
> **1716–1725** Borgard pattern (England)
> **1725–1787** Armstrong pattern (England)
> **1787–1820** Blomefield pattern (England)

Mouldings are the decorative rings around parts of the cannon. They offer clues about origin and period of manufacture. Some examples:

- **Rose and Crown (England):** single moulding either side of trunnions, and rose and crown badge on second reinforce.
- **Borgard pattern (England):** single moulding behind and double moulding in front of the trunnions. Rose and crown on second reinforce.

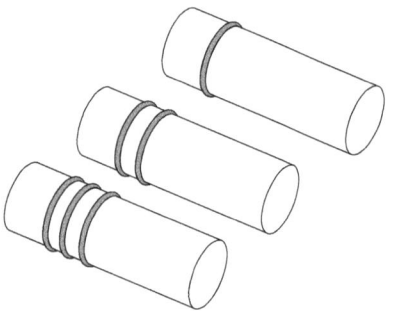

Mouldings

- **Armstrong pattern (England):** a cleaner, classical design that replaced the traditional Tudor Rose emblem with the Royal Cypher (monogram) on the first reinforce.
- **Blomefield pattern (England):** simple ring moulding either side of trunnions, loop at cascabel. Removing traditional decorative elements in favour of a uniform breech thickness improved casting quality, making it stronger than the earlier Armstrong and faster to produce under the material demands of the Royal Navy during the Napoleonic Wars. Simple, small Royal Cypher on first reinforce, gunfounder's initials and year of casting on trunnions.
- **Swedish cast iron (pre-c.1700):** steady taper from cascabel to muzzle without distinctive steps, elaborate cascabel with concentric

CANNON-AGE ARMAMENT

rings, elaborate mouldings either side of trunnions, and short sharp muzzle swell.
- **Swedish cast iron (post-c.1700):** plain single moulding bands either side of trunnions, broad and flat base ring, and short sharp muzzle swell.

Cannon carriage

- **Naval gun bed:** a large wooden beam with a longitudinal hemispherical groove carved out that matched the outside diameter of the gun, and lateral groves carved to match the cannon's reinforcing hoops and maximise contact surface. At one end of the bed the longitudinal groove was open for the muzzle face, and at the breech end closed except for a wedge cut so that the powder chamber could be fitted behind the bore. The cannon was strapped as tightly as possible to the bed. The bed was mounted on two wheels.

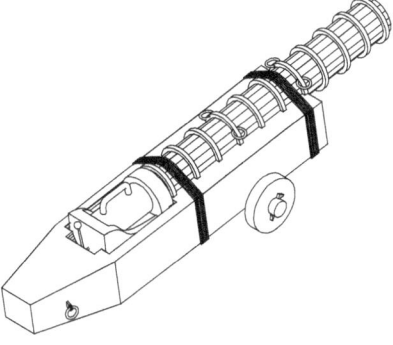

Naval gun bed

- **Naval gun carriage:** flat bed with vertical sides and four wheels that provided a stable platform for the cannon. Sometimes a block of wood was used in place of the rear wheels. At the top of each side semicircular notches and restraints (capsquares) held the trunnions. Later, the bed was dispensed with and the cheeks were fastened to the axles (or rear block).

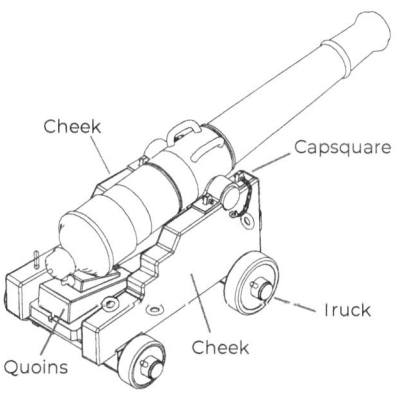

Naval gun carriage

Recoil system

- **Gun carriage block and tackle:** rope connections from through-hull ring bolts, through sides of the gun carriage and the cascabel neck. Used to (a) move the cannon between the stowed and ready positions (from within the boundaries of the hull, to the muzzle being extended outside the hull); (b) to secure the cannon in each position; (c) aim the cannon by traversing it (moving it horizontally); (d) absorb the recoil of firing; and (e) reset the cannon to the ready position after firing.

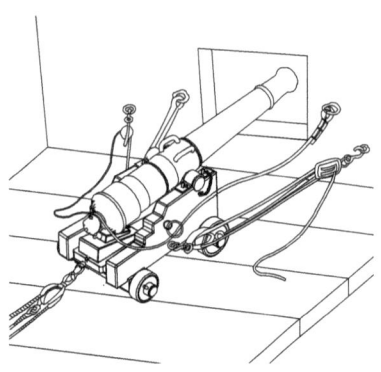

Gun carriage block and tackle

Cannon assemblage

Cannon assemblage implements were wood and copper to avoid creating sparks and accidentally igniting gunpowder.

- **Sponge:** wooden cylinder covered in lamb or sheepskin dipped in water and put down the barrel to make sure all sparks were out from previous firing.
- **Worm:** pole topped with a metal screw used to scrape out wadding and embers stuck in the barrel from the previous shot.
- **Ladle:** pole topped with a scoop to place loose gunpowder in the firing chamber as an alternative to a pre-prepared cartridge.
- **Rammer:** rigid or flexible pole with wide blunt top used to force the powder cartridge and projectile to the far end of the bore.

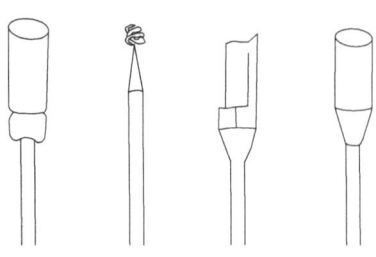

Sponge, worm, ladle, rammer

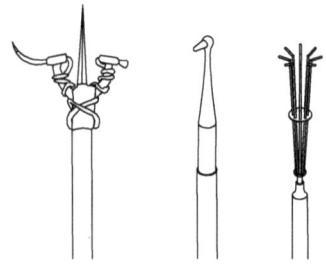

Linstock, searcher, cat

CANNON-AGE ARMAMENT

- **Linstock:** pole topped with a slow-match to ignite the gunpowder in the vent (touch hole) prior to adoption of the portfire and then flintlock, or as a backup if the flintlock failed.
- **Searcher:** pole topped with a right-angle pick to take a wax impression of bore defects. Inspection and maintenance tool that would be less common than the rest of the assemblage.
- **Cat:** pole topped with multiple wire prongs to locate bore defects. Another inspection/maintenance tool.
- **Powder horn:** funnel-shaped container used to pour a small quantity of loose gunpowder into the vent (touch hole).
- **Cartridge:** cylindrical container of paper or cloth bag of gunpowder inserted into the muzzle and pushed down the bore.
- **Gunner's pricker/priming wire:** long needle or stiletto used to clear the vent and pierce the cartridge for firing.
- **Quoins:** wooden wedges inserted under the cannon to control muzzle elevation.
- **Shot gauge:** hoop matching the calibre of the gun to confirm a projectile was the correct size.
- **Tampion:** plug to close muzzle when the gun was stowed.
- **Slow-match:** rope boiled in saltpeter solution that smouldered when lit and was hard to extinguish.
- **Handspike:** pole used as a lever to elevate the breech and insert quoins
- **Lead apron:** shaped cover for the vent when the gun was stowed.

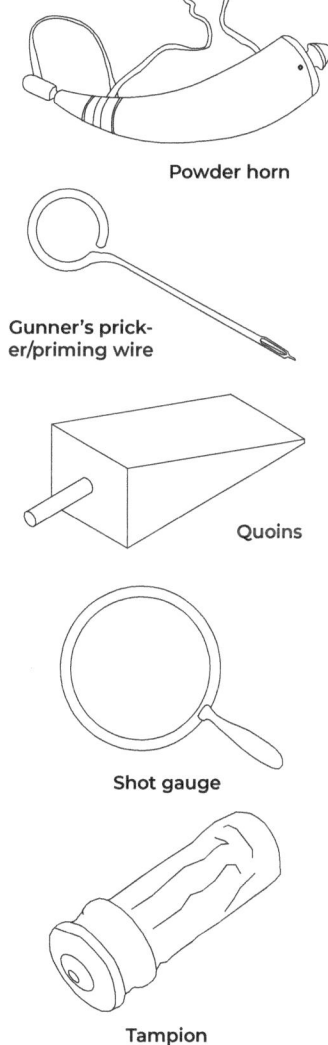

Powder horn

Gunner's pricker/priming wire

Quoins

Shot gauge

Tampion

THE SHIPWRECK DECODER

Projectiles

- **Ball/round shot:** spherical ball of iron or stone, used as a kinetic weapon against ships, walls and fortifications, and having the longest range and best accuracy available for this type of weapon.

Ball/round shot

- **Hollow/shell/bomb:** hollow spherical ball of iron, filled with explosive powder, with a hole to insert a fuze that was ignited by the explosive charge that fired the cannon. Used to damage or destroy opposing equipment.

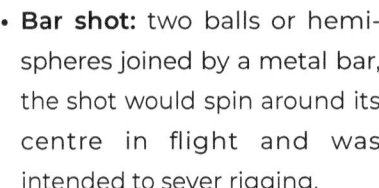

Hollow/shell/bomb

- **Bar shot:** two balls or hemispheres joined by a metal bar, the shot would spin around its centre in flight and was intended to sever rigging.

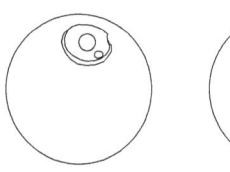 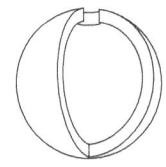

 Bar shot (hemispheres)   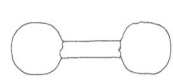 Bar shot (balls)

- **Chain shot:** two balls joined by a metal chain, with the same function as bar shot.

Chain shot

- **Expanding shot:** bar shot where each ball or hemisphere was attached to a separate metal bar, the two bars ending in a perpendicular ring wrapped around the other bar. Loaded in the collapsed position, when fired the balls or hemispheres moved apart until the two rings locked in the middle.

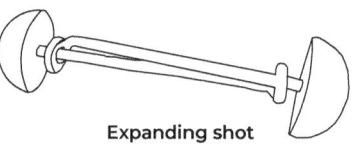

Expanding shot

- **Canister shot:** small round shot e.g. lead musket balls filling a light metal canister used for short-range anti-personnel fire. The metal canister disintegrated

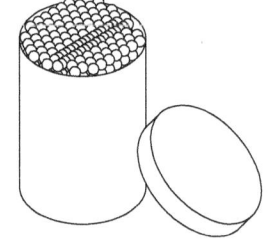

Canister shot (balls)

when fired, and the small shot inside expanded into a cone with its apex at the muzzle.
- **Grapeshot:** round shot filling a canvas bag, with the same function as canister shot, but with larger and more destructive balls..
- **Carcass:** either a hollow spherical ball of iron, or a framework of iron rings/plates bound together, filled with flammable paste or viscous liquid such as pitch, with multiple holes. Used to set fire to wooden structures.
- **Wooden bottom:** a flat wooden disk the same diameter as the shot and fixed to it, ensured that a fuzed shot remained oriented with the fuze towards the muzzle.
- **Sabot:** a collar fitted to the projectile that centred the projectile in the barrel and engaged the bore rifling.

Grapeshot

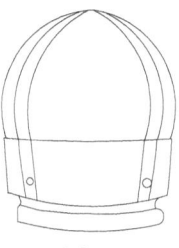
Sabot

Wreck site layouts

Cannon are one of the most durable components of a vessel, and their distribution on a site can give important information about the vessel, the wrecking event, and later salvage operations. Interpreting wreck sites is a long and complex process for professionally trained archaeologists, but we can start paying attention to how cannon are distributed on the site.
- Cannon regularly spaced along the ballast pile in two rows with muzzles facing out could mean the wreck settled intact on an even keel, and the guns fell down to the ballast pile as the decks degraded.
- Cannon regularly spaced along the ballast pile in a single row with muzzles facing in alternate directions could mean the wreck settled intact but listing to one side. High side guns slide across decks as restraining ropes degrade, guns fall to ballast pile as decks degrade.
- Cannon with or without trunnions in a dense group on ballast pile could mean old cannon used for ballast.
- Long trail of cannon could mean they were dumped in wrecking event in an attempt to lighten the vessel.

- Small number of isolated cannon could mean they were lost or dumped, or had been mounted on a smaller vessel.

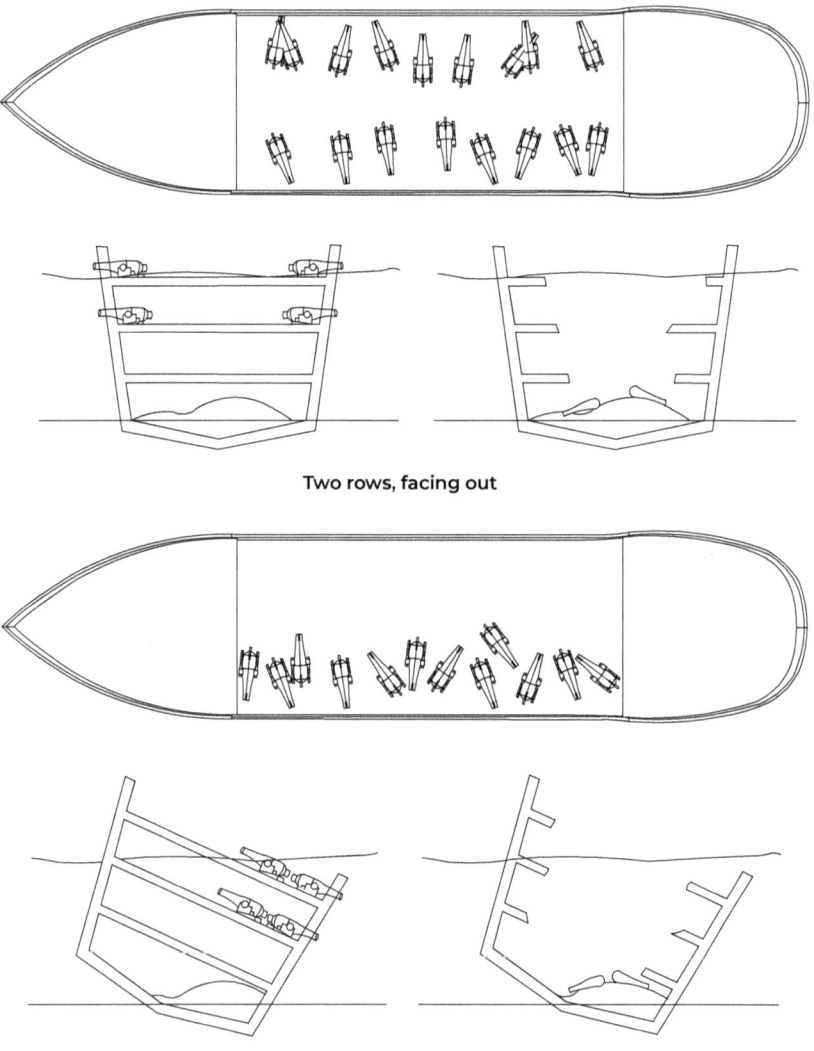

Two rows, facing out

Single row, alternative directions

These are just some of many ways of interpreting cannon layout from seabed finds. Specific circumstances, the influence of human activity since sinking (including salvage operations) and other explanations need to be considered by experts before drawing conclusions.

CHAPTER 14
MODERN ARMAMENT

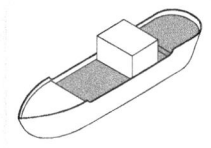

Modern naval guns and other shipborne armaments include sea mines, torpedoes, depth charges, rockets and missiles. This chapter examines the core features of these weapons, exploring their development, operational principles, and the impact they have on global naval strategy.

Modern naval guns

- Small calibre (<40 mm, up to two finger widths); pedestal or tripod mount ➤ Anti-aircraft, anti-personnel
- Medium calibre (40–150 mm, about the size of a fist); base-ring mount ➤ Dual-purpose (anti-aircraft/anti-surface) aka secondary guns
- Large calibre (>150 mm, roughly head sized); barbette mount ➤ Main guns for surface bombardment
- Note gun lengths, calibres, calibre mix, and layout

> **1861** Gun turret
> **1880** Hydraulic recoil
> **1906–1945** Gun turret—main guns only
> **1912** Gun turret—centreline layout

The traditional ship of the line achieved its firepower by stacking gun batteries. Each additional gun deck raised the profile of the vessel, presenting a larger target. Each gun port weakened the integrity of the hull and armour. Each gun had a limited range of fire brought to bear by moving the ship itself. Penetration of armoured hulls required more power than could be achieved by traditional breech-loaded guns. New designs were developed with breech-loading, large calibres, and long barrels. Longer barrels produce a higher muzzle velocity because the charge has more time to accelerate the projectile. These new guns were too large to be carried in batteries spaced along the length of the hull (broadside).

The revolving turret allowed guns to be brought to bear around a broad firing arc, independent of a vessel's movement. Removing gun decks allowed vessels to be built with lower target profiles and without compromising armour integrity. A gun turret has three main components: gunhouse, trunk, and base-ring mount or barbette.

- **Gunhouse:** armoured shelter for the gun's breech mechanism and crew. It rotates on a base of rollers contained within the upper section of the ring-mount or barbette. The gunhouse may not be secured vertically, in which case it may fall out if the vessel rolls over on sinking.
- **Base-ring mount:** heavy metal ring bolted to the deck as a secure base for medium-calibre guns.
- **Barbette:** armoured tower penetrating deep into the hull as a secure base for large-calibre guns.
- **Trunk:** mechanisms for lifting ammunition from the below deck magazine and handling rooms to the gunhouse.
- **Wing turret:** gun turret mounted either side of midships superstructure.

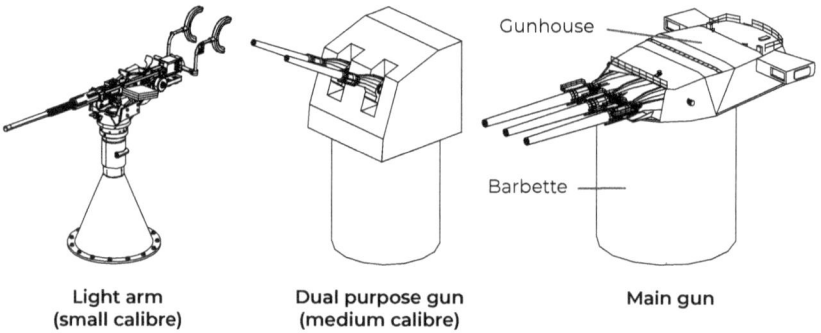

Light arm (small calibre)   Dual purpose gun (medium calibre)   Main gun

Key developments

There were three key periods of development in turreted ship design:

- **Pre-dreadnought (1861–1906):** vessels were designed for a naval combat doctrine that assumed fleets would initially engage at long range with large-calibre main guns before closing to engage at short range with small-calibre, fast-firing, secondary guns.
- **Dreadnought (1906–1912):** HMS *Dreadnought* was launched in 1906 with all her guns of the same large calibre for a new naval combat doctrine that assumed fleets would most likely engage at long range.

MODERN ARMAMENT

- **Super-dreadnought (1908–):** the USS *South Carolina* launched in 1908 with four gun turrets mounted along a centre line and no wing turrets. The firing arc for each gun turret was maximised by clear decks fore and aft (i.e. no forecastle or poopdeck). The gun turrets were split into bow and aft groups of two turrets each. In each group the centre-most turret was raised to fire over the adjacent outermost turret. This new efficient layout maximised the arc of fire for each turret and became the standard through to the modern day.

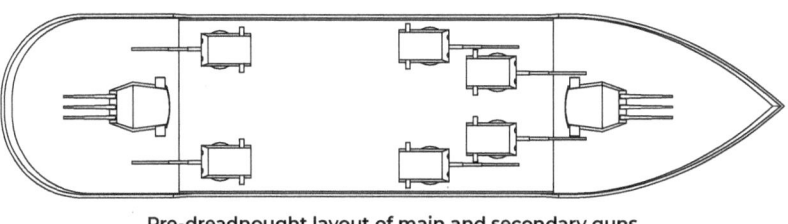
Pre-dreadnought layout of main and secondary guns

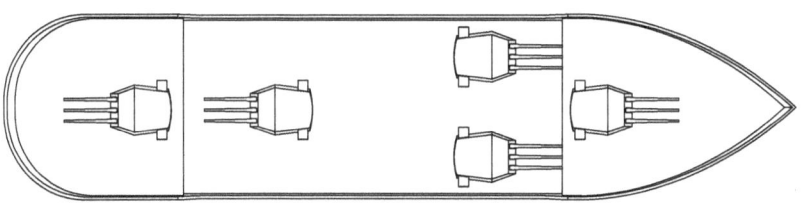
Dreadnought layout

Super-dreadnought layout

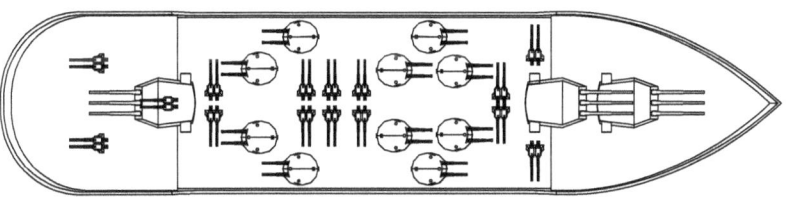
Super-dreadnought layout with dual purpose and anti-aircraft guns

Main gun sizes peaked in 1940 with the 18.1 inch calibre main guns on the Japanese battleships *Yamato* and *Musashi*. Large-calibre guns were superseded by aircraft and missile technology, and no nation has launched a warship with large-calibre main guns since the Second World War.

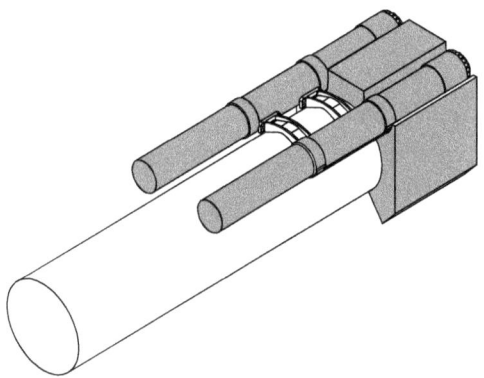

Hydraulic recoil system

- **Hydraulic recoil:** the cannon is mounted on rails, and recoil is absorbed by two connected cylinders that together form a sealed system. In the first cylinder is a piston, and a sealed chamber filled with oil in front of the piston. The first piston is rigidly connected to the cannon, and the oil chamber is connected to the second cylinder behind the second piston. In the second cylinder is a piston, and a sealed chamber filled with air in front of the piston. On firing, the cannon is driven back on the rails, dragging the first piston. The first piston compresses the oil chamber, forcing oil from the first cylinder through the connection to the second cylinder, pushing the second piston into the air chamber, and compressing the air. The force of recoil is absorbed and stored progressively as air pressure rises. Once the force of recoil is spent, the pressure of the compressed air is released, pushing the second piston back, forcing the oil from the second cylinder back through the connection to the first cylinder, pushing the first piston and attached cannon back into their original positions.

MODERN ARMAMENT

Anti-aircraft guns

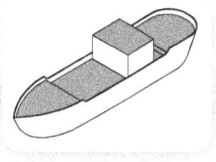

- Can be located anywhere on the main deck and superstructure ➤ Larger calibres more likely to be deck mounted
- Medium-calibre wing turrets on post-1914 warship ➤ Most likely intended for air defence

1914 Anti-aircraft guns

The earliest naval anti-aircraft guns emerged around 1914, using existing designs with modified mountings. Initially, air defence needed to compensate for relatively poor targeting systems and used a combination of explosive shells fired in groups. These combined tracers intended to strike aircraft directly with barrages of air-burst shells thrown up into flight paths. By the end of the Second World War, targeting systems had improved enough that air-burst barrages were no longer necessary.

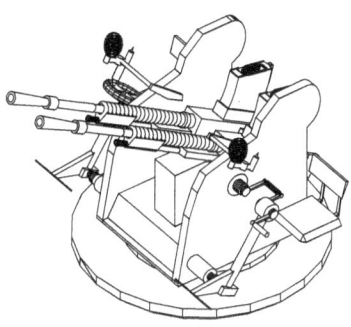

Anti-aircraft gun

Any direct-fire weapon capable of firing at high-angle elevations can be used in an air-defence role. Naval air defence usually relies on dedicated small-calibre (<40 mm) automatic guns, and dual-purpose medium-calibre (40–150 mm) guns with at least semi-automatic firing that can be used for both surface and air engagement.

Guns intended for air defence:
- Will have mountings capable of rapid traverse and high-elevation fire;
- May be unenclosed, partially shielded, or fully enclosed within a gunhouse;
- May have multiple (usually two, four or eight) barrels that cannot be separately aimed; and
- May have flash cones on the end of the muzzle(s) to suppress muzzle flash when firing.

Light arms

- Can be located anywhere on the main deck and superstructure
- Multiple barrels ➔ Pre-modern (approximately 1860–1930) design

> **1861** Multi-barrelled small-calibre gun

Light arms are small-calibre, rapid-firing weapons. They can be mounted on a pedestal fixed to the deck or gunwales, or on a tripod fixed to the deck.

From the mid-19th century, warships began carrying light arms for close-range defence against small, fast-moving torpedo boats, and later for anti-aircraft defence. Light arms were and continue to be used in an anti-personnel role during maritime interdictions.

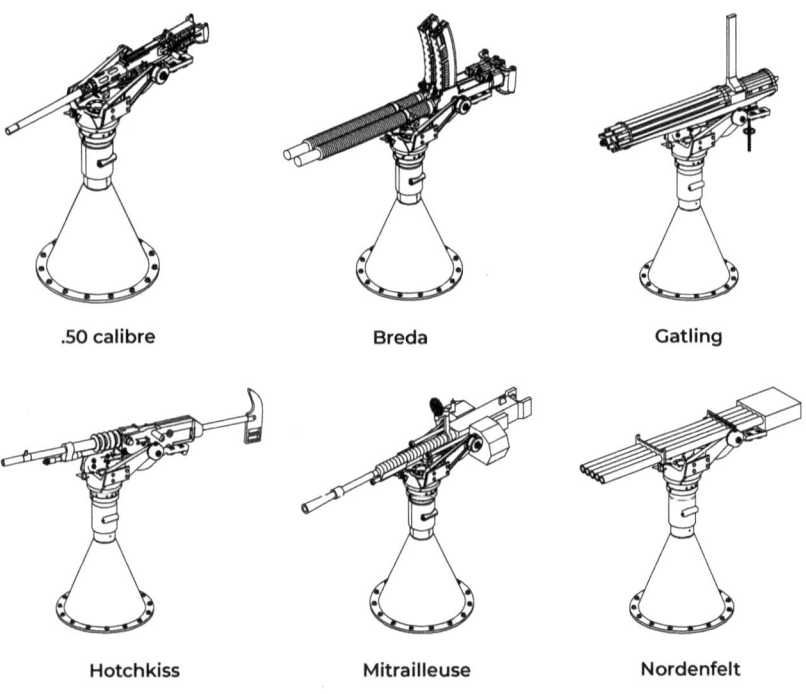

.50 calibre   Breda   Gatling

Hotchkiss   Mitrailleuse   Nordenfelt

MODERN ARMAMENT

Ordnance

> **WARNING:** Under no circumstances should divers touch or attempt to recover any ordnance they find!

- **Bomb type:** thinnest shell possible to safely contain the maximum weight of explosives for the volume. Bomb type parts are: an explosive charge; detonation fuze; and optional fins (for stability in descent through air or water).
- **Rocket type:** self-propelled rail-launched projectiles that operate by expelling propellant.
- **Guided type:** a projectile capable of altering its trajectory after launch (there are missiles, torpedoes and bombs of this type).

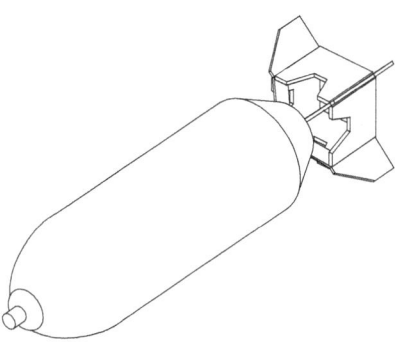

Bomb type ordnance

Gun ammunition

Gun ammunition has two parts:
- **Projectile:** the component that is expelled from a gun muzzle. Modern projectiles are elongated with a copper rotating band towards the trailing end, and narrow to a point at the leading end. The rotating band has the widest cross-section of the projectile and is wider than the rifling grooves of the barrel. When forced into the barrel, the harder material of those grooves engraves notches in the soft copper of the rotating band to seal the propellant gas behind the projectile, imparting spin as it travels through the barrel.
- **Cartridge:** a hollow cylinder that contains the charge, with a straight or bottle neck to fit the gun chamber, and a rim base to aid extraction after firing.

The projectile and cartridge are stored and assembled in three variations:
- **Bag-charge:** the projectile and multiple bag-charge sections are separate components assembled within the gun chamber. Each

bag-charge section is a cloth bag containing loose grain or bundled rods of propellant, stored within a cylindrical tank until withdrawn for use. Bag charges are necessary to break the weight of main gun (large calibre) ammunition into hand-liftable parts.

- **Semi-fixed:** the projectile and cartridge are separate components assembled within the gun chamber. Semi-fixed ammunition is used to break medium-calibre ammunition into two hand-liftable parts.
- **Fixed:** the projectile and cartridge are pre-assembled as a single unit to simplify handling (small calibre).

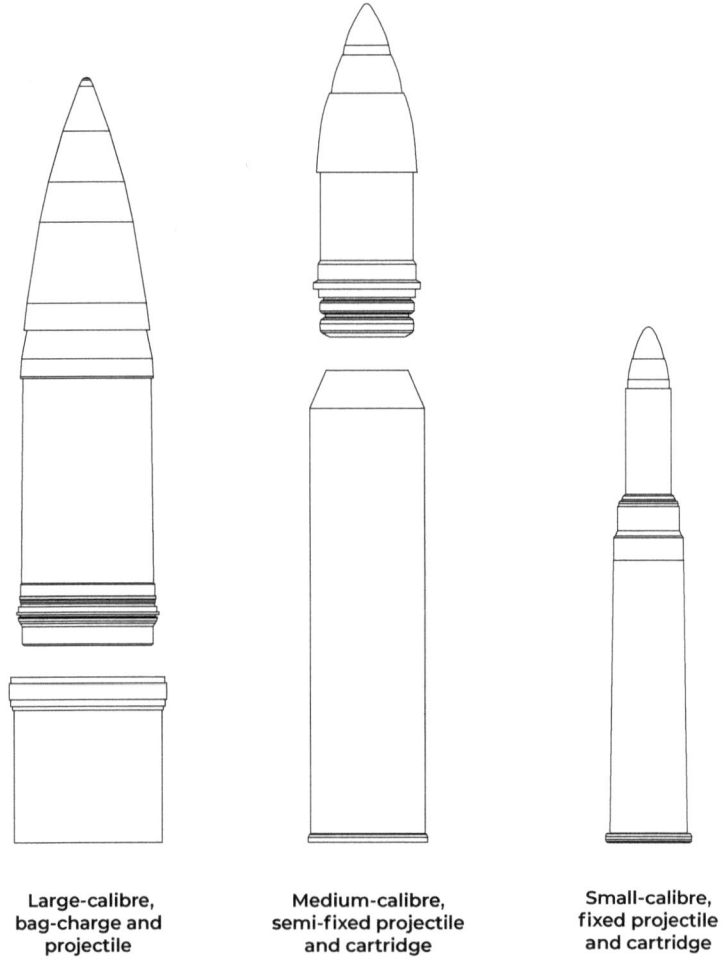

Large-calibre, bag-charge and projectile

Medium-calibre, semi-fixed projectile and cartridge

Small-calibre, fixed projectile and cartridge

MODERN ARMAMENT

Sea mines

1855 Sea mine

Sea mines are underwater munitions that are anchored to the seabed and intended to be automatically triggered by the presence of a vessel. Newer sea mines may have antennas for external control.

- **Mine case:** positively buoyant package containing the explosive charge and firing mechanism. The mine case is usually a sphere or cylinder.
- **Mooring cable:** connects the mine case to the anchor, the cable length will determine the depth of the deployed mine.
- **Anchor:** negatively buoyant base, usually with flat bottom and concave top.

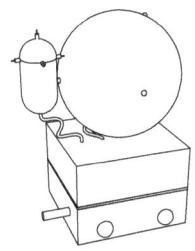

Sea mine (undeployed)

Undeployed, the mooring cable is wound on a reel within the anchor body and the mine case is cupped in the concave top of the anchor. On deployment: (1) the mine is pushed into the ocean; (2) the negatively buoyant anchor falls away from the positively buoyant mine case, spooling out the mooring cable to the maximum set length; and (3) the anchor falls to the seabed and holds the mine case floating in mid-water.

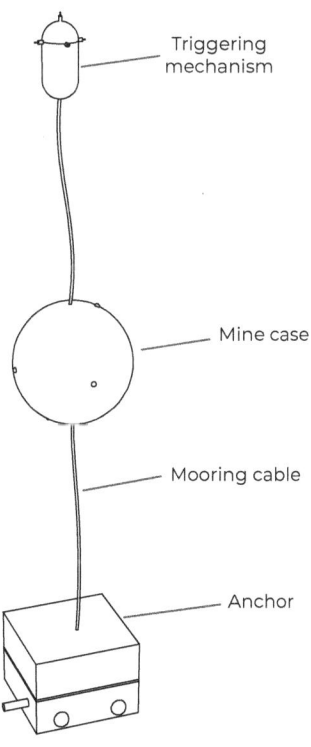

Sea mine (deployed)

Torpedoes

- Surface tubes ➜ Likely individually mounted in fixed positions on dedicated torpedo boats ➜ Swivel-mounted banks of one or more tubes on larger vessels
- Submarine ➜ Primary tubes located at the bow ➜ Any secondary tubes located at the stern in case of pursuit
- Torpedo dimensions ➜ Diameter 30–55 cm (about wide enough to wrap your arms around) ➜ Length 3–6 m (3–5 body lengths)
- Flat nose ➜ Suggests either a missing component (warhead, detonator or guidance transducer), or a supercavitating design
- Connected banks of long narrow pressurised gas cylinders on a warship ➜ May be torpedo tubes

1866 Torpedo

Torpedoes are self-propelled guided underwater munitions. The main sections are:

- **Nose:** domed end containing the warhead, detonator, and—beginning in 1943—guidance transducer. Some advanced designs utilising supercavitation may have a flat end. When a flat-nosed torpedo travels at high speeds it generates a cavity of low-pressure water around the torpedo that reduces friction and drag.

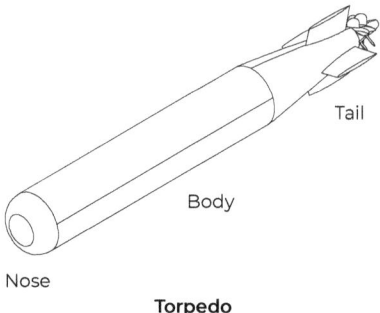

Torpedo

- **Body:** cylindrical main body containing the power supply for the engine (fuel, pressurised gas, batteries).
- **Tail:** engine, depth control and guidance mechanisms, propellers, fins and rudders.

In naval usage, torpedoes are fired from a surface or subsurface torpedo tube. The torpedo tube may be fixed (e.g. on torpedo boats and submarines) or trainable (e.g. on larger surface warships).

MODERN ARMAMENT

- **Surface torpedo tube:** tubes designed for use on the surface operate on the same principle as a gun. The torpedo is loaded into a tube of matching diameter with a sealable end (chamber) and an open end (muzzle). The chamber is sealed by closing the breech door. Pressurised gas is released into the chamber behind the torpedo, forcing the torpedo with velocity out of the muzzle.

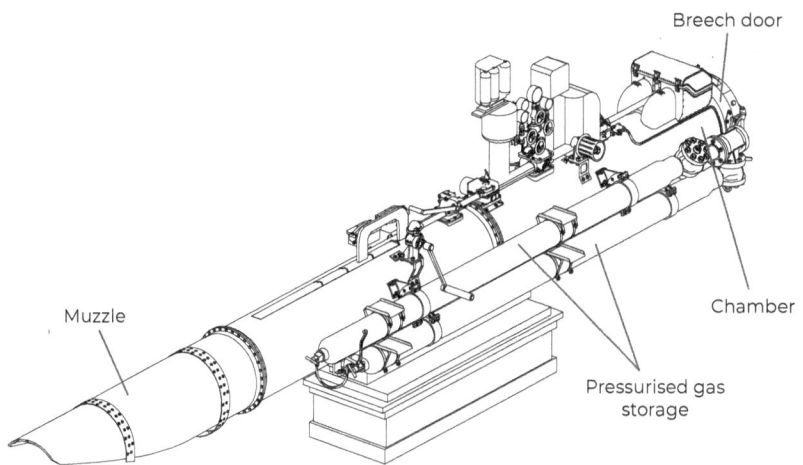

Surface torpedo tube

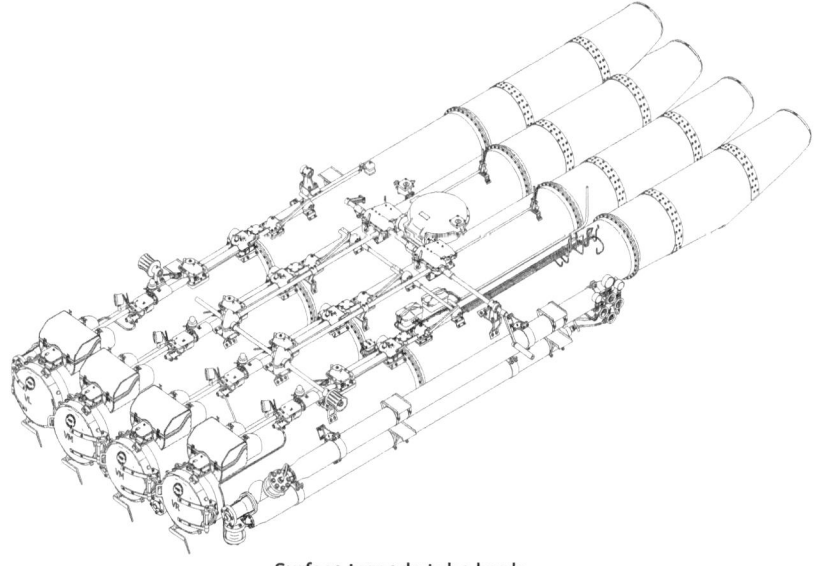

Surface torpedo tube bank

THE SHIPWRECK DECODER

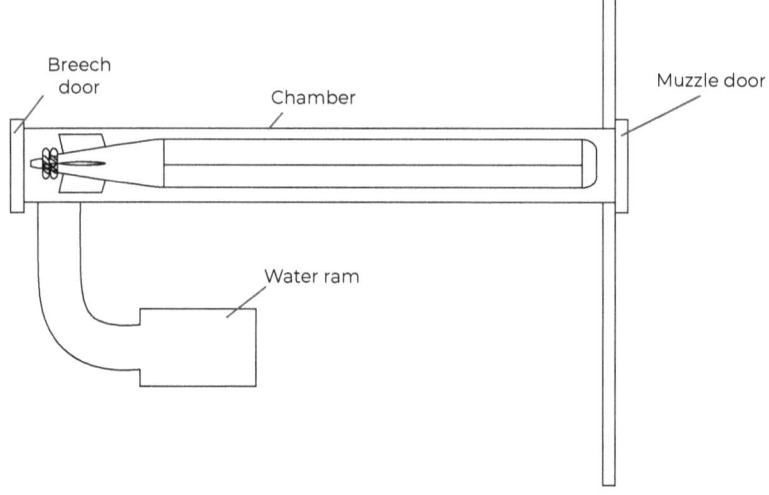

Underwater torpedo tube

- **Submarine torpedo tube:** open directly to the outside water so must be sealed by pressure doors to avoid flooding the boat. To fire a torpedo, the outer (muzzle) door must be closed to seal the chamber from the outside water before opening the inner (breech) door. The torpedo is loaded from racks through the breech door into the chamber. The breech door is sealed and the chamber flooded and equalised to the ambient water pressure before the muzzle door can be opened. Finally the torpedo is launched by water ram.

Depth charges

- Depth charges look like a small barrel or stubby torpedo

1916 Depth charge

Depth charges emerged as the first truly effective anti-submarine weapon system. A canister of high explosives detonated by a pressure trigger or timed fuze, they are intended to cause damage by generating a shockwave through the water that will impact a submarine within an effective range.

MODERN ARMAMENT

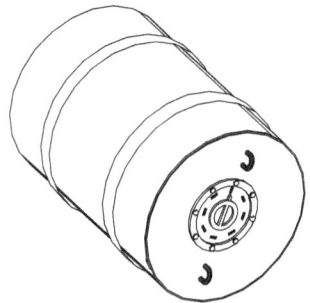

Barrel depth charge

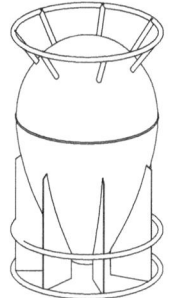

Finned depth charge

The shockwave can also damage the deploying vessel if detonation is too close, so there are three main systems used to achieve distance:

- **Stern mounted racks:** depth charges could be rolled off stern mounted racks while the vessel was in motion. Distance was achieved by moving away from the depth charge while it sank to the detonation depth. This method required the vessel to pass over the submarine.

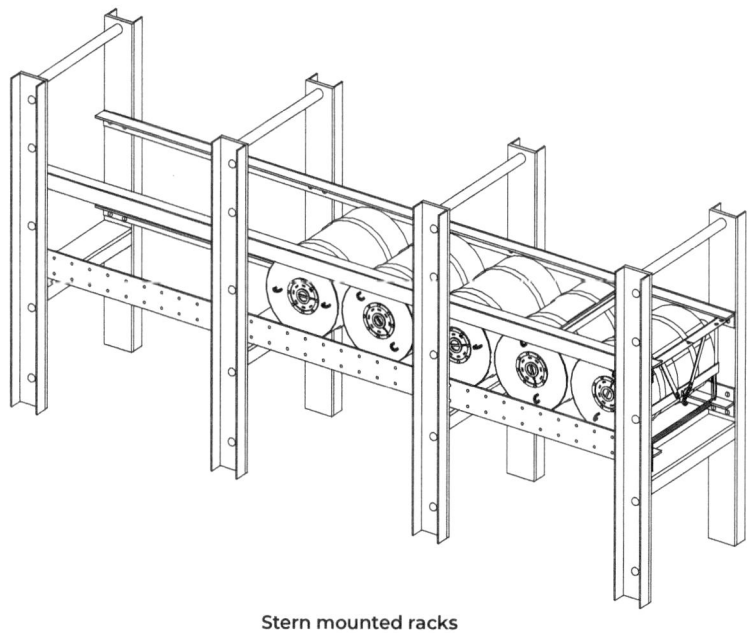

Stern mounted racks

THE SHIPWRECK DECODER

- **Depth charge mortars:** early depth charge mortars were modified from existing ground-based designs. They projected the depth charge away from the vessel. Mortars have a wide bore, very short barrel, and are fired at high elevation so that the projectile falls indirectly onto the target area. Another common design was the Y-gun which could launch depth charges to either side of the vessel. Depth charge launching mortars may be located to the sides or stern, but they did not have sufficient range to launch forward of a vessel.
- **Depth charge howitzers:** launching depth charges ahead required a greater range to avoid the vessel catching up with the effective range of the charge before it detonated. Howitzers represented a halfway point between guns and mortars. They had a wide bore and relatively short barrel, giving a stubby appearance. They were fired on a low elevation like a gun, but at a lower velocity so the trajectory was shorter range, but curved for a more indirect effect. Depth charge launching howitzers may be located at the bow of a wreck.

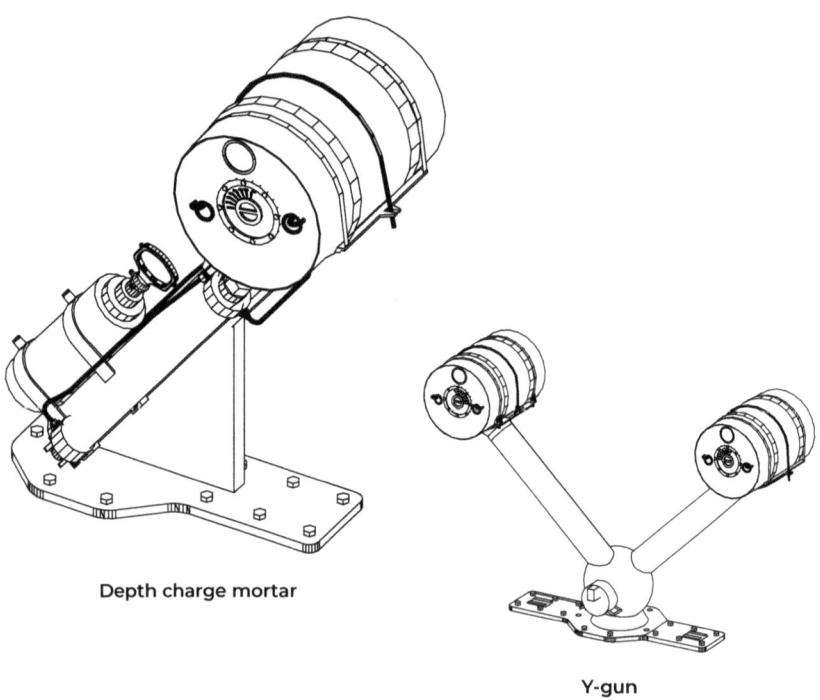

Depth charge mortar

Y-gun

MODERN ARMAMENT

Rockets and missiles

1232 Early rockets in warfare (China)
1380 Early rockets in warfare (Europe)
1780 Mysorean rocket
1808–1865 Congreve rocket
1940 Modern rockets
1952 Guided missile

The Chinese are credited with the earliest gunpowder rockets in 960, which had been adapted as self-propelled munitions for warfare by 1232. The Mysoreans (in India) developed iron-cased rockets allowing greater range and larger payloads, which they successfully deployed against the British in 1780. The British captured and adopted the technology as the Congreve rocket, introducing self-propelled munitions into European warfare.

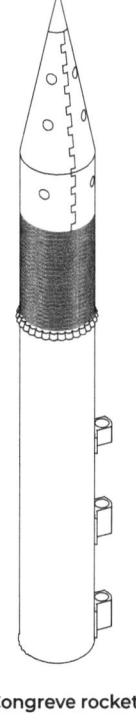

Congreve rocket

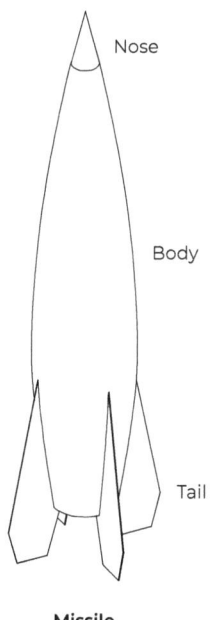

Missile

Missiles are airborne weapons, self-propelled by a jet or rocket motor, and guided to a land, sea, or air target by internal sensors or external direction. The main sections are:

- **Nose:** pointed or domed end containing the warhead, flight and guidance mechanism.
- **Body:** cylindrical main body containing fuel.
- **Tail:** straight or tapered tail for the jet or rocket engine, flight surface fins for stability.

Missile launchers vary in design and complexity according to their intended use and the naval vessel they are to be deployed from. Key characteristics include: can be hard or cold launch, rail and/or canister; fixed or targetable; and singular or combined into banks or arrays.

- **Hard launch:** the missile is launched by its own motor. Hard launch systems require an exhaust vent to dispose of propellant and heat.
- **Cold launch:** the missile is ejected from the launcher before aerial ignition of its own motor. Cold launch systems require a discharge mechanism.
- **Rail launcher:** provides initial directional guidance by restricting the missile's trajectory while it is moving on the launcher in a hard launch.
- **Canister launcher:** protective tube casing that houses a missile, from which it is hard or cold launched. The canister provides containment and initial directional guidance during the launch sequence.
- **Fixed mount:** the launcher is permanently in, or raised to, a single firing position. The whole vessel must be oriented to give the missile an initial direction.
- **Targetable mount:** the launcher is aimable to some degree independent of the orientation of the vessel.

For example: (1) A missile boat may have a relatively simple and inexpensive system for hard launch from fixed mount rail-canister launchers arranged in banked pairs; (2) a guided missile frigate may have a system for hard launch from a targetable mount rail launcher carrying two pairs of banked rails to fire up to four missiles; and (3) ballistic missile submarines are likely to have a complicated and expensive system for subsurface cold launch from vertically fixed canister launchers arranged in an array.

CHAPTER 15
SUBMARINES

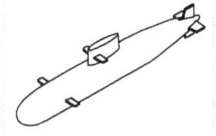

Early submarines were powered manually or by steam. The modern configuration emerged from 1900 with the introduction of electric engines. From there, submarines rapidly increased in size and operating range.

1900 Modern submarine pattern

The basic structure of a submarine is a closed reinforced tube (a pressure hull) capable of withstanding the pressure of water at its intended operational depth. Buoyancy is controlled by ballast tanks that can be alternately filled with air or water. There will be a row of small rectangular or round vents at the top of the ballast tanks that can be opened to let air escape, and a row of flood ports at the bottom of the ballast tanks to let water enter and exit.

When flooded with water, the ballast tanks alone would be neutrally buoyant. However, the fully-loaded submarine is weighted to be negatively buoyant when the ballast tanks are flooded. The submarine's buoyancy is then controlled by the addition of compressed air to the ballast tanks.

Beyond the basic structure, most submarines follow a broadly common layout dictated by size, environment and function.

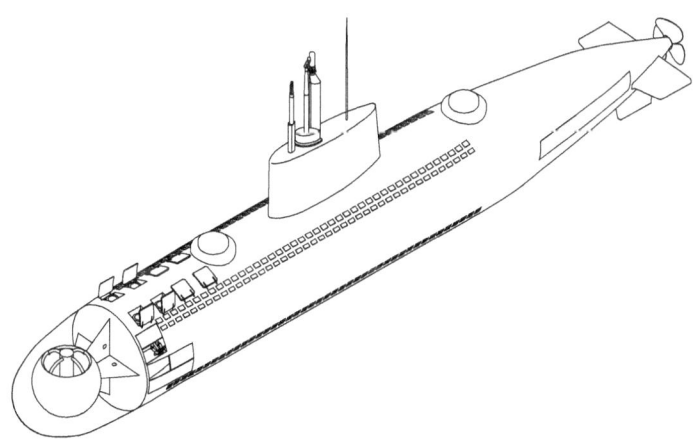

Modern pattern submarine

Bow

- Escape hatch open or closed ➤ Final actions of the crew
- Number of torpedo tubes
- Open muzzle door without any torpedo in the tube ➤ Submarine had launched a torpedo
- Open muzzle door with a torpedo in the tube ➤ Submarine was preparing to launch the torpedo
- Torpedo tube muzzle door and breech door both open ➤ Water will have flooded the bow compartment ➤ Cause of sinking

> **1929** Escape hatch
> **1922** Sonar dome

The bow will usually feature recessed anchors, any forward hydroplanes for manoeuvring, and may have a sonar dome for detecting other vessels. Other externally identifiable features may include an escape hatch, and/or net cutter.

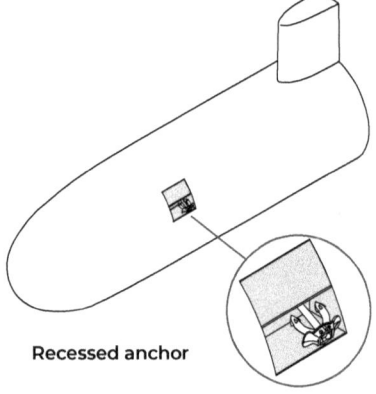

Recessed anchor

The torpedo tubes occupy the leading part of the bow compartment, with additional torpedoes stored on racks immediately behind the tubes. The next section aft will usually be crew accommodation and living space, with junior ranks closest to the bow and senior ranks closest to midships.

- **Forward hydroplanes:** shaped control surfaces mounted on either side of the bow and capable of being angled upwards or downwards. They act as horizontal rudders to direct the bow in the vertical axis (i.e. to point the sub up or down).

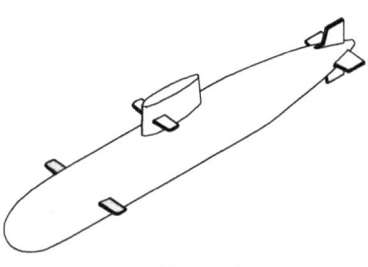

Forward hydroplanes

SUBMARINES

- **Escape hatch:** pressure hatch designed to enable escape from the forward compartments when the vessel is submerged.
- **Torpedo tubes:** externally, closed muzzle doors appear as flush panels, either round or rectangular. In normal cruising, muzzle doors are closed to maintain the regularity of the submarine's leading surface and to minimise risk of flooding.
- **Net cutter:** submarines intended to penetrate harbour defences or operate in channels may be fitted with a cutting device to counter nets. It is usually a metal bar with teeth, like a large saw, mounted atop and below the bow. One or more cables running from the top of the net cutter to the top of the conning tower ensure nets cannot slip behind the cutter and snag the superstructure.

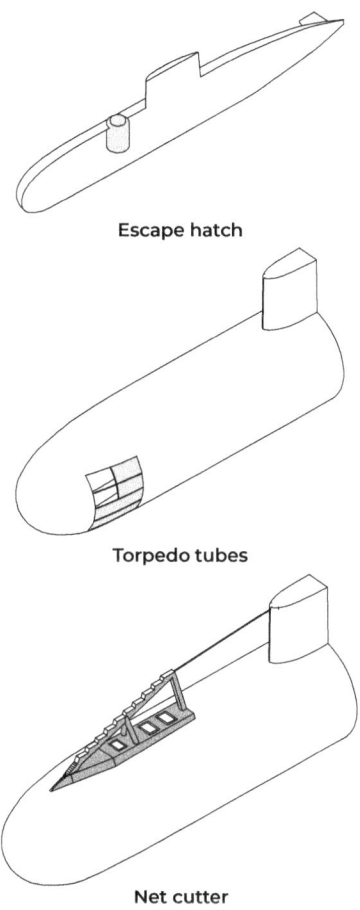

Escape hatch

Torpedo tubes

Net cutter

- **Sonar dome:** bulbous cover for an array of sound detecting and projecting transducers, mounted on the top of the bow. The sonar allows the submarine to track other surface and subsurface objects including other vessels.

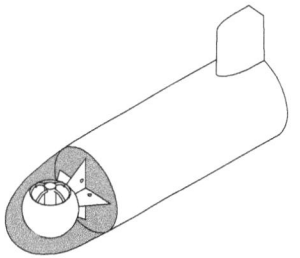 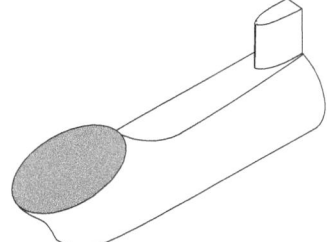

Sonar dome

Midships

- Narrow, solid pole ➤ Antenna
- Tube topped with a window or lens ➤ Periscope
- Wide tube topped with baffles or other vent structure ➤ Snorkel, diesel engines

> **1905** Periscope
> **1943** Snorkel

The midship of a submarine is readily identifiable by the presence of a conning tower. Internally, this section houses the control room, radio and sonar rooms, the galley, and officer quarters. Externally identifiable features may include saddle tanks, deck guns, railings and aircraft storage. Deck guns and railings reduce the hydrodynamic efficiency of the hull so are rare after the Second World War.

- **Conning tower:** the highest point on the hull is the primary entry and exit route for the submarine. The tower will be topped by a pressure hatch, periscope, antennas and snorkel. Over time, external features of the top deck were consolidated within an enclosed conning tower to improve hydrodynamic efficiency. There may also be hydroplanes on it.

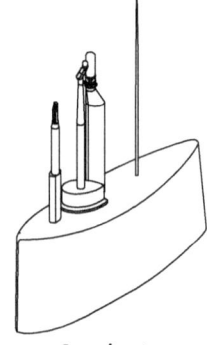
Conning tower

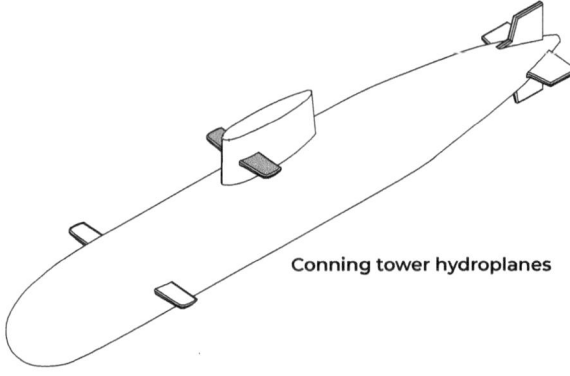
Conning tower hydroplanes

SUBMARINES

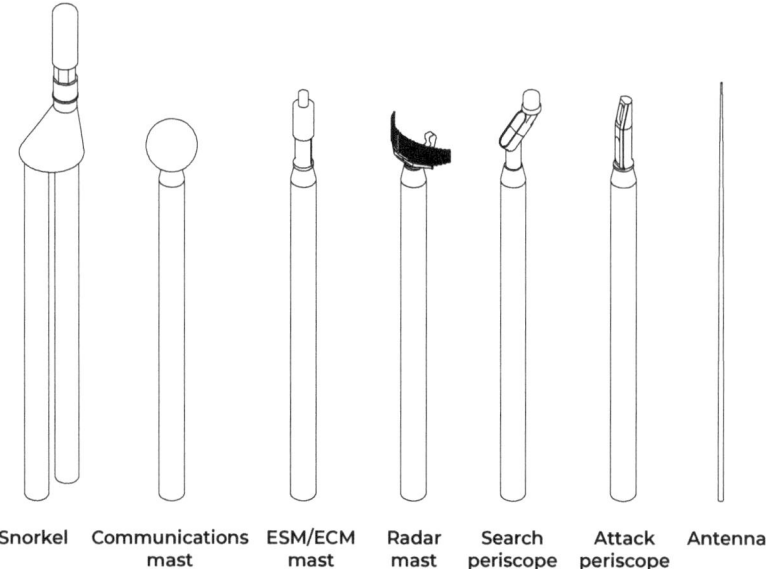

Snorkel   Communications mast   ESM/ECM mast   Radar mast   Search periscope   Attack periscope   Antenna

- **Periscope:** retractable tube that allows the crew of a shallowly submerged submarine to view above the surface.
- **Antennas:** retractable antennas for communication, navigation and targeting systems.
- **Snorkel:** paired exhaust and intake pipes to allow diesel engines to run while shallowly submerged.
- **Saddle tanks:** ballast tanks fitted on either side of the pressure hull. Saddle tanks appear as bulges on the sides of the hull.

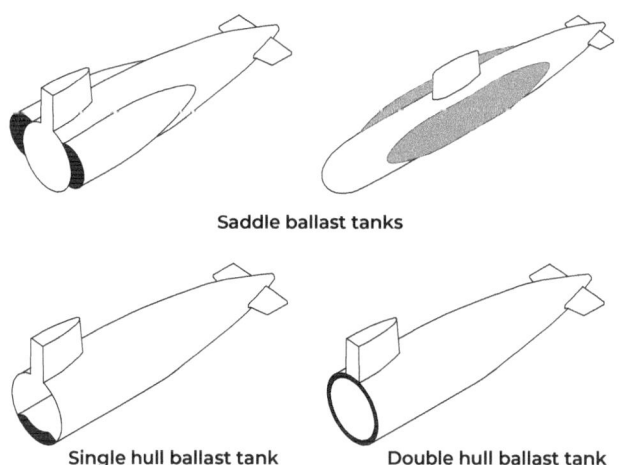

Saddle ballast tanks

Single hull ballast tank   Double hull ballast tank

THE SHIPWRECK DECODER

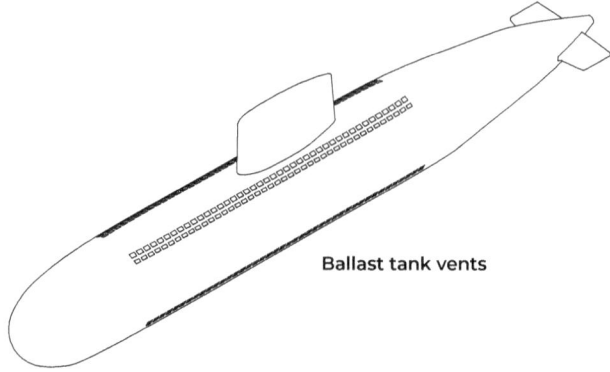
Ballast tank vents

- **Deck guns:** small or medium-calibre guns mounted forward and/or aft of the conning tower.
- **Aircraft hangar, catapult and lifting device:** some rare experimental submarines carried pressurised hangars in place of deck guns for storage of up to three aircraft. The hangar will be associated with a catapult for launching the aircraft, and a crane or derrick to lift it out of the water after landing, for recovery.

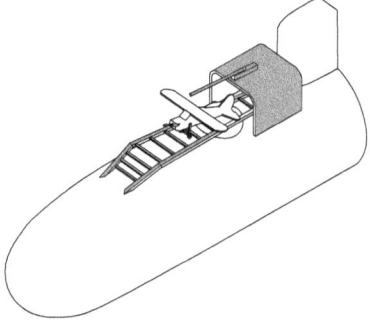
Aircraft hangar

Stern

- Number of aft torpedo tubes
- Open aft torpedo tube muzzle door ➔ Submarine was being chased
- Number and type of propellers ➔ Period of construction

The stern houses the crew quarters and engine room, including motors (petrol, diesel or nuclear), electric generators and battery banks. The stern will be fitted with propellers, rudders, hydroplanes, and may also have an escape hatch.

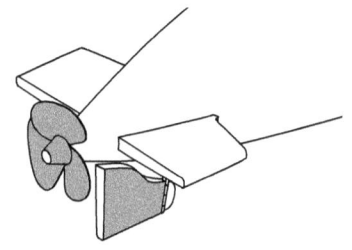
Rudder and propeller

SUBMARINES

- **Aft hydroplanes:** shaped surfaces mounted either side of the stern for stability. Some designs have a third mounted on top of the stern, like a fin.
- **Aft torpedo tubes:** cannot be reloaded at sea, so usually a weapon of last resort when being chased.

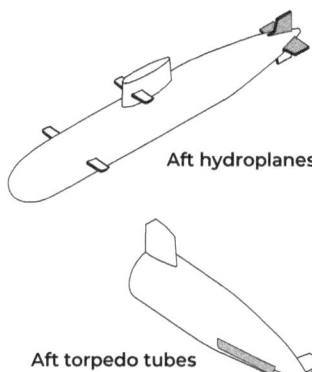

Aft hydroplanes

Aft torpedo tubes

Armaments

Missiles

- **Missile tubes (subsurface launch):** vertical tubes capable of deploying missiles while submerged using a steam cannon. In this system, an explosive charge flash-vaporises a tank of water, and the resultant high-pressure steam launches the missile out of the tube with enough momentum to clear the surface. Once the missile is clear of the surface the rocket stage ignites.
- **Missile tubes (surface launch):** vertical tubes within the main axis of the submarine, or recessed and raised for surface launches.

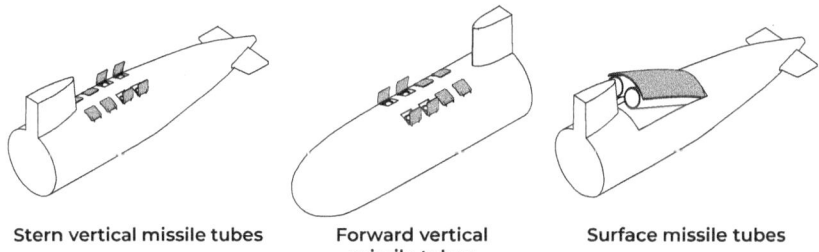

Stern vertical missile tubes   Forward vertical missile tubes   Surface missile tubes

Mines

Submarines may be designed to covertly lay mines while submerged, usually by dropping them from vertical tubes mounted in the bow or along the flanks. Externally, closed mine deployment tubes appear as a flush panel, either round or rectangular, beneath the submarine.

Mine deployment tubes

SELECT BIBLIOGRAPHY

Babicz, J (2015), *Wartsila Encyclopedia of Ship Technology*. Biuro Okretowe Baobab.

Catsambis, A, Ford, B, Hamilton, D (eds) (2011), *The Oxford Handbook of Maritime Archaeology*. Oxford University Press USA.

Dill, R and Achenbach, P (1948), "Performance of a Coal-Fired Boiler Converted to Oil", United States Commerce Department, Building Materials and Structures Report.

Friedman, N (2013), *Naval Anti-Aircraft Guns and Gunnery*. Seaforth Publishing.

Haydock, R (1918), "Military Searchlights", *Professional Memoirs, Corps of Engineers, United States Army, and Engineer Department at Large*, 10(50), p. 261–267.

Historic England (2019), "A brief history of ships' figureheads", heritagecalling.com/2019/01/31/a-brief-history-of-ships-figureheads

Jolie, E W (1978), "A Brief History of US Navy Torpedo Development", 15, NUSC Technical Document 5436.

Lavery, B (2017), *Ship: 5,000 Years of Maritime Adventure*. DK.

Mark, S (2008), "The Earliest Naval Ram", *International Journal of Nautical Archaeology*, 37(2), p. 253–272.

McCarthy, M (2005), *Ships Fastenings: From Sewn Boat to Steamship*. Texas A&M University Press.

McKee, F M (1993), "An Explosive Story: The Rise and Fall of the Depth Charge", *The Northern Mariner*, 45.

Mott, L (1991), "The Development of the Rudder, A.D. 100–1600: A Technological Tale", Thesis submitted to the Office of Graduate Studies of Texas A&M University.

Oertling, T (1996), *Ships' Bilge Pumps: A History of Their Development, 1500–1900*. Texas A&M University Press.

Rippon, P (1988), *Evolution of Engineering in the Royal Navy*. Spellmount.

Staniforth, M (1985), "The Introduction and Use of Copper Sheathing—A History", *Bulletin of the Australian Institute of Maritime Archaeology*.

Steffy, J (2017), *Wooden Ship Building and the Interpretation of Shipwrecks*. Texas A&M University Press.

Verrill, H (1916), *The Book of the Sailboat: How to Rig, Sail and Handle Small Boats*. Sothis Press.

ABOUT THE AUTHOR

Ashton East had to wait until his twelfth birthday to achieve his Junior Open Water certification and join his parents' diving adventures. In the decades since, he has progressed to underwater photography and rebreather diving, and continued exploring shipwrecks around the world. Wanting to better understand these underwater time capsules he started taking Nautical Archaeological Society short courses, reviewing maritime archaeological and engineering literature, and visiting maritime museums to study exhibits of historical maritime equipment. This book began as a personal Covid lockdown project to document and structure these explorations. At the insistence of a good friend, he sought publication so that others might benefit from a handy guide to the shipwrecks of historic vessels.

ACKNOWLEDGEMENTS

I owe endless thanks to my wife, whose mostly good-natured patience endured countless explanations about why that thing on the wreck we just saw is a marvel of maritime history rather than "another rusty lump" she dutifully poses beside for the camera.

I am grateful to my publisher, Alex Gibson, whose reviews and challenges pushed me to refine each page, and his patience throughout this journey was invaluable.

My thanks to Peta Knott from the Nautical Archaeology Society, for her patience and bemused willingness to arrange short-courses and further materials for our (very) difficult group. Further thanks to the many experts who provided suggestions for improvements and pre-publication reviews, not least Mark Beattie-Edwards, Giles Richardson, David Gibbins, Mallory Hass, Dominic Robinson and Nicholas Hall.

INDEX

Aegean *vii*
aircraft *146–147, 194*
alarm *82, 121*
aluminium *30, 70, 71*
American Civil War *153, 164*
ammunition. *See* armaments (modern): ordnance: gun ammunition
amphorae *142*
anchor *42–47*
    cable *46–47*
    mechanism *46–47*
    modern *44–45*
    recessed *190*
    rode *46–47*
    stern (kedge) *69*
    stone/composite *42–43*
ancient vessels *vii, 26, 38, 104, 111, 142*
anemometer *73*
anoxic water *vi*
antenna *87–88, 181, 192–193*
armaments (modern) *173–188, 192*
    anti-aircraft *173, 177–178*
    anti-submarine *184–185*
    barbette *173*
    calibre *173–179, 194*
    dreadnought *174–175*
    gunhouse *174, 177*
    hydraulic recoil system *176*
    light arms *178*
    ordnance *32, 147, 179–188*
        bomb *179*
        depth charge *184–186*
        gun ammunition *179–180*
        magazine *147*
        rocket/missile *179, 187–188, 195*
        sea mine *181, 195*
        torpedo *33, 67, 179, 182–184, 190*
    pre-dreadnought *174–175*
    range *173–174, 178, 184–186*
    rifling *179*
    super-dreadnought *175–176*
    trajectory *179, 186, 188*
    turret *173–176*
armour *32–33, 38, 87, 97, 147, 153, 155, 173–174*
Asia *43*. *See also* China; India; Indonesia; Japan; Korea; Pakistan
astrolabe *76*
Austria *159*
backstay *106, 111*
ballast *27, 31, 145, 171–172, 193–194*
    saddle tanks *193*
    tanks *189*
bark *110*
barometer *72*
barquentine *110*

barrel (cargo) *142, 148, 150. See also* armaments (modern): ordnance: depth charge
bathroom. *See* head (bathroom)
bathtub *vi*
battery *139–140, 182, 194*
beakhead *40, 94*
beams *19*
belaying pin *108*
bell *82*
bench *104*
binnacle *71, 76*
binoculars *72, 75*
boiler *95–100, 114, 123–131*
    Admiralty *114–115, 119*
    Babcock & Wilcox *114–115, 118, 119*
    box *114–116*
    Cornish *114–115*
    donkey *109, 120*
    fire-tube *115*
    flued *115*
    Lancashire *114–116*
    Mumford *114–115, 118*
    Normand *114–115, 117*
    Reed *114, 117*
    Schulz-Thornycroft *114–115, 118*
    Scotch *114–116*
    three-drum *115*
    water-tube *115*
    White-Forster *114–115, 119*
    Yarrow *114–115, 117*
boom *89, 106, 111, 143, 144*
boom crutch *111*

bow *14–15, 28, 35–48, 75, 89, 94, 96, 104, 175, 190–192*
    bluff bow *35–36*
    bow flare *37*
    bowsprit *40, 107, 110*
    bow thruster *41*
    broad bow *41*
    bulbous bow *38–39*
    decoration *40*
    fine bow *35–36*
    icebreaker bow *39*
    plumb bow *35*
    rake bow *35*
    reverse bow *35*
    sailing bow *40*
    sharp bow *41*
    spoon bow *37*
    square bow *35–36*
brailing ring *109*
brass *71, 82, 147*
breech. *See* cannon: breech
brick *v, 90, 92–93, 113, 114*
bridge *70–81*
    flying bridge *71*
brig *110*
brigantine *110*
bronze *30, 82, 85, 158–162*
    fastener *22, 24*
bulkhead *28–29, 31, 148*
bullseye *108*
bulwark *19, 28*
    bulwark stay *28*
buoyancy *25–26, 35–37, 49–51*
Butterworth cover *151*
cable *31, 46, 78–80, 95, 139, 143, 181*

INDEX

Canada
  Great Lakes *vii*
cannon *vii*, 32, 38, 96, 147, 153–172
  Age of Cannon *vii*, 153–172
  assemblage 168–169
  base plate 159–160
  base ring 154–155, 159–160, 167
  block and tackle 168
  bore 155, 161–162, 163–165, 169
  breech 157, 160, 162, 165–166
  button 154, 159, 160
  calibre 96, 155, 157, 162–164
  carriage 167–168
  carronade 160, 162–163
  cascabel 154, 158–159, 161, 164–167
  chase 154–156, 164–165
  classification 162–163
  dolphins 157–158
  gunlock 159
  howitzer 162–163
  loading 162
  magazine 147
  mortar 162–163
  mouldings 156–157, 166–167
  muzzle 154–157, 160–167, 169, 171
  projectiles 170–171
  range 153, 157, 162–163, 170–171
  reinforce 154, 157, 158, 164–166
  rifling 155
  swivel gun 162–163
  trajectory 155, 162–163
  trunnion 154, 157–158, 162, 166–167, 171
  types 164–166
  vent field 154, 157, 159
  vent (touch hole) 169
cannonball 163, 170
canoe 20–21
capstan 46, 82–83
carburettor 133, 136
cargo 26, 83, 87, 141–152
  handling 143–145, 148–152
  hold 141
  solid 142–145
cargo vessels *vii*, 14, 84, 87
carlings 19
casemate 32
catapult 146–147, 194
cathead 46–47
cavitation 63
ceramic 94
Chadburn. *See* telegraph (aka Chadburn)
chain 46–47, 57–58, 143, 170
chainplate 106, 108
chamber pot 94
China 52, 60, 61, 92, 111, 148, 187
chronometer 75
citadel 33
clay pot 142
cleat 108
coal 92–93, 113–116, 120, 148
  bunker 114
  chute 113
coin 105–106
Cold War *vii*
combustion engine *vii*, 133–137
  four stroke engine 133, 135

201

two stroke engine *133, 136*
communication *80–81, 82, 87–88, 98, 121, 193*
compass *71, 76*
condenser *113*
Confederate States *153, 164, 165*
control head *79–80*
control room *192*
cookfire *92*
copper *24, 26–27, 30, 85, 138–139, 168, 179*
   fasteners *22, 24*
cowls *84*
crane *83, 142–148, 151, 194. See also* davits
   gantry crane *144*
   luffing jib crane *145*
   travelling gantry crane *145*
crankshaft *65, 121, 122, 126, 129–130, 134–136*
crate *142, 148*
crew quarters *194*
crow's nest *87*
cruise ship. *See* passenger ferry/cruise ship
cutter *110*
cylinder *22, 82–83, 112–113, 121–126, 129–131, 134, 142, 152, 176, 179, 181*
   gas *93, 142, 152*
davits *99–100*
deadeye *108*
deaerator *112*
deck *17, 18, 49–51, 89, 148*
   forecastle deck *17, 175*
   foredeck camber *37*
   gun deck *46*
   half deck *17*
   landing deck *146–147*
   main deck *17*
   orlop deck *17*
   parking deck *143, 145*
   platform deck *17*
   poopdeck *16, 17, 50, 175*
   quarterdeck *17, 70*
   second deck *17*
   superstructure deck *17*
   top deck *16, 95, 192*
   upper deck *17*
   well deck/dock *143, 145*
deck prisms *95*
Denmark *157*
depth *vi*
derrick *46–47, 89, 194*
   derrick boom *143–144*
diagonal riders *25*
diesel
   diesel-electric engine *139–140*
   diesel engine *133–136, 139, 192, 194*
dive sites *vi–vii*
echo sounder *74*
efficiency *32*
Egypt *40, 111*
electricity
   electric engine *138, 189*
   electric generator *139, 194*
   electric-powered vessels *138–140, 189*
electronics *100*
elevator *102*

INDEX

engine room *32, 90, 95, 194*
escalator *102*
Europe *32, 38, 40, 52, 60, 82, 187. See also* Rome; Aegean; Denmark; France; Germany; Greece; Mediterranean; Netherlands; Portugal; Sweden; United Kingdom
evaporator *112–113*
feedwater tank *112–113*
figureheads *40*
fire chamber *92*
First World War *vii*
fishing vessels *83, 89*
flywheel *122, 126, 130*
forecastle *16, 46*
frames *16, 18–19, 20–22, 25–26, 28*
France *40, 114, 164*
full-rigged *110*
funnel *69, 120–121*
futtocks *18*
galley (kitchen) *92–93, 192*
gangway *101*
gas *93, 152, 182*
   gas turbine engine *133, 137*
gauges *70–77*
gearbox *60*
Germany *114*
girders *28, 31*
glass *71, 75, 97*
goalpost *143*
GPS *77*
gratings *95*
Greece *40, 52, 55*
greenwater *35*

gribbles *26*
gunport *96*
guns. *See* cannon; *See* armaments (modern)
gunwale *16, 20*
hangar *146–147*
hatches *28, 95, 113, 141, 150, 151, 190–192, 194–195*
hawse hole *46–47*
head (bathroom) *vi, 94*
headphones *80–81*
helicopter *146–147*
hogging truss *25*
hoist *143, 147*
holds *16, 83*
hose *78–79, 151*
hull *14–16, 18–34, 96*
   concrete *34*
   fibreglass *34*
   hull sheathing *26, 38*
   metal *26, 28–33, 38, 76, 96*
      double bottom *30–31*
      double hull *30*
      double side *30*
      single bottom *30–31*
   pressure hull *189*
   wooden *18–27, 38, 84–86, 90, 96*
      bottom based *20*
      carvel *20–21*
      clinker *20–21*
      double diagonal *21*
      double planked *20–21, 21*
      frame first *20*
      hard shell *20*

mortise and tenon joinery
  20, 22–23
sewn planking 20, 22–23
trenails 22, 23, 24
hydrodynamics 35–37, 39, 49
hydroplanes 190, 192, 194–195
icebreaker 64
inclinometer 73
India 187
Indonesia 111
injectors 133–135
instruments 70–77
iron 22, 24–26, 30, 40, 42, 85,
  92–93, 96, 156, 160, 170–171
  cast iron 92–93, 156, 160–167
  wrought iron 161–163, 164–165
Japan 176
keel 16, 18–19, 20–21, 25, 31, 105
  bar 31
  duct 31
  flat plate 31
kingpost 143
knees 19, 25–26
Korea 32
ladder 102
landing pad 147
lead 26, 42, 85, 169
  lead line. *See* sounding/lead line
leeboard 60
lever 56–57, 82, 85, 103, 124, 128, 169
lifeboat 99–100
liferaft 99
lighting 15, 95–96. *See also* signal
  flags/lamps
  oil lamp 95

searchlights 98
main deck 16–17
manoeuvrability 14, 35–38, 41, 66,
  68, 109
marine growth vi
mast
  mast step 106
mast crutch 111
masts 105–111. *See
  also* communication: masts
  bipod 111
  crosstree 106–108
  for communication 87–88
  foremast 96, 107
  mainmast 87, 96, 106–107, 110
  mast cap 107
  mast collar 106
  mast stack 105, 107–108
  middle mast 107
  mizzenmast 107
  trestletree 107–108
  tripod 111
medieval vessels 26, 52, 55, 142
Mediterranean vii, 42, 92, 142
metal vi, 42, 44, 47, 76, 87, 94, 97,
  106, 112–132, 168–170, 174. *See
  also* bronze; copper; hull: metal;
  iron; steel
microphone 80–81
Middle East. *See* Egypt;
  See Phoenicia
midships 14–15, 17, 25–26, 46, 60,
  75, 174, 190, 192–194

INDEX

military vessels *vii, 14, 32–33, 38, 69, 82, 87–88, 90, 98, 114, 153–172, 173–188, 189–195*
    aircraft carrier *102, 146*
    amphibious assault ship *146*
    dreadnoughts *96*
mines. *See* armaments (modern): ordnance: sea mine
minesweepers *21*
missile. *See* armaments (modern): ordnance: rocket/missile
moorings *48*
motorised vessels *38, 40*
muntz *26–27*
museums *vi*
nails *20, 24*
Napoleonic Wars *166*
Nautical Archaeology Society *vii*
navigation *32, 70–71, 75–77, 99, 193*
    lights *15, 96*
net *146*
    net cutter *190–191*
Norman *40*
North America. *See* Canada; *See* United States
nuclear propulsion *194*
oars *61, 103–104*
    oarlock *104*
    oar port *104*
officer quarters *94, 192*
oil *59, 113–115, 150, 151, 176*
orientation *v*
outrigger *104*
Pacific *vii*
paddleboats *60, 61, 128*

paddlewheel *61, 70*
Pakistan *111*
passenger ferry/cruise ship *14, 64, 84, 102*
pattern recognition *v*
periscope *192–193*
petrol engine *133–136, 194*
Phoenicia *40*
pilothouse *70–71*
pin rail *108*
pipes *31, 85–86, 113–114, 142, 150–151, 193*
    hawse pipe *47*
pistons *86, 90, 122–130, 134–136, 176*
pitch *35–37*
pivoting jib crane *143–144*
planks *18, 20–25*
plastic *70, 71, 142*
plates *26, 28, 30–33*
    armoured *32–33*
    keelson plate *31*
    ridder plate *31*
plumb bob *73*
poles *87, 88, 103, 105, 106, 111, 143–144, 168–169, 192*
poop *16–17*
    pooping *50*
portholes *95–97*
Portugal *157, 159*
pots and pans *92–93*
pressure relief valve *151*
propeller *39, 41, 49–50, 62–69, 90, 140, 182, 194*
    Archimedes screw *63*

205

azimuth *66, 140*
configurations *66–67*
ducted *66*
guards *68*
number of blades *64*
propeller assembly *65–66*
shaft *65–66*
Voith Schneider *68*
public address system *81*
pulley *57, 79, 100, 108, 143*
pump *59, 84, 113, 150–151*
   bilge pump *84–86*
radar *71, 87, 193*
radio room *81, 192*
radome *87*
ramp *89*
rams *38–39*
refrigeration *141*
rigging *83, 106–111, 170*
ring buoy *99*
rivets *24, 29*
rocket. *See* armaments (modern): ordnance: rocket/missile
roll-on roll-off ramp *145*
Rome *40, 52, 55*
rope *46–47, 105–106, 108, 143–144, 169*
rowed vessels *38, 103–104*
rudder *52–59, 75, 194*
   layouts *55*
   pintle/gudgeon *54*
   rudder angle indicator *73*
   rudder assembly *53–54*
   rudder plate/blade *53*
   rudder post *28, 53, 56*
   rudderstock *53–54, 56*
   rudder trunk *53*
   types *55*
runway *146*
safety *16, 95, 99–100*
sagging arch *25–26*
sailing vessels *vii, 46, 69, 70–71, 83, 105–111*
   Age of Sail *vii, 105–111*
   sails *105–111*
schooners *109–110*
screen *71, 77*
seaplanes *146*
search and rescue *98*
sensors *87–88*
sextant *77*
shipping container *142, 148*
ship's wheel. *See* steering assembly: ship's wheel
shipworm *26*
shot *170*
shroud *106, 108*
signal flags/lamps *80, 87*
skylights *95*
slamming *35, 37, 49–51*
sloop *110*
snorkel *192–193*
sonar *71, 74, 190–192*
sounding/lead line *74*
South America *111*
Spain *159*
spar *40, 106, 111*
spark plugs *133–136*
speakers *81*

INDEX

speed *14, 32, 35–37, 39, 49–51, 66–67, 78–80*
sponsons *33*
squatting *49–51*
staircase *102*
stanchions *19*
stay *106*
steam
   Age of Steam *vii*
   steam donkey. *See* boiler: donkey
   steam engine *121–131*
      compound engine *121*
      Cornish *121–122, 127*
      crankshaft *121*
      dual-action pot *129–130*
      grasshopper *122, 128*
      Newcomen *121–122, 124–125*
      side-lever *128*
      steam cycle *112*
      steam engine assembly *123*
      steam turbine *123, 132*
      triple expansion *121, 123, 130–131*
      twin pot engine *121, 131*
      Watt *121–122, 126*
   steamships *vii, 38, 58, 61, 69, 78–79, 82, 112–132, 189*
      feedwater system *112–113*
   steam whistle *121*
steel *34, 44, 105, 161–162, 165*
   stainless *30, 92*
steering assembly *56–59*
   crosshead *56–59*
   hydraulic ram *59*
   hydraulic rotary vane *59*

quadrant *56–58*
ship's wheel *57–58, 70, 75*
steering engine *58*
tiller *56–57, 70*
whipstaff and rowle *56–57, 70*
stem *18–19, 28, 35*
   angle (rake) *37*
stern *14–15, 28, 49–69, 75, 96, 175, 194–195*
   stern frame *28*
   sternpost *18–19*
stone (cut) *92*
stone (shaped) *42–43*
strakes *18, 20, 21, 28*
stringers *28*
submarines *140, 182, 188, 189–195*
   conning tower *191, 192*
   mine laying *195*
   missile tubes *195*
superstructure *14, 16, 70–71, 75, 89, 95, 146, 174, 177, 178, 191*
Sweden *156, 160–161, 166–167*
switchboard *81*
tachometer *73*
taffrail log *74*
tank *150, 152. See also* feedwater tank
targeting *162, 177, 186, 188, 193*
technology *vi*
telegraph (aka Chadburn) *78–81*
telegraph (wireless) *80–81*
telephones *81*
telescope *75*
thermometer/temperature gauge *73*
thwarts *19*

timberhead 19
timelines vi
toilet. *See* head (bathroom)
tools 90–91, 168–169
torpedo. *See also* armaments (modern): ordnance: torpedo
 torpedo belt 33
 torpedo boats 182
 torpedo bulge 33
 torpedo tube 182–184, 190–191, 194–195
torque 53–54, 60, 67, 74, 122, 126
towing point 41
tracks 143, 145, 146
 rail launcher 188
transom 49–51
 angle (rake) 50
trawlers. *See* fishing vessels
triple expansion steam engine. *See* steam: steam engine: triple expansion
tugs 55, 64, 66
turbo-electric engines 139–140
ullage port 151
United Kingdom 96, 174, 187
 England 156, 161–167
 Scapa Flow vii
United States 61, 87, 96, 153, 160–161, 164, 175
 Great Lakes vii
vacuum effect 113, 124–126
vehicles 143
vents/ventilation 84, 96–97, 189, 192, 194
Viking 40

wake 49–51
welding 29
whistle 121
winch 82–83, 89, 100, 109
windlass 46, 82–83
wire 78, 105–106, 133, 138–139, 146–147, 157, 161, 169
 arresting wire 146
wood vi
workshop 90–91
yard 106
yaw 35, 37

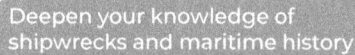

Find more books at DivedUp.com

www.ingramcontent.com/pod-product-compliance
Lightning Source LLC
Chambersburg PA
CBHW050928240426
43671CB00019B/2957